W9-DJK-222

Fight Like a Girl

MEGAN SEELY

Fight Like a Girl

How to Be a Fearless Feminist

New York University Press • *New York and London*

NEW YORK UNIVERSITY PRESS
New York and London
www.nyupress.org

Library of Congress Cataloging-in-Publication Data

Seely, Megan.
Fight like a girl : how to be a fearless feminist / Megan Seely.
p. cm.
Includes bibliographical references and index.
ISBN-13: 978-0-8147-4001-9 (cloth : alk. paper)
ISBN-10: 0-8147-4001-4 (cloth : alk. paper)
ISBN-13: 978-0-8147-4002-6.(pbk. : alk. paper)
ISBN-10: 0-8147-4002-2 (pbk. : alk. paper)
1. Feminism. 2. Women's rights. I. Title.
HQ1236.S37   2006
305.42—dc22   2006023651

New York University Press books are printed on acid-free paper,
and their binding materials are chosen for strength and durability.
Manufactured in the United States of America

c 10 9 8 7 6 5 4 3 2 1
p 10 9 8 7 6 5 4 3 2 1

Dedicated to all those who came before me, those who stand with me, and those who will come after me.

And to my sisters, Aimee and Amanda

Contents

Acknowledgments	ix
Preface: How I Became a Teenage Activist	xi
The F-Word: An Introduction	1
1. Fight Like a Girl	15
2. Catch a Wave	27
3. A Movement for Everyone	59
4. At the Table	93
5. Good Enough	122
6. Knock 'Em Up ... Knock 'Em Down	147
7. Fighting Back	185
8. ... Like a Girl	218
Appendix A: Timeline and Checklist for Action	227
Appendix B: Building an Activist Kit	231
Appendix C: How to Write a Press Release	233
Appendix D: Guidelines to a Good Media Interview	235
Appendix E: Guidelines to Creating and Earning Effective Media	239
Appendix F: Feminist Shopping Guide	243
Appendix G: Where to Donate Stuff	247
Notes	251
Bibliography	263
Index	275
About the Author	279

Acknowledgments

I would not have been able to write this book—or to think the way that I do—without the women who came before me, who fought for my rights before I even existed. From my grandmothers and mother to the women of the movement, I owe a debt of gratitude to all those who fought to allow me to grow up in a world knowing the possibility of equality. May my voice, my commitment, my activism be my contribution to this legacy.

To my editor, Ilene Kalish, you took a conversation and turned it into a book. Thank you for educating me about the world of publishing, thank you for protecting me in this endeavor, and thank you for being such an amazing advocate. You honor your profession and readers everywhere. And thank you to everyone at NYU Press!

To Jonathan—thank you for being my partner and friend, for encouraging me, and for helping this dream come true.

To my mom—who read everything I wrote before anyone else saw it. Who would I be without you? You are brilliant! I promise to return the favor . . . when you write your book.

To my dad—thank you for being the kind of dad men can look up to. Thank you for never apologizing that you had only daughters. And thank you for encouraging us to be the best we could be, not in spite of but because of our gender.

To my sisters—how lucky I am to have two sisters . . . you are my inspiration, my laughter, and my best memories. That we have become friends beyond sisters is icing on the cake!

To Helen—a mentor who became a friend and who told me that if the process of creating this book wasn't at least a little bit painful, the book would never become a feminist classic. I am thankful every day that our paths have met.

To good friends who listened endlessly to my ideas, rants, highs, and lows—thank you for your confidence and encouragement throughout this journey.

To Aidan, Adam, Emma, Devon, Ella, Gwendolyn, Sarah, Owen, Kate, Josie Jane, Taylor, Riley, Cian, Ashley, and all children—may my generation do our work to leave you a better world.

To Nikki, Elena, Mandy, Rosemary, Beth, and Rachel—you are all fabulous feminists. Thank you for your input and encouragement. You honor the movement with your contributions.

To all those in the field, working every day to secure our rights and safety—where would we all be without you?

In memory and honor of Dido Hasper . . . and to everyone at Women's Health Specialists/Feminist Women's Health Centers—thank you for all that you have taught me, for empowering me to see my body in a new and healthy way, and for your contributions, directly and indirectly, to this book.

To my students, past and present—thank you for helping to create an environment where education is a shared experience, an exchange of ideas where I have learned as much from you as I hope you have learned from me.

To Dr. Judith Levy, my acupuncturist—thank you for undoing the damage I do to my body in the name of activism and for guiding my body back into balance after weekend flights to DC, sleepless nights planning actions, and living with a mind that doesn't rest.

To all those who responded to my questionnaire and to those who passed it along to others—it was an honor to read your responses and to hear your impressions of feminism today. Thank you for your time and input, and thank you for supporting the book.

I have gathered information from many sources throughout my life. I have learned from teachers, activists, advocates, practitioners, and many others who have come into and through my life. My interaction with these people has shaped who I am and what I think, to such an extent that I sometimes question where my ideas and knowledge distinguish themselves from those that belong to others. A collective consciousness has been shared with me, and I now pass it on. Thank you for allowing me to be a part of this process.

Preface
How I Became a Teenage Activist

For the most part, I grew up in the small town of Aromas, California, a largely agricultural area. Early in high school, I was introduced to the United Farm Workers movement and the work of activists like Cesar Chavez and Delores Huerta. In 1987, when I was fourteen, my friends and I joined Chavez's hunger strike during the grape boycott.[1] I had to answer a lot of questions about not eating grapes, particularly after I passed out in the pool during swim practice. But once I learned about the dangers of using pesticides on foods and about the plight of most farm workers, I had to act.[2] I believed that if people only knew of the working and living conditions of the people who provide our nation's food, then something would change.

During the time of my hunger strike, I made a grocery trip with my mother. I entered the store and saw grapes in the produce section. I asked to see the managing grocer. I wanted to know where the grapes had come from and to educate the grocer about the plight of the farm workers. It took a bit of persuading, but finally someone came out to speak to me. I told him about the working and living conditions, the pesticides, the harassment, and the discrimination. Quite a crowd of shoppers had formed, unnoticed by me. I vividly remember catching a look in his eyes and realizing that not only was he not interested in what I was saying but he was irritated, and, to my surprise, I realized that I was the source of his irritation. How could he not care? I was in disbelief. I was frustrated. I was upset. But, more than anything, I was outraged. He was saying something, but I could barely make sense of it through my cloud of confusion. He wanted me to leave. I was causing a disturbance. So I did the only thing that I could think of. I grabbed a bunch of grapes and raised them above my head. Shaking them in my fists, and in the deepest, most serious fourteen-year-old voice I could muster, I yelled, "These grapes have blood on them!" I slammed the grapes against the floor. Only then did I notice the crowd. I spun around and marched out of the store. I wasn't sure where I was headed, but I had to move. A few minutes later, my mom was at my side, saying it would be a long time until we would or could go back to that store. I wasn't sure if she was speaking in support of me or out of embarrassment because of what I had just done. I didn't care.

It wasn't until just a few years ago that I found out that the grocer had tried to make my mother pay for the grapes. Not only did she refuse, but she left her shopping cart in the middle of the produce section and left the store. We never shopped there again.

My early stages of activism were so filled with passion and outrage that I was often unsure of what to do with myself. I was angry a lot and embraced the saying "If you're not outraged, you're not paying attention." Many people told me that I overwhelmed them, that I turned people off to what I was saying because I yelled. I never thought that I yelled; I thought I spoke with passion. These responses were hard to understand because I thought I had a message people needed to hear, quite frankly, whether they thought so or not. I was learning so much, and my awareness of the issues was growing, perhaps faster than my diplomatic skills. I was searching for my voice and a way to use it effectively.

Around this time, my mother began to find her voice—or at least a new one. At forty-one, she became a re-entry student at the University of California, Santa Cruz, and took classes with, and later became a teacher's assistant to, Bettina Aptheker, a women's studies instructor and a long-time activist. And, while the experience and transformation was hers, as her daughter, I was deeply affected. I would often beg my mother to take me to class with her. I had grown up in a predominately female family, one that supported strong women, but I had not been widely exposed to the political nature of being female in a male-dominated society. I grew up on a ranch with two sisters where there were no boys to do the "boys' work" and with a father who had no sons and who didn't see that as a deficiency. I grew up being told that I could do anything that I put my mind to and that my voice mattered. This, as I began to learn in Aptheker's class, was not the norm. I sat in huge lecture halls, and, while I learned about women's empowerment and many political victories, I also began to learn about violence, oppression, racism, sexism, and homophobia. And, again, I was outraged.

Four years later, when I left my mother's college for my own, I looked around for the feminist community, and I found NOW, the National Organization for Women. I began a relationship that would change the course of my life. Not in my wildest dreams did I ever imagine that, a few years later, at age twenty-eight, I would become California NOW's youngest president, leading the largest statewide feminist organization in the country. I soon found myself a part of an active, vocal, and diverse group of young women and men who considered ourselves third-wave feminists. We were (and are) in a unique position of working alongside many second-wave feminists, those who came of age in the 1960s and 1970s. I am indebted to the people who mentored and guided me, women who fought similar battles before me, who had an understanding of the "big picture," and who could guide me to more effective ways of using my voice. At the same time, I believe that those of us who consider ourselves "third wavers" have something unique to offer. As a result of the efforts of our foremothers, we came of age with many of the rights and advantages that they did not have. We didn't have to fight for the right to be educated or to have a career; we could choose to obtain a safe and legal abortion, if we wanted one; we did not have to fight these struggles because the women and men who came before us already had. With these battles already waged, many of us were all the stronger, which in turn informed our experience with feminism. As third wavers join with second wavers, we need to build intergenerational partnerships in which we incorporate the knowledge and experience of the women who came before us and the knowledge and experience of women who are now coming of age.

Today, there are a variety of organizations working for women's rights, in the United States and worldwide. I continue to work with a number of these organizations, but I initially chose NOW because I appreciate its longevity and its focus on a variety of social justice issues. NOW addresses the many concerns that we face as women—from economic justice to reproductive rights. Joining gave me the invaluable experience of "hands-on" work in the women's movement. I was trained to work with the media on political and public education campaigns. I learned how to lead and how to make change happen. As a result of my involvement, I have had tremendous opportunities to work with, and to learn from, other feminist leaders.

These experiences have taught me more than I could ever learn from a book. Education is more than what you read or what occurs in a

classroom. One of the great possibilities of women's studies and feminism is the opportunity they present for action-based learning. Intern-
ships, chapter leadership, and community activism all provide "hands-
on" experience and offer the opportunity to learn by doing. Through activism, we can learn from the experience of communities and develop
community-based solutions to change the world.

One of the most significant aspects of the women's movement is
that it gives validity to women's voices and to women's experiences.
Throughout history, women have fought against the notion that they
have little or nothing to contribute to politics or society. They have
fought to have their voices heard, their experiences recognized, and
their leadership respected. But, even within the context of the women's
movement, our voices have sometimes been misrepresented. For example, in the 1960s, when middle-class white women like Betty Friedan
began to talk about the frustration of being relegated to the home and
their desire to be in the paid labor force, they represented only one part
of women's experiences. At the same time, women of color and poor
women who had long been in the paid labor force were working without fair wages, safe work environments, or recourse for rampant sexual
harassment. All of these women represented the struggles that became
part of the women's movement. Who got the attention, which stories
were told, and which women were recognized as leaders became a political choice both within and outside the movement that created an
image of feminism that did not fully recognize all its contributors. I
point this out not to be politically correct or to unnecessarily chastise
but rather to suggest that we must embrace the experiences, perspectives, and leadership of all women if this movement is to continue to
move forward and effect positive change. That's the kind of movement
that I envision and that I hope to give voice to here.

As president of California NOW, I had the opportunity to benefit
from reputation, history, and global recognition, but I had also been
called on to address criticism and explain the relevance both of NOW
and of the feminist movement. I recognize that many see feminism as
unnecessary, or too radical, or not radical enough. Many view NOW as
a "white woman's organization" or as a lesbian organization or as
strictly an abortion-rights organization. However, feminism and NOW
represent women of color, poor women, young women, disabled
women, mothers, working women, lesbians—all women. But the
media, and those who actively oppose feminism, have created a cam-

paign against our movement. From the 1998 *Time* magazine cover claiming that feminism is dead to the radio talk shows of Laura Schlesinger and Rush Limbaugh to the writings of conservative women like Christine Hoff Sommers and Anne Coulter, the so-called horrors of feminism have been force-fed to a new generation. This media hype has had a lasting imprint on the women's movement and continues to divert attention from the true goals of feminism—ending discrimination against all women and girls, securing our safety, protecting our health, ensuring equal opportunities, and respecting our sexual identities.

I began to write this book after many conversations about the relevance of feminism today and after answering seemingly endless questions about young women in the movement. Questions came from active feminists, media interviews, friends, and family, all wanting to know, where are the young people in feminism today? Do they care? Are they active? Are they apathetic? I wrote this book because I see a great deal of activism among young people, but also a generation that doesn't feel that this movement belongs to them or that there is a seat at the table for their ideas and leadership. On the other hand, I see a generation of women who benefit from the gains of the feminist movement, who align themselves with the tenets of feminism but reject the term and any association with the movement. It is an interesting phenomenon that these empowered young women have little, if any, understanding of the fight that was necessary to win their rights and little connection to the fight that must continue to protect and advance rights for all women. Like the generations before us, young women must be able to draw on our experiences, critique our political, social, and economic environments, and create a plan of action for instituting change. As young women, we enter into a movement that has a great deal of history, and as a result we are confronted with the challenge of making a place within feminism to call our own.

OUTREACH FOR *FIGHT LIKE A GIRL*

While I have a tremendous amount of respect for those who came before me, this book focuses upon the voices of a younger generation. I wanted to write a book that explores where my peers, and those coming up behind me, enter the feminist movement—what are the issues today, and how is my generation addressing them? I wanted to create a venue to speak about our concerns and about the movement. In classes, bookstores, meetings and through the Internet, I distributed questionnaires with the hopes of capturing the thoughts and ideas of those ages thirty-five and under. I realize that this focus targets a specific population—primarily those who frequent feminist and political listserves or attend feminist meetings. And, as with any questionnaire, I was subject to receiving responses from those who chose to submit. Despite all this, I was thrilled and surprised to see how far my questionnaire traveled. I received responses from all over the United States—from urban and rural areas, from coastal and mountainous regions, from universities and colleges, from community centers and after-school programs. Most of my respondents were college-age, though not always in college. Most were activists, but many were not involved in formal organizations. Some teachers and professors made the questionnaire a requirement in their classes or gave extra credit for its completion. Respondents passed the questionnaire on to friends and to members of other listserves and book groups and to attendees at various meetings. The questionnaire found its way to people in Canada who were eager to respond. I used this information to help me in my understanding of today's young feminists and also have pulled quotes that you'll find scattered throughout the book. I asked each respondent to self-identify, which, as you will see, led to a great variety of self-definition. It was important to me to use the respondents' language despite the risk of appearing "politically incorrect," as well as to show our diversity as a generation and as a movement. There is no single third-wave voice but rather a multitude of ideas and a commitment among us to respect differing perspectives.

This book focuses on the voices of my generation. I share my experiences as someone who is thirty-something, involved in the movement, and a self-proclaimed third-wave feminist. I discuss my thoughts and my fears for the world we live in today. Beyond my voice, you will hear from women, men, and trans individuals who have volunteered their opinions and views on social-justice issues and the meaning of feminism in their lives.

This book is a rebuttal to the message that feminism is dead and that young people are apathetic. It is a call to action. Dispelling the myths of feminism and detailing what is at stake for women and girls today, I outline the steps for taking action toward political, social, and economic equity for all. Exploring the issues of body image and self-acceptance, education and empowerment, health and sexuality, political representation, economic justice and violence, this book looks at the challenges that women and girls face, while emphasizing the strength that we, both independently and collectively, embody. Additionally, I delve into the politics of the feminist movement from both inside and outside the movement, exploring both history and current realities. With an emphasis on young women, I discuss what the movement and activism mean to youth today. I look at how and where we encounter feminist ideas and activism—including the challenges to building multiracial, multicultural bridges and to forging intergenerational partnerships.

Perhaps more important, I want the book to be used, not just read. I have included a variety of resources to aid in taking action, including an "On My Bookshelf" section that includes titles for further reading; "Fabulous Feminist Web Resources," with lists of Web sites that offer more information and an organizational community; "Spotlight" sections that are designed to give the reader more information about a specific issue or campaign; and sections that suggest actions that call for varying degrees of involvement—Getting Started, The Next Step, and Getting Out There. But this book is far from an exhaustive list of activism. My hope is that you will use this as a reference and begin to build your own set of books, resources, and organizations you can work with and to develop your own activist strategies. For the fight for justice belongs to us all. We must educate ourselves, empower one another, and unite under a common vision of creating a just society.

I write this book with this vision, looking critically at the issues that impact our lives, putting women at the center, and defining issues from the perspectives of those most affected. My focus is on self-exploration, self-discovery, and self-definition. I believe that we must speak up for what we believe in, work to end discrimination and oppression, question that which already is and envision what is still to come. Women and girls must be shown that they are valuable, strong, beautiful, and capable. I believe in the assertion that we are entitled to equal rights—including the right to be respected in our homes and workplaces and in our choices. I believe we must learn our history so that we know the contributions of our foremothers. I believe in the safety, health, education, economic security, independence, and free will of all. In this book, I want to reclaim the idea of fighting like a girl—a phrase that is usually meant to suggest that those who fight like girls, as opposed to fighting like men, don't really know how to fight and that their struggle is not real, not intense, not legitimate—just hair pulling and nail scratching. I don't agree with that characterization at all. I know how to fight, and I know plenty of women whose struggles are all too real, all too harrowing, all too dangerous. I'm here to say that not only can we fight like girls; we can win.

The F-Word
An Introduction

FEMINIST.
Bitch.
Fat.
Ugly.
Dyke.
Man hater.
Bra burner.
Hairy.
Butch.
Loud.
Militant.
Radical.
Angry.

These are some of the negative words that regularly surface when I ask people what comes to mind when they hear the word "feminist." But, for me, "independence," "strength," and "equality" come to mind when I think of feminism. After thirty-plus years of the modern feminist movement, many young people have negative ideas about feminism. Ironically, these same people reap the benefits of feminism in their own lives. From Title IX[1] and educational equity to political representation, women in the United States have greater social, political, and economic equality today than their mothers experienced a generation ago. First and foremost, feminism simply means that women are the equals of men. A feminist is someone who supports this principle. Study after study tells us that the majority of people in the United States agree with this, but fewer and fewer want to identify with feminism. "Feminism" has thus become a bad word, the "f-word."

> **fem·i·nism,** *n.* **1. a doctrine advocating social, political, and economic rights for women equal to those of men. 2. a movement for the attainment of such rights.**
>
> **(Definitions, unless otherwise noted, come from *Random House Webster's College Dictionary*)**

I come to feminism from a different view, a view that suggests that feminism is about equality and also empowerment, strength, self-definition, and self-determination. It is an assertion that all women and girls can have not just equality in their lives but also quality of life—in the United States and around the globe. Feminism is about advocacy, activism, standing up, and speaking out. It is about fighting for social justice. And it is about working toward a solution to the continued discrimination and violence we as women face in the world—rape, sexual harassment, trafficking, sexual assault, and domestic violence. Feminism is about eradicating not just sexism but also racism, ageism, ableism,[2] sizeism,[3] and homophobia. Most of all, feminism does not have a static definition but encompasses and encourages many types of feminisms. So why do some turn away from feminism today?

THE MYTHS ABOUT FEMINISM

Many myths surround the term "feminism." The word has been distorted, diluted, misrepresented, stolen. So let's take a moment to break a few of these myths down.

Do All Feminists Hate Men?

No. It's more complicated than that. Take my friend "Jane." When Jane was five, the boys in her school wouldn't let her play on the big playground. She wanted to climb and pretend to be a firefighter like the boys did, but they teased her and pushed her off the jungle gym every time she tried to participate. When she was seven, she wanted to play football, but there was only a boys' team in her town. She was not allowed to play. When she was in high school, she was frequently frustrated that the boys' athletic teams had more resources—better equipment, new uniforms, and better practice times—than did the girls' teams. These inequities have long been a source of frustration for Jane. Does this mean that Jane hates all men? No. Does she realize that there have been times in her life that her gender has caused her to be discriminated against? Yes. This awareness is disturbing and makes her apt to speak up about her experiences, but it doesn't

> The word "feminist" has a lot of negative stereotypes, for example the term "femi-nazi" and the fact that feminists are depicted as fat, angry, bitter, butch lesbians who hate men & probably couldn't get one if they tried.
> Christina, 21, Korean-Irish American, heterosexual, California

make her hate men. Jane is now married, a successful attorney, and a mother. She is also a feminist. She continues to confront gender inequity, but, like most women, over time, she has learned that what we are up against is not just men—individually or collectively—but a system that values men over women, a system that promotes men over women, and a system that allows and, some would argue, encourages the violation of women. This system is called patriarchy. Patriarchy—the rule of the father—is at the root of a society that exalts men and the male experience—often at the cost of women and women's experience.

> **Pa·tri·arch·y** *n.* **1. a. a** form of social organization in which the father is the head of the family, clan, or tribe and descent is reckoned in the male line. **b.** a society based on this social organization. **2. a.** an institution or organization in which power is held by and transferred through males. **b.** the principles or philosophy upon which control by male authority is based.

My generation doesn't seem to want to talk about patriarchy—it is too boring, too political, and too 1970s. But, like it or not, we must name the system that orders our society if we have any hope of changing that system.

Patriarchy sets a tone for society—a tone that allows for the devaluing of women and our experiences and encourages the interpretation of society through male eyes. Patriarchy allows for the overall—covert and overt—privileging of men and their experiences. As a set of spoken and unspoken rules or codes, patriarchy permeates the world's religions, political systems, and sociocultural structures, which allows for, and supports, the power of men. This explains everything from why for more than 225 years there have been only male presidents in America, to why most Fortune 500 companies are led by men, to why male movie stars often get top billing and are paid more than women. As a system, it's important to understand that patriarchy is also connected to race, class, and sexual orientation. That is, if patriarchy were a pyramid, sitting at the top would be straight, white, rich men. And they would most likely be smiling, because they have had it made for a long time. Women, depending on their race, class, and sexuality, are usually not at the top—yes, there's Hillary and Oprah—but they are the exception and not the rule.

Instead, we live in a time when self-empowerment is sold to women and girls as packaged, magazine-cover "beauty" and when "acceptance" is defined through male attention. As a result, we have women raised in an environment where far too many quietly question their strength, their value, their contribution, and their voice even as they, at times, project a public image of control. Women often embrace a belief that the sexes are treated equally, while accepting the notion that women are on display, and in existence, for male use and pleasure. American society teaches girls that their value and success are tied to their appearance and convince them to embrace this concept as their own self-definition. Playing into the patriarchy, girls dismiss feminism, all the while claiming equality as their right. The "I'm not a feminist but . . ." generation has emerged, denying feminism but embracing its rewards. And thus, in combination with the ongoing attack on feminism, the myths about the movement thrive.

Are All Feminists "Bra Burners"?

The idea of "bra burning" is still commonly associated with the women's movement, although bra burnings never happened, at least not as many were led to believe. In 1968, feminists protested the Miss America pageant and, as Ruth Rosen writes in *The World Split Open*, "into a large 'Freedom Trash Can,' they threw 'instruments of torture'— girdles, curlers, false eyelashes, cosmetics of all kinds, wigs, issues of both *Cosmopolitan* and *Playboy*, and, yes, bras."[4] At the request of city fire officials, the trash can was not lit on fire. The *New York Times* quickly began referring to the event as "bra burning." And, as Rosen writes, "by then, the media, all by itself, had ignited what would prove to be the most tenacious media myth about the women's movement—that women 'libbers' burned their bras as a way of protesting their status in American society."[5] The irony is that a vast number of the world's women do not wear bras, and dare I say that many American women have forgone the experience. But the world has not fallen apart, at least not yet, and when and if it does, I venture to argue that women and their bras will not be at the center of its demise. But, even today, girls and women equate feminism with bra burning and fear an association with such a "radical" movement.

> I don't look like a feminist. I do my hair, wear light make-up, and don't preach anti-men. Kathryn, 32, white, queer, Michigan

But Aren't Feminists Fat, Ugly, and Hairy?

In the tradition of Rush Limbaugh, who called feminists "femi-nazis" and said that "feminism was established to allow unattractive women easier access to the mainstream," this is classic name calling. We might as well be on the playgrounds of elementary school or the quads of high school. The goal of this type of name calling is to attack a woman's self-esteem, to have control over her actions, and to knock her down. If being a feminist means being fat, ugly, and hairy—traits women fear most in a culture that sets a limited definition for women's acceptable beauty—then it is no wonder that many women don't want to be labeled as such. In this sense, Limbaugh and his conservative friends, including women like Christine Hoff Sommers and Anne Coulter, have successfully stolen this word. As Bono once said, we're stealing it back.

From the early stories of "bra burners," the media and our society continue to marginalize women and their intellect, convincing many that our issues are individual, rather than structural and political. The attempt is to convince us that relationships, exercise, weight loss, clothing, and, of course, make-up are the critical issues of our lives. Make-up per se is not the issue. In fact, many women who consider themselves part of today's feminist movement are embracing their lip gloss and demanding equality in spite of it—or maybe because of it! The problem is that society places a higher value on women's appearance than on anything else, including the fight for our social, political, and economic equality. As a result, our energies are diverted, we question, or deny, our worth, and patriarchy lives on.

In 2001, when I was first elected president of the California National Organization for Women (NOW), I was asked to do numerous interviews. Much attention was paid to the fact that I was the youngest woman ever elected president of California NOW, and reporters had great interest in why someone in her twenties would embrace not only NOW but feminism. Perhaps not surprisingly, what most reporters questioned me about was whether a feminist can wear make-up. I had been prepared to talk about economic justice, health care, reproductive freedom, GLBTQQI issues, and violence against women, but they wanted to talk make-up. The more important question is whether this emphasis helps women to identify with feminism. Or does it dilute the perception of its importance? The issues of make-up, or other popular magazine cover topics like relationships and weight loss, certainly should not replace or overshadow our opinions about policy, economics, or politics. Nor should it refute the importance of feminism and a feminist analysis of society.

> *I gave my little sister a book called Feminism Is for Everyone by bell hooks and she told me she couldn't read it because she likes men. Allison, 21, white, pansexual, Colorado*

GLBTQQI: *Gay, Lesbian, Bisexual, Transgender, Queer, Questioning, and Intersex*

Transgender: *as an umbrella term used to describe anyone who is gender different: someone born of one gender, but having either a casual affinity for clothing and/or affectations of the opposite gender; or someone with an innate identification as the opposite gender. Transgenders can range from female impersonators, to crossdressers, to transsexuals—both male to female, and also female to male.*

Intersex: *people who are born with "sex chromosomes," external genitalia, or internal reproductive systems that are not considered "standard" for either male or female.*

(Definitions for "transgender" and "intersex" are provided by the National Transgender Advocacy Coalition.)

Are All Feminists Dykes and Butch?

Let's face it, society is uncomfortable with women's sexualities. Perhaps nothing is more frightening to men, and to some women, than a woman whose sexuality is defined outside the context of straight men. Moreover, when women are butch—strong, tough, and unfeminine—they are also threatening because they are seen as not needing male help. If women can take care of themselves and each other—physically and sexually—then what do they need men for? The irony is that we have a culture obsessed with lesbianism—well, faux lesbianism, at least. Sexual pairing of women is common in male-centered porn and advertising. Of course, these women are not there for the enjoyment of other women—but for men, they are the ultimate male fantasy. Calling all feminists lesbian, dyke, or butch is to equate women with these notions of being unfeminine and sexually independent from men. This negative labeling reinforces a narrow definition of woman and femaleness. It is true that many feminists are lesbian, dyke, and/or butch. It is also true that many are not. The more important and disturbing point is the widespread belief of this myth and the acceptance of the notion that homosexuality is an accusation. Homophobia is the problem, not feminism.

Is Feminism Needed Any More?

As I previously mentioned, we are often confronted with the sentiment "I'm not a feminist but. . . ." Many believe today that feminism is no longer necessary, that equality has been achieved and that any hardship women encounter must be the result of their own actions. I suppose that this is an understandable reaction, given the feminist message that women can do anything. In other words, if women believe this message but have difficulty in achieving their dreams, then it must be their failure. The myths that surround feminism play into this feeling of failure and discourage women from aligning themselves with feminism. This makes it much more difficult to recognize that discrimination against women is real and that often gender serves as the source of the barrier, rather than personal "failures." Making feminism the enemy redirects our attention away from that which serves to hold us back. Instead, we need to be able to celebrate our successes and be proud of ourselves even while appreciating that feminism helped open the way to our opportunities. I have known many women friends who are talented and who work very hard in their careers but who have faced challenges because of their gender. My sister, an audiologist who works with people with hearing difficulties, frequently confronts the assumption that since she has had children and is married, her career is no longer important or has become secondary to that of her husband and colleagues. She confronts a lack of support with regard to her childcare needs, lack of flexibility with her schedule, barriers to advancement, and attitudes of resentment from colleagues. She is a strong feminist and fortunately recognizes that her work situation is the result of gender bias and discrimination. She also recognizes that solutions to this work-life integration lie in feminist tenets. It is feminism that asserts that we need better support for the multiple family models that exist today—stay-at-home moms, moms in the workplace, dual-parent-earner households, single parents, and all the many combinations we create that constitute family. We still need the support of feminism in our lives and in achieving our many goals.

Aren't All Feminists Angry?

A few years ago, I was invited to speak in a classroom at San Francisco City College. The discussion was great—we covered topics from health care and reproductive rights to pay equity and the glass ceiling. And then . . . the inevitable. From the back of the room, a young man raised his hand and said something to the effect that he understands all the "stuff" we were talking about but just can't get over the "fact" that most feminists he meets are so angry—"Not you, Ms. Seely," he quickly added. I asked him, and the class, why, given all that we had been discussing, they thought that feminists get an angry label? I guess this young man could see where I was headed, and he blurted out, "Well, I can understand the anger, but why are they so bitchy?" Here we have it—feminists are "angry bitches." Why is it that a woman who gets angry is immediately called a bitch? Why, when people are speaking of angry women, are these two terms synonymous? A man may put his fist through a wall, and, while we may think him foolish, we rarely demean his character. But we are extremely uncomfortable with women's anger. Are people afraid that if women get angry enough, they might revolt? Indeed, our collective anger might cause a stir—to say the least. But, instead, we women learn to control ourselves, not speak out of turn, keep our voices and our heads low, and ask for qualifiers for our speech.

Of course I'm a feminist—everyone should be, if they believe that all people are equal. Cassie, 19, Caucasian, straight, California

But my question is: Why *aren't* we angry? All of us—female, male, trans, intersex alike? And why aren't we speaking up and acting out? I believe that the stereotypes I have described were assigned to feminists because of fear—fear of women collectively speaking out and standing up to the gross inequities and atrocities we face daily and globally. Years ago, Robin Morgan said that sisterhood is global, and it is timely to remember this and that collective sisterhood is even more powerful. What would the world look like if we said "no more"? No more to violence, no more to inequity, no more to lack of representation. What if women stood together, joined forces, and understood the common thread of oppression we collectively face? What if we realized our power? What if?

We live in a culture where women are not safe in their homes, workplaces, or schools, or on the street, where a woman is sexually assaulted every two minutes,[6] where 1.9 million women are physically abused every year in the United States,[7] and where 40 to 90 percent of women experience sexual harassment on the job[8] and 85 percent of girls report experiencing sexual harassment at school.[9] Women are stalked, intimated, humiliated, violated in their everyday lives and also in their "make-believe lives" of entertainment—on television, in movies, and in video games.

Only 15 percent of the members of Congress are women.[10] Women hold only 14.7 percent of all Fortune 500 board seats[11] and "hold decision-making leadership positions equivalent to chief executive officers in only three national unions."[12] Women still experience pay inequity based on both gender *and* race. According to the National Women's Law Center, women earned on average 77 percent of what white men made in 2004.[13] When race is considered, these statistics change dramatically; African American women earn 67 percent and Latina women 56 percent of what white men made in 2004.[14] According to the National Committee on Pay Equity, individual earnings data for Asian/Pacific Islanders and Native Americans are based on samples that are too small to be reliable.

Women have to fundraise with benefits, walks, runs, and the like to raise money for health research and services because our issues are disproportionately ignored by the National Institute of Health and other research arms. Women pay 68 percent more than men in out-of-pocket medical costs,[15] one in five women of reproductive age is uninsured,[16] and, although abortion has been legal for more than thirty years, women still travel extended distances, suffer shame and blame, walk through dangerous picket lines, and put themselves at risk—not because of the abortion itself, which is ten times safer than childbirth[17] and even safer than a tonsillectomy[18]—but because of anti-choice extremists who believe that picketing, violence, and fire bombing are "pro-life" acts. And, yes, this makes me angry.

If all this were not enough, in the year 2006, we still have no constitutional amendment securing rights on the basis of sex—or sexual orientation, for that matter. To the contrary, efforts to pass an ERA (Equal Rights Amendment) are minimal, and we have a U.S. president who is actively trying to amend the Constitution to "protect" heterosexual marriage, as opposed to securing equality for all. I don't know what is more disturbing—these facts or the fact that the majority of people today believe that the ERA is passé or that there is any kind of threat to heterosexual marriage that needs defending against—not to mention the absurdity of a government, or a population, that believes that the country can legislate who people love.

With violence in our lives, pay inequity and a lack of equal representation at work, challenges in balancing family demands without adequate support or accommodation, inadequate access to and research on women's health issues, politics that define our rights without our being fully represented in the decision-making process, women continue to fight for their equality. We have made many gains, but we are not there yet. Better, yes; equal, no. Perhaps more disturbing than all these realities is that so many people today believe that women are equal—that it's all good, no worries. Well, there are worries, and perhaps the first and most significant worry is that people—particularly women—continue to believe that equality exists even in the face of so much evidence to the contrary.

Why am I a part of the feminist movement? Me, a generation Xer? Because my anger is legitimate. And because I believe that passivity is exactly what the Radical Right wants from us so that it can continue to violate our rights and limit our resources. I also believe that anger is useful when we channel that energy into creating positive social change and improving lives. I believe that women are fierce—we are leaders, role models, and visionaries. I believe that we deserve more; we deserve better. I am a part of the feminist movement because I want girls to learn our history, to know our strength, to appreciate the gains made, and to pick up the fight. I am part of this movement because women have no secure future without feminism. I benefited from the work of feminists before me, and I will continue that work until all women everywhere enjoy a life of true social, political, and economic equality. And I am a part of this movement because, when the next generation of children ask me what I did to help, I want to be able to tell them that I did do something, that I thought of them in my actions and fought for their safety, their health, and their right to equal opportunity.

So what about these myths and labels? There's no question that the backlash that writers like Susan Faludi have written about is real. But there is also no question that women and girls are at risk. I believe that it is more important to counter these attacks on feminism with the truth of our lives. The biggest truth is that feminism, in its true definition, is supported by a majority of women. Ask women to tell their stories. Talk to your mothers and grandmothers. Learn our history—particularly the history that has been left out of our school books. Tell your story. One of the greatest gains of the feminist movement was that it recognized the legitimacy of women's voices. Use yours. Stand up. Speak out. And speak often.

WOMEN HAVE THE FEMINIST MOVEMENT TO THANK IF . . .

You vote.

You read.

You wear pants, skirts cut above your ankle, short-sleeved shirts, or any clothing that shows your skin.

You travel without a male chaperone or you drive a car.

You use, or have ever used, birth control. Or your birth control is covered by your insurance company or by state or federal funds.

You have had, or anyone you know has had, a safe and legal abortion.

You have given birth at home; developed a birth plan that was utilized during your hospital birth; your partner was present for the delivery; you have adopted a child; or you have chosen not to have children.

You own property or have credit cards or a bank account in your name.

You participate in sports.

You have run for and/or held elected office, worked on the campaign of a woman who was running for office, or voted for a woman candidate.

You have a job in the paid labor force or actively choose to stay home in the unpaid labor force to raise children.

You go to college.

You are studying religion or have become a member of the clergy.

You are openly lesbian, living with a partner; you share domestic partnership; or you were married as part of a same-sex couple.

You choose to marry, to keep your last name, to build an egalitarian marriage, or to cohabitate or remain single; you have the right to divorce.

You marry whom you want to (almost, we're still working on this one!).

You leave an abusive husband or report a rape or sexual harassment—you have legal recourse for violence against you.

Wearing corsets is a choice, not a mandate, as is wearing make-up, a bra, or high heels.

You serve in the armed forces and receive veteran's benefits.

You decide to cook or become a chef.

You pierce or tattoo any part of your body.

You climb trees, run, jump, do somersaults, or skin your knees.

SPOTLIGHT ON FEMINISM

Sometimes I feel like my whole life has been a process of coming into feminism and being a feminist. Mandy, 27, white, queer, New York

Women want equal rights ... who wouldn't be for that besides people who are threatened by a strong willed woman who doesn't need to depend on a man? Katrina, 22, African American, lesbian, Virginia

I think that I've always been a "feminist," even before I knew it or knew what the term meant. Morgan, 27, white, heterosexual, California

It would be foolish for me to NOT identify as a feminist since the educational, social and career opportunities that I enjoy are a direct result of past feminist struggles. Mingzhao, 21, Chinese American, heterosexual, California

As a feminist, I am often teased. People have called me a "femi-Nazi," a term I abhor and, as a Jew, find repulsive. Amy, 23, Washington, DC

Personally I love the word and am proud to identify as a feminist. The word has been stolen from us and we need to reclaim it, redefine it for our generation and what's going on in our world now. Katherine, 23, Caucasian, bisexual, Florida

I am a feminist because I never liked hearing camp counselors ask for "big strong boys" to help set up the bonfire and "nice young ladies" to set out the picnic. I am a feminist because I got sick of reading textbooks written by white/heterosexual/able-bodied/middle-class men about themselves, and the god-like role they had played in shaping the whole human history. I am a feminist because I am scared to think that men can pass laws that limit my reproductive freedom. I am a feminist because I believe in compassion for all living things, and damn a world that says might makes right. Elspeth, 22, bisexual, Michigan

It was with extreme trepidation that I decided to become a self-declared feminist. I was very familiar with the implications of such a declaration in terms of how society would perceive me ... In reality, I had always been a feminist because I have always believed in the equality of men and women. Marina, 21, Cuban, California

There's no, "I'm a feminist but ..." for me. I'm a feminist. Period. Cynthia, 33, white, heterosexual, Massachusetts

ON MY BOOKSHELF

Paula Gunn Allen, ed., *Studies In American Indian Literature* (New York: Moderna Language Association of American, 1983).

Gloria Anzaldua, ed., *Making Face, Making Soul/Haciendo Caras: Creative and Critical Perspectives by Women of Color* (California: Aunt Lute Books, 1990).

Gloria Anzaldúa and Analouise Keating, eds., *This Bridge We Call Home* (New York: Routledge, 2002).

Margaret Atwood, *The Handmaid's Tale* (Boston: Houghton Mifflin, 1986).

Patricia Hill Collins, *Black Feminist Thought: Knowledge, Consciousness, and the Politics of Empowerment* (New York: Routledge, 1991).

Angela Davis, *Women, Race and Class* (New York: Vintage Books, 1981).

Susan Faludi, *Backlash: The Undeclared War Against American* (New York: Anchor Books/Doubleday, 1991).

Barbara Findlen, ed., *Listen Up: Voices for the Next Feminist Generation* (Seattle: Seal Press, 2001).

Estelle Freedman, *No Turning Back: The History of Feminism and the Future of Women* (New York: Ballantine Books, 2002).

Susan Jane Gilman, *Kiss My Tiara* (New York: Warner Books, 2001).

Daisy Hernández and Bushra Rehman, eds., *Colonize This! Young Women of Color on Today's Feminism* (New York: Seal Press, 2002).

bell hooks, *Feminism Is for Everybody* (Cambridge, MA: South End Press, 2000).

bell hooks, *Feminist Theory: From Margin to Center* (Cambridge, MA: South End Press, 1984).

Gloria Hull, Patricia Bell Scott, and Barbara Smith, eds., All the Women Are White, All the Blacks Are Men, But Some of Us Are Brave: Black Women's Studies (New York: Feminist Press, 1986).

Marcelle Karp and Debbie Stoller, eds., *The Bust Guide to the New Girl Order* (New York: Penguin Books, 1999).

Joan Morgan, *When Chicken-Heads Come Home to Roost: A Hip-Hop Feminist Breaks It Down* (New York: Touchstone, 1999).

Robin Morgan, ed., *Sisterhood Is Forever: The Women's Anthology for a New Millennium* (New York: Washington Square Press, 2003).

Ruth Rosen, *The World Split Open: How the Modern Women's Movement Changed America* (New York: Penguin Books, 2000).

Jessica Salmonson, *Encyclopedia of Amazons: Women Warriors from Antiquity to the Modern Era* (New York: Anchor Books, 1992).

Miriam Schneir, ed., *Feminism in Our Time: The Essential Writings, World War II to the Present* (New York: Vintage Books, 1994).

Sonia Sanchez, *Homegirls and Handgrenades* (New York: Thunder's Mouth Press, 1984).

Bonnie Smith, *The Gender of History: Men, Women, and Historical Practice* (Cambridge, MA: Harvard University Press, 1998).

Starhawk, *The Fifth Sacred Thing* (New York: Bantam Books, 1993).

Gloria Steinem, *Outrageous Acts and Everyday Rebellions* (Texas: Holt, Rinehart, and Winston, 1987).

Rebecca Walker, ed., *To Be Real* (New York: Anchor Books Doubleday, 1995).

1

Fight Like a Girl

In my work as an activist and teacher, I hear people ask, "What can I do?" One of the main goals of this book is to answer that question. Activism can often seem out of reach, but in truth the best part of activism is that anyone can do it. Activism can easily be incorporated into our daily lives—from the conversations we have with friends to where we decide to shop. Activism is individual, but it is also collective. The action we take impacts those around us directly and indirectly. Whether small and individual or large and in a group, the steps we take to change the world connect us with others. True equality and respect have not yet been achieved; activism is still necessary. Sharing our realities to educate one another on the challenges that persist is an important step to politicizing our lives and recognizing that the issues we face are shared by others. The largest hurdle to activism is finding commonalities with one another so that we share the common goal of ending all discrimination and creating a world where we are not only treated but also regarded as equal. Beyond this hurdle, we learn that all of our voices are valid, that activism takes many forms, and that activism can be incorporated into every aspect of our lives.

As young adults today, we are confronted with the challenge of how to strike a balance between our desires and our social responsibilities. We have inherited a sense of equality that leads us to believe that the fight for justice is complete. We are told that feminism and social change are no longer necessary. Unfortunately, the emphasis on individuality, along with the misconception that equality has already been achieved, leads to the failure to fully appreciate the necessity of activism and feminism.

Let there be no mistake—equality is not yet enjoyed by all, and feminism is not dead. Indeed, we have achieved many rights and made many gains, but we are not there yet. The fight for true political, social, and economic justice continues. And, while we often enjoy the benefits of a fight for equality that we were not required to undertake, we must realize that this equality is not universal and that it is this generation that must take up the fight. This movement belongs to us all. We each have a stake; we all can contribute. All voices, experiences, perspectives, and visions can be incorporated and represented, for we all benefit from shared and practiced equality. We can raise our voices to speak against injustice at every level—individually and institutionally. We can elect people to office at every level of government who will honor and protect us all. We need to make sure that women are represented in leadership in every social institution within our global society—so that women are represented in any and all decision-making bodies. Women must have control over their bodies, sexualities, choices, and lives. Women must be safe at each and every turn—no exception. We can join together, work together, protect and support one another. We can be individuals who also find a common ground from which to speak collectively. We can share our stories, lead by example, and be activists in our daily lives. This is what it means to fight like a girl.

> *It is terrifying how many gains have been undone or have come under serious attack in just that last two years. It serves as a powerful reminder of how much work remains to be done.*
> Jen, 30, white, heterosexual, Colorado

Grass roots *n.* 1. ordinary citizens, esp. as contrasted with the leadership or elite. 2. the people inhabiting these areas, esp. as a political, social, or economic group. 3. the origin or basis of something.

Ac·tiv·ism *n.* the practice of vigorous action or involvement as a means of achieving political or other goals, as by demonstrations, protests, etc.—ac·tiv·ist, *n., adj.*

HOW TO FIGHT LIKE A GIRL

No act is too small; you may never know the full extent of your impact. Activism is contagious. While you may be one person, your voice and actions can touch others, whose voices and actions can touch still others, and so forth until we experience change. This is how activism works. This is how Title IX was achieved, how sexual harassment was recognized, how laws are passed and policies created. Social change begins on a small level with a small group of people who envision a new way. But before we get too far, let's get right to it. Here are some actions you can take:

- Talk to friends, family, students, and/or co-workers about political or social issues that concern you. Gather information to share with them from organizations, Web sites, books, or classes.
- Make a phone call to an elected official, advertising sponsor, business, or school to let them know how you feel about their policies, practices, or products.
- Write a letter to the editor of your local newspaper in response to an article about women, health care, politics, or any issue that interests you.
- Set up a table to give out information in your community or on your campus. You may need to get permission from your campus or community business, or check into using a free-speech area. Make sure that you stand in front of the table to hand out materials and answer questions—don't hide behind the table; be accessible. Let the table hold your materials, not you! One variation to a table is sidewalk chalking. When I was in college, we did a sidewalk chalking where we wrote meeting and event information on the sidewalk in front of the student union and main buildings—requires less people power and still gets your message out!
- Host a consciousness raising group—bring together friends, family, or colleagues to discuss an important issue.
- Organize a house party to educate and mobilize your friends to vote or to support a feminist candidate running for office. Invite people to come over to discuss an upcoming election—have each participant research a different issue and bring the information to the group. Make it a potluck, or meet over coffee.
- Work on a voter registration campaign; register people in your community to vote in the next election.
- Offer to watch the children of someone you know so that the person can go to the polls and vote.
- Give testimony at your local city hall or before the state legislature or Congress.

- Organize a human billboard action—gather some friends to line a main street in your town with signs that have a message, each sign carrying a portion of the message: for example, "Honk . . . if you . . . support . . . equality."

- Organize a candlelight vigil to raise awareness about an issue or to commemorate an important event/date. After a series of clinic bombings in northern California, I participated in a candlelight vigil that served a dual purpose—the vigil raised awareness about violence directed toward our reproductive healthcare providers and also provided some much-needed protection for a specific health center. We surrounded the building in shifts and camped out to protect the health center from attack that night.

- Organize a speakout, like the Take Back the Night rallies where women have the opportunity to speak about their experiences with violence in a safe and supportive environment. This can be done with any issue.

- Organize an informational picket—make signs, bring together a bunch of people, and walk back and forth in front of a business, courthouse, or legislature, sharing information with people passing by.

- Boycott—a boycott is the withholding of financial support (e.g., by refusing to buy a particular product) as a form of protest against the policies or practices of a business, institution, or organization. There are many legal guidelines for a boycott, so make sure to get legal advice before calling for one.

- Plan a girlcott or a "boycott" related to a specifically woman-centered cause. Sometimes, a "girlcott" is defined as bringing resources into an organization, business, or institution to support their efforts—in other words, the opposite of a boycott.

- Organize street theater. Dress up and act out your concerns in a public venue. During the 2000 elections, I was one of nine people who dressed up as the Supreme Court justices and then held a press conference about what we saw as a threat to the Court.

- Organize a benefit—for example, a walk-a-thon, a concert, a comedy night, an art show.

- Organize a rally—small, medium, or large. Have people come together in a central location to hear speakers and receive information about a given event.

- Organize a march—small, medium, or large. Have people gather in one place, hear speakers, and then walk in an organized fashion to another location. People carry signs with political messages and sign and shout chants to raise awareness about an important issue. Most notably, in April 2004, the feminist movement hosted the March for Women's Lives in Washington, D.C., to emphasize the critical issues that women are facing today. The march has been called the largest march in U.S. history, with approximately 1.15 million participants![1]

The possibilities for action are endless; I've provided just a few ideas that I've taught. Talk to organizations, talk to friends, and come up with your own ideas. Don't let taking action overwhelm you; start at the level you are comfortable. Throughout this book, I offer suggestions for actions you can take related to the issues discussed in the book. Again, this list is not exhaustive. Be creative. Have fun.

Regardless of the type of action you plan, there are a few guidelines that always apply:

Don't try to do it all on your own. Involve others—delegate responsibility.

Develop a realistic time line and follow it.

Imagine all the things that could go wrong, and plan for contingencies in advance.

Develop a media strategy from the beginning.

Fundraise and recruit new people to help with future actions.

STEPS TO TAKING ACTION

Activism is critically important, and it should be fun. Participants, observers, and the press all respond better to something that is creative and fun. You don't have to do activism on your own; invite others to join. Share the planning and the responsibilities. Look for creative funding to support the event—remember, there are many useful donations besides just money. Don't be afraid to ask. Many grocery stores and shops are happy to support your work, and they can donate supplies, food, drinks, advertising, or prizes. When asking a company, make sure that it is a company with which you want to be associated. For example, given Wal-Mart's consistent opposition to unionizing and its track record of treating women workers unfairly, I don't want to be connected to the store in any way. I particularly don't want to give it recognition for donating to my event.

The following are twelve steps to help you in taking action.[2] I include these steps to give you the full range of assistance for the largest event you can take. Note, however, that not everyone will plan a major event. Depending on the size and extent of your action, you may not need all twelve steps. Remember, activism has many levels; start where you are comfortable and build from there.

1. *Define the issue that you want to raise awareness on.* Does the problem concern reproductive rights, motherhood, economic justice, ending violence against women, the environment, the media or young feminist issues, or something else?

2. *Work with other activists, and dialogue the issue to clarify the feminist analysis of the problem and the solution.* Keep in mind everyone's perspective, and be inclusive: How does this issue affect young women, women of color, lesbians, mothers, disabled women, or older women?

3. *Decide what action to take.* Should you picket, create street theater, host a speak-out or a candlelight vigil, organize a mass rally, or present testimony to your local government on the issue? What action would best address the issue you want to raise awareness on?

4. *Decide where to hold the action.* Try to make the place of the action symbolic of the issue you want to raise. If the issue concerns the courts, demonstrate at the courthouse. Scout the location to anticipate any needs or problems with the site. Check to see if you need permits or insurance. Make sure you check to see that the date you choose does not conflict with holidays or other community events that will diminish your success. And make sure

the site is accessible to the disabled and to public transportation. Is there childcare or activities for children?

5. *Decide whom to invite to speak on the issue on which you want to raise awareness.* Make sure you represent the community affected by the issue, as well as a good spectrum of supporters. Don't have too many speakers, and don't let the speeches go on too long; two to five minutes is a good amount of time. If you have a main speaker, you can give that person a bit more time. Get someone to provide sign language for your action. Invite entertainers like musicians or poets, if you can. Make sure you have the appropriate equipment needed—for example, a microphone, a sound system.

> *Without young voices demanding an open, informed, and fair dialogue, the moneyed status quo will always prevail.*
> Kemble, 26, male, California

6. *Make it a visual action.* Brainstorm on slogans for posters and signs. Think about what props you could bring or create. Also, think about what you all will wear—are there costumes that would relate to your topic and create a point of interest? The goal is to stand out!

7. *Create a great name for the event that is clever and media savvy.* Write up chants to use at the action or songs to sing. Get a bull horn(s), and assign someone to lead the chants!

8. *Write a press release and mail, e-mail, or fax it to the appropriate staff person at all your local media.* Contact newspapers, radio, television/cable stations, and any Internet sites that would be appropriate. Work on your short statements to the media, called sound bites. They are usually fifteen- to thirty-second statements that the press will use to represent your action for broadcast. I'll talk more about how to handle the press later in this chapter.

9. *Plan to set up a table or tables for information, and have sign-up sheets for future meetings or actions.* Always table at your own events—it is a great way to get more information out about your activism. Assign a person or two to attend to the table while the event is going on. Choose someone who can answer basic questions—why are you having the event? What is the

goal of the event? When is the next event or meeting? How can someone get involved?

10. *Think about everything that needs to be done* from the start to the finish of your action and assign activists to those tasks. We call that logistics! Write it down. Create a check list.

11. *Make sure you have some fundraising at every action.* As a good friend of mine always says, "The movement won't move without money." Donations = actions! Have a donation jar, or make pledge envelopes for people to take home so they can send in a contribution. Have someone get up and make a pitch for the participants to give donations. Sometimes it can be very intimidating to ask for money, but, remember, you are not asking for yourself; you are asking for the movement.

12. *Once the action is over, have a meeting to debrief on how it went.* Be open, and listen to everyone's feedback. Follow up on any final details—such as returning anything you borrowed or paying outstanding bills. And always make sure you thank everyone involved.

WORKING WITH THE MEDIA

My first opportunity to deal with the media was in college. My college chapter of NOW was hosting a Take Back the Night event. The lead organizer on the event quit about two days before the event, and I was left to organize speakers, lead chants, and handle the media. Before I knew it, there was a camera from a local news station in my face, and I had become the "spokesperson" for the event, my campus, and my NOW chapter. I was overwhelmed, and I can't even remember what I said. I learned how to give a media interview the hard way. Fortunately, I knew the significance of the event and could articulate our goals. In the end, the march was successful, and we received good press. But giving an interview to the media can be intimating and a bit tricky. Sometimes you give a good interview, and sometimes the coverage you later see barely resembles the interview you gave! I certainly have had both experiences.

Activists need media skills. We need to know how to do an interview, talk in sound bites, and hold the attention of our viewers if we are to get our message across and make an impact on the lives of women and girls. People turn to newspapers and television to get their news—53 percent consider the television the most trusted source of information.[3] We must be a part of that—if for no other reason than that feminism puts women at the center of the story,

I'm just not into the whole "girly power," "girls rule," "girls kick ass thing." I'm more concerned with achieving equality rather than denying inequality even exists. Kara, 20, heterosexual, Virginia

making us the subject of news rather than the objects of it. It's the difference between having a voice and being told what to do.

There are two types of media coverage—media coverage you pay for and media coverage you earn. Media coverage you pay for is air time or ad space that you have purchased. The reality is that purchasing media coverage is often cost prohibitive and limiting for activists, since an average ad can cost $50,000 and even more during peak times. Media outlets are also controlled by a select few who decide what is to be aired or published. If the ad is not favorable to the owners, the likelihood that the ad will be published or aired is minimal, as we saw with MoveOn.org's attempt to get its anti-George W. Bush ad aired by CBS during the Super Bowl in 2004. MoveOn.org is a Web-based organization "working to bring ordinary people back into politics."[4] It gained quite a bit of recognition during the 2000 presidential elections, and again in 2004, by creating a number of thought-provoking ads regarding elections, candidates, and policy issues. A cornerstone to the group's work is the on-line communities it facilitates to connect people to do political advocacy work. Often its advertisements are controversial, which, even if the ads are not aired or published, can earn them unpaid media coverage.

Unpaid media attention is a favorite goal of activists because it can be much more accessible to the average activist. Your success rate is dependent upon how media savvy you are and how effective you are in getting the media's attention. Whether writing public service announcements (PSAs), writing letters to the editor, giving an interview, or inviting the press to cover an event, you have to catch the media's attention. You need to create a message or event that is enticing enough to get the press not only to show up but also to publish or air your efforts. In the appendix, I have included some guidelines to help you create and earn effective media attention.

The media are a powerful resource for gathering and delivering information. Activists need to know how to use the media to get their messages across to the public and to influence policy. After all, as activists, our goal is to create effective social change. Activism is a vital method for creating awareness and changing perceptions. This will not happen unless people are aware of our efforts.

ACTIVISM IN DAILY LIFE

You can easily incorporate activism into your daily life. Opportunities are everywhere. No act is too small. Each day I look for ways to be active. I believe that going to acupuncture and utilizing alternative health care is a political act. I believe that phone calls to my sisters and my friends about current events are activism. Arguments with my partner about household chores or debates about whether or not to have children are political. Where I buy my clothes, my books, my food, are all choices that support my beliefs. The classes I teach, the curriculum I author, the events I plan are activism. I write letters to legislators, I work phone banks for important ballot measures, I work to get feminist candidates elected to office, I work in coalition with other progressives, I vote, I speak out against injustice, I may run for office someday. I live my life as an activist. I live my life politically. We can all do this. We all have it in ourselves; titles don't make us leaders. It is our actions that mean something and impact our community. It is our voices that inspire. And our commitment to justice that makes a difference.

I've found that I take my feminism for granted. Kate, no identifying information given

WHAT DO YOU THINK ARE THE GREATEST GAINS OF THE FEMINIST MOVEMENT?

The greatest gain made by the feminist movement is the equal rights we women get and people get to hear our voices. Xuo, 20, Mien

We have more control over our own bodies, we are more self-sufficient, and in many ways feminism is 'in the water.' Elizabeth, 22, white, bisexual, Michigan

To let everyone know that you have a voice, mind and spirit and that you are fully capable of doing anything and everything a man can do. MaLinda, 25, Hispanic/Native American

Freedom to vote and be heard. . . . Mireya, 30, Mexican, heterosexual, California

Credit in our own name. Veronica, 28, Latina, Illinois

Freeing up women's roles and allowing them greater access to professional lives and thereby forever changing the basic structure of the patriarchal nuclear family. Ruby, 30, white, transgender queer, Ohio

The biggest achievement of the feminist movement, in my opinion, is simply getting people to realize how prevalent discrimination against women was and remains. Karen, 29, white, straight, Queens, New York

Economic freedom and reproductive choice. Tanya, 23, Chinese-American, Minnesota

An acknowledgement of the vast problem of violence against women in the world. Crystal, 25, Caucasian, Virginia

Definitely, the Roe v. Wade Supreme Court decision. That has to be the greatest gain by far. Ben, 32, Asian, Republican, heterosexual, California

When the movement suddenly realized—on a number of occasions—that it still had its own "isms" it needed to confront. Class issues. Race issues. Sexual orientation issues. Only upon those realization did any changes begin. Kyle, 33, transsexual FTM, Irish Canadian

. . . female world leaders . . . our own powerful women in government and business . . . Nicole, 20, hetero, Maine

Education for girls. Marianna, 26, white Caucasian, California

The awakening of multiple generations and the empowering of my fellow women. Claire, 20, mixed—white, Mexi, Indian, hetero w/live-in boyfriend, California

My reality, and every opportunity I have ever had, are a direct result of the feminist movement. It's hard for me to pinpoint the greatest gain of all because I have trouble imagining what life was like before. Hannah, 22, Caucasian, heterosexual, Washington, D.C., metro area

GREAT FILMS FOR WOMEN

The Abortion Ship (2003)
*Action for Justice: Making a
    Difference for Women and
    Girls* (2002)
Amélie (2001)
Antonia's Line (1995)
Beloved (1998)
Boys on the Side (1995)
Citizen Ruth (1996)
*Como Agua Para Chocolate/Like
    Water for Chocolate* (1992)
The Contender (2001)
Eat, Drink, Man, Woman (1994)
Fried Green Tomatoes (1991)
*From the Back Alleys to the
    Supreme Court and Beyond*
    (Dorothy Fadiman's
    trilogy, 1999)
G.I. Jane (1997)
Girl Interrupted (1999)
Go Fish (1994)
How to Make An American Quilt
    (1995)
If These Walls Could Talk (I and II)
    (1996 and 2000)
I'm the One that I Want
    (Margaret Cho, 2000)

The Hours (2002)
Iron Jawed Angels (2004)
The Joy Luck Club (1993)
Killing Us Softly 3 (2000)
A League of their Own (1992)
Magdalene Sisters (2002)
Million Dollar Baby (2004)
Mi Vida Loca (1993)
Muriel's Wedding (1994)
North Country (2005)
*Passion for Justice: 21st Century
    Feminism* (2002)
Poetic Justice (1993)
Prey for Rock and Roll (2003)
Rachel's Daughter (1998)
Real Women Have Curves
    (2003)
Set It Off (1996)
Shakespeare in Love (1998)
Small Justice (2002)
Tea with Mussolini (1999)
Thelma and Louise (1991)
The Vagina Monologues (2002)
Votes for Women (1996)
Vera Drake (2004)
Whale Rider (2002)

2
Catch a Wave

I was an exchange student in Sweden during my junior year of high school. At my school at home, junior year included a class on U.S. politics and history. So while living in Sweden was great and I could take corresponding literature, math, and sciences classes, learning about American political history wasn't so simple. My parents and teachers decided that I would take a correspondence class to make up this work, but when they gave me my textbook, my mother discovered a problem. There were virtually no references to women. She suggested to my school a textbook change but met a great deal of resistance. Most disturbing, she read their resistance as rooted in an undervaluing of women's history and the belief that a knowledge of women's contributions was unnecessary in studying American history. While she lost the battle with the school, she instituted her own curriculum for me that I was required to complete in a correspondence course with her. Yes, more homework for me, but work that was well worth it. We also did a bit of subversive activism—we added our own commentary in the margins of all the textbooks that my school sent, hoping that whoever got the textbooks after me would learn about women's history, too. That year, I learned a great deal about American political history. I learned the valuable lesson that claiming our place in society has always been a fight. I also learned that women's history is American history and that our contributions help to shape the world we live in today.

The feminist movement has a rich history—a history full of struggle, sacrifice, justice, resistance, and many victories. But, unfortunately, feminist activism is often left out of our textbooks, the halls of our educational institutions, and, as a result, far too often, our consciousness. Far too many move forward without a complete understanding of the past—without a full accounting of the struggles both within and outside the movement. We talk of the future with little emphasis on the present. But if we are to create a future, we need to build upon the past. And to do so, we must know, respect, and understand our history.

Fortunately, there is a commitment today to reclaiming the past contributions and stories of women and to teaching women's *herstory* to the current and future generations—so as not to lose this heritage. Great writers like bell hooks, Ruth Rosen, and Estelle Freedman have chronicled this history. From the women who fought for more than seventy years to win the right to vote to the women who work today to further advance women's quest for equality, American women have a tremendous tradition of fighting for justice. I have included a chronology of these women, their efforts, and the history of American feminism. I believe that we need to know our history to understand the present and in order to plan for the future. Women's history is American history. Knowing this, knowing what women have done in the past, can empower women today. I include the following chronology as both information and inspiration.

> *The greatest gain in the movement was when women noticed that they had power, both as a group and individuals.*
> Andrea, 22, white, straight, Washington state

CHRONOLOGY OF THE U.S. WOMEN'S MOVEMENT

March 31, 1776—Abigail Adams writes her now-famous "Remember the ladies" letter to her husband, John Adams, asking him to "remember the ladies" and not to "put such unlimited power into the hands of the Husbands."

1790—Judith Sargent Stevens Murray publishes *On the Equality of the Sexes,* advocating that women and men should have equal education.

1792—Mary Wollstonecraft publishes *Vindication of the Rights of Woman,* advocating equal opportunity for women.

1821—Troy Female Seminary is started in New York by Emma Hart Willard, the first endowed school for girls.

1832—The Female Anti-Slavery Society of Salem, Massachusetts, is founded.

1833—Oberlin College, in Ohio, becomes the first coeducational college in the United States.

1837—Mount Holyoke College is founded by Mary Lyons, in Massachusetts, the United States's first four-year college for women.

1839—Mississippi is the first state to pass a Married Women's Property Act, allowing married white women to own property in their own name.

1848—Lowell Female Labor Reform Association is organized by female textile workers in Massachusetts. The first women's rights convention in the United States is held in Seneca Falls, New York. Married white women are allowed to own property in the United States.

1850—"Bloomers" cause controversy in the United States as Amelia Jenks Bloomer introduces knee-length pantaloons as women's clothing.

1851—Sojourner Truth, a former slave, delivers her famous "Ain't I a Woman" speech at Akron, Ohio's women's rights convention.

1865—The Thirteenth Amendment is passed, ending official slavery in the United States.

1866—Elizabeth Cady Stanton and Susan B. Anthony organize the American Equal Rights Association, an organization that worked for universal suffrage.

1868—The Fourteenth Amendment, defining "citizens" and "voters" as male, is ratified.

1869—Elizabeth Cady Stanton and Susan B. Anthony form the National Woman Suffrage Association, while Lucy Stone, Henry Blackwell, and Julia Ward Howe found the more conservative American Woman Suffrage Association.

1872—Victoria Woodhull becomes the first woman to campaign for the U.S. presidency.

1873—Myra Bradwell, an attorney from Illinois, sues in the U.S. Supreme Court for the right to practice law. Her case is rejected by the Court because she is married.

1878—A Woman Suffrage Amendment is introduced in the U.S. Congress. This amendment eventually becomes the Nineteenth Amendment, which, in 1919, gives women the right to vote.

1890—National Woman Suffrage Association and the American Woman Suffrage Association join together under the leadership of Elizabeth Cady Stanton, forming the National American Woman Suffrage Association.

1892—A nationwide antilynching campaign is launched by Ida B. Wells after the murder of three black businessmen in Tennessee.

1893—The National Council of Jewish Women is founded by Hannah Greenbaum Soloman. Colorado becomes the first state in the U.S. to allow women the right to vote.

1895—Elizabeth Cady Stanton publishes *The Woman's Bible,* criticizing churches for their narrow definition of women's roles within the church.

1895–1899—Rosa Sonnenschein publishes *The American Jewess,* the first Jewish women's magazine.

1896—The National Association of Colored Women is founded by Fanny Jackson Coppin, Charlotte Forten Grimké, Frances E. W. Harper, Josephine St. Pierre Ruffin, Mary Church Terrell, Harriet Tubman, Margaret Murray Washington, Frances Ellen Watkins, and Ida B. Wells-Barnett.

1903—The Women's Trade Union League of New York is formed, later becoming the forerunner of the International Ladies' Garment Workers' Union.

1911—Opposition to women's suffrage formalizes with the creation of the National Association Opposed to Women's Suffrage.

1913—Alice Paul and Lucy Burns organize the Congressional Union, which becomes the National Women's Party in 1916. Using more radical means, such as hunger strikes and White House pickets, they work to publicize the importance of women's suffrage.

1915—The Women's Peace Party is formed.

1916—Jeannette Rankin of Montana becomes the first woman to serve in the U.S. House of Representatives.

1919—The Nineteenth Amendment passes in Congress and moves to the states for ratification.

August 26, 1920—The Nineteenth Amendment is ratified by the necessary three-quarters of the states on August 18 and is officially added to the Constitution on the August 26. The National American Woman Suffrage Association closes but becomes the foundation for the League of Women Voters.

1921—Margaret Sanger founds the American Birth Control League, later to become Planned Parenthood.

1923—The National Women's Party introduces the Equal Rights Amendment, proposed to eliminate gender discrimination. The Equal Rights Amendment still has not been ratified.

1932—Amelia Earhart is the first woman to fly solo across the Atlantic. Frances Perkins is the first woman to hold a Cabinet position, when Franklin D. Roosevelt appoints her as the Secretary of Labor.

1933—Katherine Hepburn wins her first Oscar for her performance in *Morning Glory.* Hepburn goes on to win three more Academy Awards, making her the winner of more Oscar awards for performance than any other actor.

1935—Mary McLeod Bethune organizes the National Council of Negro Women.

1936—Birth control is no longer classified as "obscene" following the modification of a federal law prohibiting the dissemination of birth control information through the mail.

1943—The Equal Pay Act is introduced in Congress.

1955—Rosa Parks refuses to give up her seat on a bus in Montgomery, Alabama, which leads to the Montgomery Bus Boycotts. Del Martin and Phyllis Lyon found the first U.S. lesbian rights group, Daughters of Bilitis.

1960—The birth control pill is approved by the U.S. Food and Drug Administration (FDA).

1961—Eleanor Roosevelt is appointed by President Kennedy as the chair of the first President's Commission on the Status of Women. Pat Maginnis founds the Society for Humane Abortion in California.

1962—Delores Huerta helps to found the United Farm Workers. Fannie Lou Hamer, a Mississippi sharecropper, is beaten and jailed for leading efforts to register neighbors to vote. She co-founds the Mississippi Freedom Democratic Party.

1963—The Equal Pay Act passes Congress, prohibiting sex discrimination in pay. Betty Friedan publishes *The*

Feminine Mystique. The Commission on the Status of
Women reveals widespread sex discrimination against
women in employment and under the law in its first
report, *The American Woman.*

1964—The Civil Rights Act passes, Title VII of which
includes a clause prohibiting discrimination on the
basis of sex. Casey Hayden and Mary King address
sexual inequality within the civil rights movement. The
Homosexual League of New York / The League for
Sexual Freedom stages its first protest in New York
City.

1965—The U.S. Supreme Court decision *Griswold v.
Connecticut* permits the use of birth control devices by
married couples on the basis of a constitutional right to
privacy. President Lyndon B. Johnson signs Executive
Order 11246 requiring companies that do business with
the government to utilize affirmative action in hiring
minorities.

1966—Out of frustration at the Equal Employment Opportunity Commission's lack of enforcement of the Civil Rights
Act of 1964, the National Organization for Women (NOW)
is created. NOW then petitions the EEOC to end sex-
segregated employment ads.

1967—Affirmative action is extended to women. The Chicago
Women's Liberation Group is founded. New York Radical
Women forms. NOW adopts a Bill of Rights for women.
Alicia Escalante begins the East Los Angeles Welfare
Rights Organization (she later founds the Chicano
National Welfare Rights Organization). Johnnie Tillmon,
Etta Horn, and Beulah Sanders start the National Welfare
Rights Organization to educate women about negotiating
the welfare system.

1968—Shirley Chisholm is the first African American woman
elected to Congress. Women's Liberation, New York
Radical Women, and New York NOW protest the "Miss
America" pageant in Atlantic City. National Domestic
Workers Union is formed.

1969—Cornell University in New York offers the first
women's studies course.

The Boston Women's Health Collective begins publishing its pamphlet *Our Bodies Ourselves* (later published as a book in 1973 and still widely referred to for woman-centered health information). National Abortion Rights Action League (now NARAL Pro-Choice America) is formed. Redstockings, a radical feminist activist organization combating derogatory and discriminatory attitudes about women, is formed. The first full women's studies program is established, at San Diego State University. The Stonewall Riots occurs in New York City, protesting discrimination against the gay community.

1970—Pat Mainardi proposes "wages for housework," bringing awareness to the unpaid work of women. North American Indian Women's Association is formed. Bella Abzug is elected to Congress. Maggie Kuhn creates the Gray Panthers to address older women's rights. Hawaii, Alaska, and New York are the first states to liberalize abortion laws. Barbara Seaman, who published *The Doctors' Case against the Pill* in 1969, disrupts a Senate subcommittee's hearing on the birth control pill, arguing that women are being used as "guinea pigs." The Lavender Menace Action is one of the first actions fighting for the rights of lesbians. The Gay Liberation Front Women is formed.

1971—The Feminist Women's Health Center is founded by Carol Downer and Lorraine Rothman in Los Angeles, California. The National Women's Political Caucus is formed to encourage and support more women to run for office. The National Press Club allows women members.

1972—Title IX is passed by Congress to enforce sex equality in education. *Ms.* magazine is launched. (*Ms.* first appeared as an insert in *New York* magazine in 1971.) Charlotte Bunch, Rita Mae Brown, and Joan E. Biren found *The Furies,* a collective lesbian newspaper. Margo St. James starts COYOTE (Call Off Your Old Tired Ethics) in San Francisco to improve working conditions of sex workers. The Equal Pay Act of 1963 is expanded to include administrative, executive, and professional employees. Juanita Kreps becomes the first woman director of the New York

Stock Exchange (she is later appointed as the first woman
Secretary of Commerce). The first U.S. battered women's
shelters open in California and Minnesota. *Free to Be . . .
You and Me* is published, providing an entire generation
nonsexist, multiracial songs, poems, and stories for kids.
The Older Women's Liberation holds its first conference in
New York City. Sally Priesand becomes the first ordained
woman rabbi.

1973—*Roe v. Wade* is decided in the U.S. Supreme Court, legal-
izing abortion in the first trimester. Helen Reddy wins a
Grammy for her song "I Am Woman." The National Black
Feminist Organization is formed. Billie Jean King defeats
Bobby Riggs in the much-publicized "battle of the sexes"
tennis match. The U.S. Supreme Court rules against
sexually segregated classified employment ads. The AFL-
CIO nationally endorses the ERA.

1974—The Equal Credit Opportunity Act is passed in
Congress, allowing married women credit in their own
names. Helen Thomas is the first woman reporter to be
named a White House reporter for UPI. Girls are allowed
to play in Little League. Domestic workers are covered by
the minimum wage law. The National Women's Football
League is formed. The first All-American Girls' Basketball
Conference is held. The Coalition of Labor Union Women
(CLUW) is formed.

1975—The United Nations sponsors the First International
Conference on Women, held in Mexico City. For the first
time, under Title IV-D of the Social Security Act established by Congress, federal employee wages can be
garnished to pay child support and alimony.

1976—The United Nations Decade for Women begins. The
National Alliance of Black Feminists organizes in Chicago.
The Organization of Pan Asian American Women is
founded. Barbara Jordan is the first African American and
the first woman to give the keynote address at the Democratic National Convention. NASA begins accepting
women for astronaut training. Joan Nestle and Deborah
Edel found the Lesbian Herstory Archives—the largest
and oldest of its kind in the world. Sarah Caldwell

becomes the first woman to conduct at New York's Metropolitan Opera House. *Lilith Magazine* is founded. Nebraska enacts the first marital rape law—setting a precedent that it is illegal for a husband to rape his wife. Military service academies begin to admit women.

1977—The National Association of Cuban-American Women is founded. The National Coalition Against Domestic Violence is founded.

1978—The Pregnancy Discrimination Act passes Congress prohibiting job discrimination against women who are pregnant. Women Against Pornography is formed in New York City. The group later sponsors the first Take Back the Night march and rally protesting violence against women.

1981—Sandra Day O'Connor is the first woman appointed to the U.S. Supreme Court.

1983—Sally Ride is the first American woman in space. Byllye Avery founds the National Black Women's Health Project, now the Black Women's Health Imperative.

1984—Geraldine Ferraro runs as the Democratic Party's vice-presidential candidate, with the presidential candidate Walter Mondale.

1985—Emily's List is started. The group gives campaign donations to Democratic, pro-choice candidates (EMILY stands for Early Money Is Like Yeast). Wilma Mankiller becomes the first woman chief of the Cherokee Nation of Oklahoma.

1987—The Feminist Majority is founded by Eleanor Smeal, past president of NOW. Congress designates March as "Women's History Month."

1989—Reverend Barbara C. Harris becomes the first woman consecrated as a bishop in the Episcopal Church.

1990—Congress passes the American with Disabilities Act. Dr. Antonia Novello becomes the first woman and the first Latino to serve as U.S. Surgeon General.

1991—Anita Hill bravely testifies at the Senate Supreme Court Confirmation Hearings about sexual harassment by her former employer and then-nominee to the U.S. Supreme Court, Clarence Thomas, setting off a national conservation about sexual harassment in the workplace.

The U.S. Senate overturns the "gag rule," which barred federally funded family planning clinics from discussing abortion as an option. Sharon Pratt Dixon becomes mayor of Washington, D.C., and as such becomes the first African American woman to serve as mayor of a major U.S. city. Susan Faludi publishes *Backlash*, detailing the attacks on the women's movement throughout the 1980s and introduces a whole new generation to the importance of feminism. *Thelma and Louise* is released in theaters.

1992—Rebecca Walker and Shannon Liss create the Third Wave Direct Action Corporation to address the issues of a new wave of feminists. The Third Wave Direct Action Corporation later becomes the Third Wave Foundation. An estimated 750,000 people converge on Washington, D.C., for the Pro-Choice March. More women are elected to political office than any time in U.S. history, prompting some to name 1992 "the year of the woman" in U.S. politics. Carol Moseley-Braun (D-IL) is the first African American woman elected to the U.S. Senate (she later runs for president, in 2004). The Supreme Court reaffirms a woman's right to abortion in *Planned Parenthood of Southeastern Pennsylvania v. Casey*. Mae Jemison becomes the first African American woman astronaut.

1993—Congress passes the Family and Medical Leave Act. *Bust* magazine is published.
The Center for Young Women's Development is founded in San Francisco, California. Ruth Bader Ginsburg is appointed to the U.S. Supreme Court.

1994—Congress passes and President Clinton signs the Freedom to Access Clinic Entrances Act, making it illegal to obstruct the entrances to abortion clinics. Congress passes the Violence Against Women Act, providing services and funding for victims of rape and domestic violence.

1995—The United Nations Fourth World Conference on Women is held, in Beijing, China. Shannon Faulkner becomes the first woman to be admitted to the Citadel, the formerly all-male South Carolina military college.

1996—Rape is officially recognized as a weapon of war and as
a human rights violation, thus as a war crime. The
Feminist Expo is held in Washington, D.C. Hosted by the
Feminist Majority and sponsored by nearly 300 organizations, it brings thousands of feminists together to create a
feminist vision for the future. Andi Zeisler and Lisa Jervis
found *Bitch* magazine. The U.S. Women's National Soccer
Team wins the first-ever Olympic gold medal for
women's soccer, at the Atlanta Olympic Games.

1997—Madeline Albright becomes the first women to serve as
the U.S. secretary of state, making her the highest-ranking
woman in the history of the U.S. government. Sarah
McLachlan kicks off Lilith Fair, with a full lineup of
women musicians. The Women's National Basketball
Association (WNBA) is formed. The Lusty Lady, in San
Francisco, unionizes, taking an important and historic
step toward sex workers' rights. (For more information on
sex workers' unionization efforts, see Julia Query and
Vicki Funari's film *Live Nude Girls Unite*.)

1998—Congress passes the Violence Against Women Act II,
extending funding to sexual assault programs. Eve Ensler
hosts *The Vagina Monologues* in New York, launching the
V-Day campaign to end violence against women.

1999—Carly Fiorina becomes the president, CEO, and, in
2000, chairperson of Hewlett-Packard, becoming the first
woman to hold all three positions in a Fortune 500
company. Lieutenant Colonel Eileen Collins is the first
woman astronaut to command a space shuttle mission.
Nancy Ruth Mace becomes the first woman to graduate
from the Citadel, the formerly all-male military school in
South Carolina.

2000—The Second Feminist Expo is held, in Baltimore,
Maryland. Jennifer Baumgardner and Amy Richards
publish *Manifesta: Young Women, Feminism and the Future*.
Hillary Rodham Clinton is elected to the U.S. Senate to
represent the state of New York, making her the first U.S.
First Lady ever to hold public office. Beijing +5, "Women
2000: Gender Equality, Development and Peace for the
Twenty-first Century," takes place in New York. The

World March for Women is held in Washington, D.C., and
in New York City.

2002—Nancy Pelosi becomes House Minority Leader, making
her the highest-ranking woman in the U.S. House of
Representatives and the first woman to lead a major political party in the U.S. Congress. The California State
Legislature passes SB 1301, codifying *Roe v. Wade*
language into state law, further securing abortion rights in
California.

2004—An estimated 1.15 million people march on Washington, D.C., for the "March for Women's Lives"—the
largest march (of any kind!) in U.S. history. Susan
Hockfield becomes the first woman president of the Massachusetts Institute of Technology (MIT). Massachusetts
becomes the first U.S. state to legalize same-sex marriage.

2005—Condoleezza Rice becomes the first African American
woman to serve as U.S. secretary of state. The California
legislature becomes the first in the United States to pass a
marriage equality bill (AB 849) (unfortunately, the bill is
vetoed by Governor Arnold Schwarzenegger).

THE WAVES OF A MOVEMENT

The American women's movement is often discussed in terms of
"waves," but it is important to understand that the presumed boundaries of these waves can be misleading. For example, these waves are
not entirely separate from one another but rather blend into one other.
There is no true stopping point where one wave ends before another begins. Rather, the triumphs and the setbacks of one wave becomes the
starting ground for the succeeding waves, passing from one generation
to the next. Each wave of the feminist movement builds upon efforts of
previous generations. Suffrage and the right to vote, a gain made in the
first wave, which most scholars designated as occurring in the late
1800s through the early 1900s, became an accepted reality for women of
the next generation, who then began to work on additional issues of access, representation, and equality. The second wave, which most designate as beginning in the 1960s, emphasized the importance of personal
politics. Under its classic banner, "The personal is political," the second

wave led the charge for abortion rights, child care, recognition of unpaid labor, access to health care, and equal pay for equal work. While many of these battles have not yet been won, the fight continues. Subsequently, along with the gains of the first and second waves, the challenges also carry over. Significant criticism of the first and second waves—such as concerns about racism, generational tensions, and relevance of issues—continue to be central to the dialogue about the women's movement. This dialog has been passed onto the next generation, the third wave, which gained momentum in the 1990s. The third wave is challenged to look critically at our collective past and to build a more diverse, inclusive, and integrated movement.

> *A second-wave feminist professor told me that the Third Wave does not exist. I was like, thanks for denying me my identity.* Sally, 25, Caucasian, bisexual, Colorado

The American feminist movement is often seen as occurring in waves. The *first wave* was characterized by the fight for suffrage and the right to vote for women. The *second wave* was characterized by the concept of "personal politics" and the fight for full recognition of women in society. And the *third wave* is characterized by multicultural, inclusive feminism.

Arguments, both within and outside the movement, focus on a debate about whether or not we should even look at the American women's movement in terms of waves. Questions have arisen about the risk of isolating and pigeon-holing generations of women's-rights activists and thus diluting the strength of the movement. There are also questions about those who don't generationally fit into the waves as commonly defined, such as those who were born in the mid- and late 1960s, who are too young to have been at the center of second-wave activism but who are too old to be included with the activists of the third wave. They are often stuck between the experiences and consciousness of the second and third waves and find themselves not belonging to either group. Active in the movement, they often express frustration at being ignored in the dialogue of intergenerational feminism. On the other hand, I would argue that looking at the women's movement in this country in terms of waves can help us to organize, understand, and build upon efforts of the past. Further, for many young feminists, the term "third wave" is a way to identify with today's feminism and not just with a movement that has been presumed to belong only to our foremothers. Recently, a new question is arising about the possible emergence of a fourth wave—teens who are now entering the scene of feminism and the feminist movement, starting feminist clubs at high school, doing activism on campus, and participating in national events like the 2004 March for Women's Lives in Washington, D.C.

The greatest achievement made by the feminist movement is to collectively raise the consciousness of women regarding the inequalities of their social condition. Ilun, 23, Taiwanese-American, asexual, New York City

Whether or not you believe in the "waves" of this movement, there is no question that the contributions of people who took, and continue to take, action to improve the lives of women and girls is valid and critically important.

SUFFRAGE AND THE FIRST WAVE OF FEMINISM

The first wave of the women's movement is characterized as the suffrage movement and occurred primarily during the 1800s and early 1900s. Originating in the abolition movement to end slavery, women began working toward winning the right to vote. Hosting the first American women's rights convention, in Seneca Falls, New York, in 1848, women came together to create the Declaration of Sentiments, a document that asserted true gender equality. Women won suffrage in 1919 with the passage of the Nineteenth Amendment, and the final state approval necessary for the ratification of the amendment came on August 26, 1920—recognized today as Women's Equality Day.

Winning the right to vote is a cornerstone to the women's movement because it gave women political power through representation for the first time in modern history. The 2004 HBO film *Iron Jawed Angels* introduced a new generation to Alice Paul, Lucy Burns, and the fight for women's suffrage. Recalling the challenges, pickets, arrests, and hunger strikes, the film gives today's generation a more realistic look at the intense struggle endured by the suffragists. Often we underestimate the sacrifices and struggles that women endure for their freedom. *Iron Jawed Angels* leaves us with a graphic memory of Alice Paul being force-fed during her hunger strike in prison and an understanding that the right to vote was not readily granted to women. Indeed, the fight for suffrage lasted for more than seventy years. Many who began the struggle—Susan B. Anthony, Elizabeth Cady Stanton, and Sojourner Truth, for example—did not live to see their life's work achieved. But their legacy lives on. The fight for suffrage began a modern movement to change the regard in which women were held. It challenged the way in which women were treated and the resources to which they had access. However, while the women's movement was touted as a movement for all women, in fact race divisions within the movement were strong. These divisions have long been glossed over by historians, the media, and the movement itself, undervaluing the importance and truth of this history. We need to examine the racism that permeated the first wave in order to understand its ongoing influence in the movement. If we are to strengthen the feminist movement today, then we need to fully recognize and understand the contributions of all while learning from the mistakes of the past.

The fact is that women of color, like Ida B. Wells, were instrumental to suffrage and to the consciousness that women's rights must include all women. Wells protested the "back of the bus" politic of the women's movement by refusing to march at the back of the 1913 suffrage parade, as was the plan for delegations of women of color. Further, in response to segregated and exclusionary suffrage groups, Wells established Chicago's Alpha Suffrage Club, perhaps the first suffrage group for black women. White Christian feminist groups of the time refused to join antilynching campaigns, address anti-Semitism, or fight discriminatory immigration policies. With few exceptions, divisions among activist women began as women of color looked to create new venues to recognize and address issues ignored by "mainstream" women's organizations. Women of color have been forced to fight for their place in history and for their inclusion on the movement's agenda. Tragically, this fight continues today.

In addition to the challenge of racism within the U.S.-based women's movement, American women were largely unaware of feminist activity that was occurring in other regions of the world. At the time of our Seneca Falls convention, women throughout Europe, Asia, and Latin America were arguing for gender equality.[1] Suffrage, education, political representation, property rights, labor rights, and pay equity were all central issues for women activists in Japan, Germany, England, France, Mexico, and other nations. Women around the globe contributed significantly to the structure of their home country's gender dynamic. They also contributed to a wider understanding of globalization and imperialism and their impact on the status of women worldwide.

While the first wave of feminism left us with intense racial divisions and little understanding of women of the world, the suffragists made a critical contribution to American women's liberation and set into motion a movement that continues to change the lives of women for the better. With the right to vote, we have a voice in our democracy and a better opportunity to impact the system.

Personal Politics and the Second Wave of Feminism

The second wave of the women's movement was characterized by economic and personal power. Beginning in the early 1960s, the second wave took on the issues of advancement for women in the workplace (e.g., pay equity, the glass ceiling, sexual harassment); recognition of women's labor in the home; contraceptive equity and legality and access to reproductive health care; constitutional equality; women's safety; and political participation among women, from voting activity to holding elective office. Fortunately, there has been no noted end to the second wave, as this generation's activists are still vigorously working to end discrimination against women.

Perhaps one of the most important gains of the second wave was to identify a sexism so pervasive that it could no longer be ignored. By identifying sexism, in the courts to the household, the second wave taught us the importance of ending discrimination, not just on a political level but also on a deeply personal one. Coining the phrase "the personal is political, the political is personal," the second wave of the women's movement championed the fight to bring recognition to women's lives, arguing that our collective experience is a legitimate part of the American experience. With this recognition came consciousness-raising groups, speak-outs, marches, rallies, demonstrations, feminist publishing houses and publications, research, women's studies programs at colleges and universities, court battles, and legislative efforts to bring women closer to parity with men. The second wave is noted for its great victories, such as Title IX, which instituted a vision of gender equity in education. Title IX made sexual harassment in school illegal and outlined the goal of a fair and level playing field in sports and in the overall pursuit of academic excellence. Additionally, the second wave championed important court wins for women's health and reproductive rights, most notably *Griswold v. Connecticut* (1965), in which the U.S. Supreme Court invalidated a Connecticut statute that prohibited the use of contraceptives by married persons; *Eisenstadt v. Baird* (1972), in which the Court extended the right to privacy to include both married and nonmarried persons with regard to reproductive health decisions; and *Roe v. Wade* (1973), in which the Court legalized abortion in the first trimester. Indeed, the second wave championed the issues that impact women's lives—including the right to be safe from violence at work, on the street, and in our homes; the right to equitable pay and career advancement; the right to attend military academies as well as to serve; and the right to accessible, affordable, and representational health care.

The second wave helped launch women's studies programs and departments across the nation, creating a venue for women's contributions. Women's studies classes are often the first, and sometimes the only, place we learn women's side of history and perspective on current issues. Beyond women's studies, the second wave began the massive effort to put women into mainstream studies, so that our history textbooks, and sociology, psychology, history, anthropology, science, and books on every area of study, do not exclude women's perspectives or contributions. For the first time, women were able to widely publish and to be recognized as contributors to their fields. Chronicling and critiquing our past, as well as evaluating our present and visioning our future, women's studies professors and writers introduced a discourse that is woman-centered. This legacy continues today, as younger generations are now afforded the opportunity to earn degrees, and build careers, specifically in women's/feminist studies.

Women's studies further gave rise to much of the activism of the feminist movement. While certainly women have raised awareness and called for change in multiple arenas of society, including factories, offices, and community centers and within religious institutions, colleges and universities have been a central training ground for activism. Typically places that encourage the questioning of the status quo and fosters new ideas, college campuses are a prime locale for feminist organizing. This is a tradition that continues to live on as classic second-wave organizations such as NOW, the Feminist Majority, and Gloria Steinem's Choice USA have student chapters and campus task forces established throughout the nation.

The women's health movement also saw its rise during the second wave. Reclaiming our bodies, demanding research and knowledge, and calling for affordable and accessible health care are cornerstone issues for the feminist women's health movement. Key organizations began in the second wave and continue to work today to provide comprehensive health care information and services for all. Among these organizations are the Feminist Women's Health Centers, which put women back into the center of our health care and empower women in the choices they make; the Boston Women's Health Collective, which made woman-centered health information widely available through classic publications like *Our Bodies, Ourselves;* the National Women's Health Network, which lobbies for women's health priorities and is often the only voice women have on Capitol Hill; and the National Black Women's Health Project (now the Black Women's Health Imperative), which is leading the way on education, advocacy, research, and leadership training for African American women's health initiatives. These organizations, and many others, have changed the face of health care for women. And, while the fight to protect women's health is still being fought, the second wave put into motion the idea that women, and only women, must control their bodies.

Perhaps the most classic battle of the second wave was the fight for an Equal Rights Amendment (ERA). Drafted in 1923 by the first-waver Alice Paul, the ERA battle was picked up by the second wave in the 1970s—a great example of intergenerational work. The Equal Rights Amendment simply reads,

> *Section 1. Equality of rights under the law shall not be denied or abridged by the United States or by any state on account of sex.*
>
> *Section 2. The Congress shall have the power to enforce, by appropriate legislation, the provisions of this article.*
>
> *Section 3. This amendment shall take effect two years after the date of ratification.*

The quest for constitutional equality has been a long, controversial battle, with the most notable opposition coming from Phyllis Schlafly, of the Eagle Forum. She effectively argued against the ERA, claiming that feminists hated "men, marriage, and children."[2] Despite tireless efforts among members of the feminist movement, congressional approval, and ratification in thirty states, the ERA never achieved approval in the necessary three-quarters of the states to be adopted as an amendment to the Constitution. Perhaps the third wave will continue the intergenerational efforts of the ERA by picking up this fight for constitutional equality—not just for women this time, but for all those who are marginalized and oppressed.

While much of the second-wave agenda has yet to be realized, there is no debate that the second wave established an expectation of equality. The second wave took the once-extreme notion of economic, political, and social equity for women and brought it into mainstream consciousness. The second wave taught my generation that we could do, and be, anything. But, despite their best efforts, they have not achieved every goal. Now, the fight continues with another generation joining in. We have a stake, too. While the vision, knowledge, and activism of the second wavers remains central to the movement, a new generation joins them—bringing with them all that they have learned from the second wave while also introducing their own vision, knowledge, and activism to the movement.

THE THIRD WAVE

In the early 1990s, the next wave, the third wave, of feminism began to emerge. Frequently referred to as "third wavers," third-wave feminists are dispelling the myths of feminism, claiming feminism for a new generation, and embracing and incorporating our diversity as people in a movement to bring gender equity throughout the globe. Third wavers confront the sentiment "I'm not a feminist, but . . . ," the attitude that young women want the benefits of feminism—fair pay, contraceptive equity, access to higher education, protection from sexual harassment—without recognizing the fight that was necessary to win these rights. Third wavers benefit from the gains of the previous waves but also recognize the importance of continuing the work and the legacy of a feminist movement. Third-wave feminism is a movement that is working alongside the activists of the second wave.

As I mentioned earlier, I consider myself a third waver. I grew up in the feminist movement. This means that I grew up in a time of possibility and was frequently told that I could do anything. I was taught that my voice is powerful, that women's voices are powerful. But, as I grew up, I began to realize that not all little girls are told these messages and that even when they are, the world doesn't necessarily support them. One definition of "third-wave feminists" is that they are the children of the second wave of feminism—literally and/or figuratively. Either you were, as Rebecca Walker claims, a "movement baby" who was carted around to meetings, marches, and rallies or you simply grew up in a time that benefited from the efforts of second-wave feminism. Third-wave feminists, for example, were born, or came of age, after the passage of Title IX, the Supreme Court win of *Roe v. Wade,* and the general fight for equality for all women. Walker introduced the notion of a third wave through a 1992 article for *Ms.* magazine and later edited an anthology, *To Be Real,* which highlighted the perspectives of young women. She, along with others, built an organization dedicated to funding and sponsoring young women's projects. The Third Wave Direct Action Corporation was founded in 1992 and became the Third Wave Foundation a few years later. Walker set the tone for recognizing the energy and activism of a new wave of feminists. For while we may have more freedoms today than ever before, we still live in a time when our political, economic, and social representation is marginalized. We live in a global community where our lives are in danger, we do not have adequate access to health care, our home labor is rarely recognized, and our paid labor jobs bring us inequitable salaries. While many of the issues are the same as those that faced earlier generations, third-wave feminists are adding their perspectives to the discussion. And young women are working to address the criticisms of the first and second waves to build a stronger movement.

One way in which the third wave is working to build a stronger movement is by diversifying its approach to activism and social change. Organizations like the Riot Grrrls and the Third Wave Foundation have brought youth culture into a political context and traditional organizations (i.e., the Feminist Majority and NOW) are following suit. One approach is through zines—independent, low-budget publications that have few or no rules. Zines are an "anything goes" approach to creating a venue for young voices. Often seen as radical, zines and their publishers focus on personal experiences while connecting political thought about issues ranging from abortion to rape to poverty to war. Not unlike the first and second waves, as young women come into the feminist movement, they try not only to find their voices but to also understand the political nature of their experiences. Coming of age with the Internet has also affected the approach to activism taken by third wavers. Not only has the Internet been instrumental in the production and dissemination of zines, but the Internet has been a key source of outreach, education, consciousness raising, advocacy, and organizing in today's feminist activism.

In conjunction with the politics of inclusiveness, another critical contribution of the third wave is the appreciation of and the emphasis on the intersection of race, class, sex, gender, sexual

I think my family background played a huge part in forming my feminist identity as I was raised by a very old-fashioned Mexican mother. Judith, 20, Mexican American, bisexual, Massachusetts

orientation, disability, and age. Through anthologies like *To Be Real, Colonize This!, Listen Up!,* and *The Fire This Time* and with writers like Rebecca Walker, Jennifer Baumgardner, Amy Richards, Michele Serros, Daisy Hernández, and Joan Morgan, we are beginning to hear the diverse voices of young women critiquing the movement and addressing how we view feminism. Among these writers, as well as among young feminist groups throughout the country, a debate is alive about the effectiveness of identifying the waves of the feminist movement, the importance of claiming feminism or the idea of creating new terminology, and the errors of the past and proposals for the future. Forums are addressing white privilege in the movement and the lack of connectedness to feminism among women of color. As Daisy Hernández and Pandora Leong write, in an April 2004 article titled, "Feminism's Future Young Feminists of Color Take the Mic,"

> Many women of color, like their Anglo counterparts, eschew the term "feminism" while agreeing with its goals (the right to an abortion, equality in job hiring, girls' soccer teams). But women of color also dismiss the label because the feminist movement has largely focused on the concerns of middle-class women. . . . Attempts to address the racism of the feminist movement have largely been token efforts without lasting effects. Many young women of color still feel alienated from a mainstream feminism that doesn't explicitly address race. . . . Feminism in the United States has stagnated in part because it has largely neglected a class and race analysis.[3]

It is precisely this analysis that the third wave embraces in its feminist discourse and activism. Learning from the movement's collective past, third wavers today include a racial consciousness in every aspect of gender discrimination.

Similarly, the third wave includes an internalization of a broader definition of gender, actively avoiding a limited male-versus-female dichotomy. A growing understanding of and focus on transgender issues is increasingly central to the work of third-wave writers, activists, researchers, and CR groups. Today's gender activists turn to writers like Amy Bloom, author of *Normal;* Kate Bornstein, author of *Gender Outlaw* and *My Gender Workbook;* Jennifer Finney Boylan, author of *She's Not There;* and Judith Halberstam, author of *In A Queer Time and Place,* to delve into a wider understanding of gender and gender oppression. While a great deal of understanding is still to be gained and there is a tremendous amount of work to do before we legally and socially recognize multiple genders, more of the movement is incorporating challenges to gender within the fight for equality.

> The main issue of feminism that I fear is under-represented is the issue that race and class are seen as separate issues. There should be no separation.
>
> Yun Jin, 21, Korean-American, bisexual, California

Whether over issues of race, gender, or economics; levels of activist experience; ideas for change, feminist discourse, and/or agenda, the third wave is intersecting with the second wave in a challenging, yet meaningful way. While we may not define every problem the same way or come to the same conclusion about what action to take, we must hear one another and commit to working together. For we cannot do this work alone; we need one another if we are to realize the goals of feminism.

MENTORING THE MOVEMENT

Today, the women's movement is in an interesting position—one that allows for direct involvement of women of different generations. This presents opportunities and challenges. In the movement today, second and third wavers face one another in the same room and work collectively in the fight to end discrimination. We have the opportunity to share experiences with, and learn from, one another intergenerationally. We have the opportunity to change the misconceptions about feminism and to learn from criticism, bringing all women to the table. I have personally experienced both the challenges and the triumphs of intergenerational leadership. On the downside, I have experienced the marginalization that accompanies being a young feminist who is trying to legitimize her vision and leadership in a community of second-wave feminists who believed that I was too young to lead. But, on the positive side, I spent four years leading California NOW in an intergenerational partnership. My executive director, Helen Grieco, is twenty years older than I, and together we created a model of leadership that valued and honored our experiences as activists with respect to our age differences. Intergenerational leadership is a relatively new concept, for, as I mentioned, the waves of the movement are merging in way we have not previously experienced.

For my generation in urban California, I feel feminism tends to just be accepted as something our mothers did and we ignorantly reap the benefits of the struggle. Susannah, 32, white, straight, married

The challenge today is in learning how to share the movement—and to share leadership within the movement. Sadly, we face significant barriers to achieving this—both from outside and within the movement itself. From outside, there is a widely publicized perception that young people are apathetic or that they don't get "it." Often there is a lack of reporting or representation of young people working for social justice—or, when such activities are reported upon, the young activists are reported as representing an exception to the norm. From within the movement, we see a struggle between the older generation and the younger generation of women's-rights activists. Young activists who join this movement often express feelings of being excluded and patronized and feel pigeonholed into specifically "young" issues, despite their expertise on a wide array of feminist issues. Veteran feminists—those who have been in the movement for a significant period of time—often feel threatened by the growing movement of young feminists and sense that they are being replaced and unvalued. Occasionally, I hear an expression of relief that young women are picking up the proverbial baton and that veteran feminists can finally "retire." To be fair, there are those veterans who have truly committed themselves to working with the next generation, but, unfortunately, this is too seldom the reality. Instead, I often hear stories of young women being told to sit on the side and learn from the older women as opposed to being integrated into the leadership of the movement. Subsequently, we see young women disregarding the women's movement because they don't find a place or see themselves reflected within it. Veteran feminists are frustrated because they cannot seem to recruit young activists. As a result, we confront a disconnect between generations of women and the women's movement. And we face the challenge of learning to share leadership intergenerationally in order to continue this movement and achieve the goals for which we strive.

SO HOW DO WE DO THIS?

Speaking to the next generation, the veteran feminist, author, and activist, Phyllis Chesler writes in her book *Letters to a Young Feminist:* "you are entitled to know our war stories. We cannot, in good conscience, send you into battle without giving you a very clear idea of what may happen there."[4] Not only must young activists hear these "war stories," but veteran feminists must also hear those of younger activists, for we too have been in battle. Through these experiences, we have both something to share and knowledge to gain. To foster intergenerational leadership is to recognize the contributions that young activists have to bring to the table while honoring the work and perspectives of those who have built the modern movement. It is both of these sets of experiences and perspectives that collectively strengthen and further the women's movement. I believe that, as we move further into the twenty-first century and face the future of feminism, it is imperative that we hear the multitude of women's voices. In order for this movement to be relevant to the next generation, we need to engage, empower, educate, and train young women—and men—as activists committed to making a difference. We need to mirror their experiences, address their concerns, and validate their perspectives. Going beyond their general participation, we must respect their leadership and encourage their position within a movement that belongs not just to their mothers—or grandmothers—but also to themselves. Young women can be incorporated into the movement today and not just be seen as the future. We can also recognize and celebrate the gains of the women's movement— learning about both our history and the fight that achieved our rights today. We need to clarify and emphasize what is at stake for women and girls under conservative and anti-woman political administrations (such as that of George W. Bush and the legislators who follow him). Young voices must be raised; the feminist movement needs be passed onto the future, and its leadership must be shared intergenerationally. Today, we need to look at the criticisms of the past in order to build for the future. We can learn to mentor while supporting the efforts of the next generation. And we can honor the efforts of the second wavers without dismissing their relevance in current activism. Most important, we must never forget that we come from a continuum—that women who came before us fought for the rights that we enjoy today and that women today must fight for the rights of future generations. We need to recognize these contributions and the immense value of "veteran" feminists. And we need to learn how to mentor young women, while recognizing the importance of their roles in leadership of the feminist movement today. Most of all, we must recognize that we can join together in this movement—for its future and ours.

SISTERHOOD IS INDEED GLOBAL

We are experiencing an interesting contradiction today, one that is not all that new to the United States. On the one hand, we fight for boundary recognition, debate who can immigrate and under what circumstances, and wage war under the guise of protecting democracy and nationalism. On the other hand, the Internet has broken barriers down in ways our foremothers never imaged; as governments, we export and import products among nations and involve ourselves in the governing of others; in the name of business we establish multinational corporations that employ host-country citizens, use (and abuse) host-country natural resources, and dictate local and global markets; we share medical knowledge and resources worldwide; we travel extensively; we forge personal relationships; and in many other ways we break the boundaries between nations. The contradiction lies in our quest to be independent and separate while also being an integral part of the global community. The reality is that what one does in one area of the world does affect another area—we are all interrelated on both the personal and the political levels. Nowhere is this truer than in relation to the issues of political and social justice.

As we become a more globalized community, our feminism has moved to a greater recognition of women around the world. There is much debate about the role of Western women in the lives and battles of women worldwide. Is the discussion about feminism too focused on the United States? What role should U.S. women take in the battles for freedom that are fought in Asia, Latin America, Eastern Europe, and

Africa? Do U.S. women involve themselves ineffectively in global feminism—taking leadership in fights that belong to women elsewhere? Do U.S. women focus on international issues to avoid the realities of struggle within their own country? These are all critical questions to address when exploring global feminisms and revisiting Robin Morgan's sentiment that sisterhood is global.

I believe that there are many issues to be addressed in our country—many fights still to be fought, much discrimination to be eradicated, and many people to lift up. But I also believe that sisterhood is global and that we must also realize and appreciate that when women are oppressed anywhere in the world, their oppression contributes to an overall devaluing of women everywhere. Not only do these actions of oppression impact the global attitude about women, but they devastate the daily lives of women around the globe. From honor killings, dowry deaths, domestic violence, and female genital mutilation to rape and sexual servitude around the globe,[5] women are fighting battles for their lives. While I believe there is much to do and focus upon within the United States, when we hear the cries for help from women around the world, I believe that we have no other choice than to answer with action.

The action we take can be multifaceted. From influencing U.S. policies on foreign relations to joining global efforts, American women can play an important role in eradicating global gender discrimination. We can explore the bias that we bring as American women into the debate about the status of women worldwide, listen to the voices of women from cultures different from our own, and honor the leadership from women in individual regions, joining their efforts as supporters and not in an effort to replace them as leaders. We can participate with women-led efforts such as the Beijing Conference and the fight to ratify the Convention on the Elimination of All Forms of Discrimination Against Women (CEDAW)—both here in the United States and worldwide.

In 1995, women from around the globe gathered in Beijing, China, for the United Nations World Conference on Women. The intent of the meeting was to reaffirm the conventions of the 1993 World Conference on Human Rights in Vienna and to "put women's human rights even more firmly on the world agenda."[6] Addressing the critical issues of health care, poverty, violence against women, armed conflict, economic inequalities, environmental degradation, and governance, the women in attendance argued not only for understanding and recognizing women's rights as human rights but also for implementing such rights.[7]

One important measure to support the rights of women is the Convention on the Elimination of All Forms of Discrimination Against Women (CEDAW). Adopted by the U.N. General Assembly in December 1979, CEDAW is the first international human rights treaty to define discrimination against women. CEDAW "laid the foundation and universal standard for women's equal enjoyment without discrimination of civil, political, economic, social and cultural rights. . . . CEDAW seeks to advance women's human rights protection by applying a gender perspective to principles enunciated in the Universal Declaration of Human Rights. . . . CEDAW holds governments responsible for taking steps to modify practices based on stereotypes about women's roles as well as beliefs about women's inferiority."[8] As of March 2006, 183 counties, including more than 90 percent of the United Nations membership, most of our European allies, and many of our trade partners, have ratified CEDAW.[9] The United States has not.

> **CEDAW: The Convention** defines discrimination against women as "any distinction, exclusion or restriction made on the basis of sex which has the effect or purpose of impairing or nullifying the recognition, enjoyment or exercise by women, irrespective of their marital status, on a basis of equality of men and women, of human rights and fundamental freedoms in the political, economic, social, cultural, civil or any other field."

To support the activism of women around the world and to eradicate global gender discrimination, we must start at home. We can call on our government to stop profiting off the backs of women worldwide. We can call on our government to support the efforts of women's organizations, the United Nations, microcredit unions, nongovernmental organizations, women leaders, grassroots activism, and any efforts to accord women safety, respect, and equality. And we can call on our government to ratify CEDAW.

BUILDING THE MOVEMENT

The gains of the movement to date are the foundation for our future. We still have challenges—both within and outside the movement—to overcome before we are truly a diverse, inclusive, and widely successful movement. We each bring something unique and dynamic to the table, and with this we may realize a collective power that is immeasurable. But this power will be realized only if we set aside our fears, learn from our mistakes, and build upon our diverse strengths. We must be willing to get honest—not just about our struggles in society but also about those struggles within the movement and among our greatest allies. We must all be vested in this quest, for the outcome—good or bad—deeply impacts each of us. The movement, and feminism, belongs to us all.

SPOTLIGHT ON MENTORING

I have to recognize Helen Grieco, the Executive Director of California NOW. In 1999, I directly benefited from Helen's commitment to passing the torch to the next generation. I became California NOW Young Feminist Coordinator for the state, the first position of its kind, under Helen's presidency. Helen has been working in this movement for more than twenty years, and she is a veteran feminist, if you will. She has dedicated her life to the empowerment of women, and she has lived her commitment to bringing young women into positions of leadership. She has been a mentor to me in a way that I never knew was possible. And watching her vision for the future, and working beside her, has been a learning experience like no experience in my life. We need more mentors like Helen to teach us about the past, about our collective history, and about making positive social change. Helen is a tribute to what feminism truly stands for—mentoring, empowering, and improving the quality of life for women and girls. And she is the ultimate Fabulous Feminist.

TAKE ACTION

Getting Started

Read *Ms.* magazine, *Bitch,* or any other great feminist magazine.
Ask libraries and bookstores to make feminist magazines available.
Learn our *herstory.*
Take women's or gender studies courses (either at your current college or university or at your local community college).
Search the Web and research feminist organizations, nationally and in your local area.

The Next Step

Attend a meeting of a feminist organization; check out several and see which group best suits your philosophy.

Honor our foremothers, and register to vote. Make a commitment to vote in every election.

We need a two-thirds vote in the U.S. Senate to ratify CEDAW. In 2002, the Senate adjourned without time to take a vote on ratifying CEDAW, which went back to the Senate Foreign Relations Committee for consideration. In June 2002, President George W. Bush stated his refusal to sign the treaty. As of June 2006, the United States still has not taken an official position on CEDAW, despite the State Department's making recommendations in favor of CEDAW to the Senate Foreign Relations Committee. Contact your U.S. senators and urge them to fight for CEDAW. To track the status of CEDAW, visit www.womenstreaty.org.

Many U.S. states are working on state-based CEDAW initiatives. Contact your state representative to find out what your state is doing to support CEDAW.

Getting Out There

Donate time or money to an organization that works to support feminist work.

Volunteer with a feminist organization.

Host a discussion group to discuss what is at stake today for women and girls. Create a plan of action on how you can make a difference.

Participate in a march or rally. Organize one around an issue that you are passionate about.

Investigate international exchange programs, or consider spending a summer working for an international aid group.

ON MY BOOKSHELF

Julia Alvarez, *How the Garcia Girls Lost Their Accents* (New York: Algonquin, 1991).

Isabel Allende, *The House of Spirits* (New York: Bantam, 1986).

Maya Angelou, *I Know Why the Caged Bird Sings* (New York: Bantam, 1983).

Jennifer Baumgardner and Amy Richards, *Manifesta: Young Women, Feminism, and the Future* (New York: Farrar, Straus and Giroux, 2000).

Jennifer Baumgardner and Amy Richards, *Grassroots: A Field Guide for Feminist Activism* (New York: Farrar, Straus and Giroux, 2005).

Anna Bondoc and Meg Daly, eds., *Letters of Intent: Women Cross the Generations to Talk About Family, Work, Sex, Love and the Future of Feminism* (New York: Free Press, 1999).

Mary Brave Bird, *Lakota Woman* (New York: Harper Perennial, 1991).

Mary Brave Bird, *Ohitika Woman* (New York: Grove Press, 1993).

Anne E. Brodsky, *With All Our Strength: The Revolutionary Association of the Women of Afghanistan* (New York: Routledge, 2003).

Phyllis Chesler, *Letter to a Young Feminist* (New York: Four Walls Eight Windows, 1997).

Margaret Cho, *I'm the One That I Want* (New York: Ballantine Books, 2002).

Barbara Ehrenreich and Arlie Russell Hochschild, *Global Women: Nannies, Maids, and Sex Workers in the New Economy* (New York: Metropolitan Books, 2002).

Barbara Findlen, ed., *Listen Up: Voices from the Next Generation.* (Washington: Seal Press, 2001).

Guerrilla Girls, *Bitches, Bimbos and Ballbreakers: The Guerrilla Girls' Illustrated Guide to Female Stereotypes* (New York: Penguin Books, 2003).

Charlotte Perkins Gilman, *The Yellow Wallpaper* (New York: Feminist Press, 1973).

Deborah Gray White, *Too Heavy a Load: Black Women in Defense of Themselves 1894–1994* (New York: Norton, 1999).

Leslie Heywood and Jennifer Drake, *Third Wave Agenda: Being Feminist, Doing Feminism* (Minnesota: University of Minnesota Press, 1997).

Loraine Hutchins and Lani Kaahumanu, *Bi Any Other Name: Bisexual People Speak Out* (New York: Alyson, 1990).

Harriet Jacons, *Incidents in the Life of a Slave Girl* (New York: Signet Classics, 2000).

Marcelle Karp and Debbie Stoller, eds., *The Bust Guide to the New Girl Order* (New York: Penguin Books, 1999).

Jane Katz, *I Am the Fire of Time: The Voices of Native American Women* (New York: Dutton, 1977).

Audre Lorde, *Sister Outsider* (California: Crossing Press, 1984).

Rigoberta Menchú, *I, Rigoberta Menchu* (New York: Verso, 1984).

Rigoberta Menchú, *Crossing Borders* (New York: Verso, 1998).

Joan Morgan, *When Chicken-Heads Come Home to Roost: A Hip-Hop Feminist Breaks It Down* (New York: Touchstone, 1999).

Daphne Scholinski, *The Last Time I Wore a Dress* (New York: Riverhead Trade, 1998).

Michele Serros, *How to Be a Chicano Role Model* (New York: Riverhead Books, 2000).

Assata Shakur, *Assata: An Autobiography* (Chicago: Lawrence Hill Books, 1999).

Michael Stevenson and Jeanine Cogan, *Everyday Activism: A Handbook for Lesbian, Gay, and Bisexual People and Their Allies* (New York: Routledge, 2003).

Amy Tan, *The Joy Luck Club* (New York: Putnam, 1989).

Alice Walker, *The Color Purple* (New York: Harcourt Brace Jovanovich, 1982).

Rebecca Walker, *Black, White and Jewish* (New York: Riverhead Books, 2001).

Rebecca Walker, ed., *To Be Real* (New York: Anchor Books Doubleday, 1995).

Virginia Woolf, *A Room of One's Own* (New York: Harcourt, 1989).

FABULOUS FEMINIST WEB RESOURCES

Amnesty International   www.amnesty.org
An international campaign working for human rights and peace. Web site includes a wealth of information, including information on campaigns to end violence against women, protect refugee rights, end torture, and control arms.

Black Women in Sisterhood for Action www.feminist.com/bisas1.htm
Founded in 1980, Black Women in Sisterhood for Action is a nonprofit organization providing education and career development; scholarship assistance; social assistance; and information and resources geared toward black women.

Black Women Organize for Political Action   www.bwopa.org
BWOPA is a great organization. I have worked with it many times. It is committed to training black women in the political process. It works to increase the presence and voice of black women in the political system.

California National Organization for Women   www.canow.org
The California chapter of the National Organization for Women. Provides up-to-date information about the status of women and girls, including legislative and grassroots activism.

CEDAW   www.womenstreaty.org
Web site tracks status of U.S. action on CEDAW. Also addresses critical issues regarding CEDAW. Great source of information.

Center for Women Policy Studies   www.centerwomenpolicy.org
A great source of information! The Center for Women Policy Studies is a research organization working to achieve justice and equality for women.

Feminist.com Activism Links   www.feminist.com/activism
A great site for links to a variety of feminist activism nationwide.

Feminist Majority   www.feminist.org
National and international information, resources, and activism. The Feminist Majority Web site is a great source of information on how to get involved and make a difference in the lives of women worldwide.

Gender PAC   www.gpac.org
The Gender Public Advocacy Coalition works to bring awareness to gender stereotypes while working to end gender discrimination and violence. Web site has great information and resources about legal cases and activism regarding gender identity.

Guerrilla Girls   www.guerrillagirls.com
Web site gives information about Guerrilla Girls' history and current activism. Site also includes publications, stickers, and posters.

Human Rights Watch   www.hrw.org
Campaigns to ensure that human rights apply to all. Organization engages in fact-finding research to determine the treatment of peoples around the globe. Web site includes information about the status of human rights abuses throughout the world, organized by region and by issue.

MANA (a national Latina organization)   www.hermana.org
Emphasis on the empowerment of Latinas through leadership development, community service, and advocacy.

National Organization for Women   www.now.org
Nationwide organization working on a wide range of women's-rights issues. Web site includes resources, links to other organization, activist campaigns, and a store of feminist goods.

National Women's History Project   www.nwhp.org
Great resources for educators! A wealth of information and resources about women's history.

Third Wave Foundation   www.thirdwavefoundation.org
Great source for grants and scholarships for third-wave work. Web site also includes resources and public-education programs.

United Nations Women Watch   www.un.org/womenwatch/
A great source for resources and statistics on the status of women globally.

The Women's Media Center   www.womenmediacenter.com
A great resource for feminist journalists and anyone seeking news through a feminist lens.

3

A Movement for Everyone

Extraordinary work is being done by women—internationally, nationally, and locally—that has changed policy, politics, programs, and perspectives. Women have changed not only their lives and the lives of girls today but also the lives of future generations. Women have broken barriers, set records, and established their worth, their ability, and their strength. Tremendous dedication, time, commitment, and sacrifice have gone into raising consciousness and ending discrimination. But, in the history of the feminist movement, there seems to be a divide among women ourselves—a disconnect that keeps us from unifying our efforts and achieving our collective goals. This disconnect, I believe, is based upon the very issues against which we are fighting—racism, classism, ageism, homophobia, ableism, and the like. Our disconnection is the result of a long history of oppression and segregation, of being socialized to gravitate toward those who are most like us.

I am saddened by the historical roots that have served to keep us from truly unifying, and I wonder whether we can ever resolve them. Even after three waves of the feminist movement, we are still divided as women in this country and worldwide. Can we ever come together? I have been a feminist all my life. I have been active in the feminist movement for fifteen years. And, while I am incredibly grateful for the gains that have been made and the work that has been done, there is still much to be done to make this a movement for everyone.

> Rac·ism, *n.* 1. a belief or doctrine that inherent differences among the various human races determine cultural or individual achievement, usu. involving the idea that one's own race is superior. 2. a policy, system of government, etc., based on such a doctrine. 3. hatred or intolerance of another race or races.

RACISM

Of the criticisms of feminism and the women's movement, the most poignant is that of racism. It is a myth that women of color are not involved in the women's movement. They are and always have been. Unfortunately, a division formed that served to separate women of color from white women. As a third waver, I have many questions about this division—did white women honor the perspectives of women of color? Were women of color incorporated into the leadership of the movement? Whose issues were of primary focus? How did racism infiltrate itself into a movement determined to fight for equality? I feel as if I have inherited much of this strain and daily confront the past when mobilizing for change today. But, as a white girl, it is a challenge to talk about race. What do I know about being "of color" in this culture? How can I speak to the issue of racism, not having lived it myself? I used to want to be colorblind, not to see race, but then I realized that this was essentially ignoring the role of race in a society that is far from colorblind. I realize that to try not to see color in this culture is to ignore the challenges of race and ethnicity, to undervalue the struggle that has been waged to end racial discrimination, and to distance myself from the ongoing fight to end racism. To do so also ignores the importance of celebrating our differences as a means of expanding our individual and collective knowledge.

I recognize the power of growing up white in a racist society. And, in that, I recognize that I say and do prejudicial things without fully knowing the impact of my actions or words. While I work every day to unlearn racism, to listen without prejudice, to hear the realities of my sisters, I also recognize that in a global culture with such tense race relations, I am seen first as a white woman. The assumption by some, I believe, is that I have no greater commitment to diversity than that assumed by my foremothers. So, how do we break through this? How do we create a venue to get real with each other? To have a dialogue that understands that, while we may not say the right words, while we may not fully understand the realities of living with racism, we come into the conversation with honest intentions? How do we have a dialogue about the multitude of oppressions we face without valuing one over the other? How do we get to a respectful understanding that, while a person of color knows racism in a way that a white woman can only imagine, the oppression of sexism is also real? I believe that we need to come to a place of understanding that no longer asks people to define narrowly who they are primarily—a person of color *or* a woman *or* a lesbian *or* a gay man *or* a person with a disability—but that recognizes our diversity and the importance of eradicating all discrimination and oppression. I own the fact that because I grew up white in a racist society, on some level I will have prejudice, and, though without the intent to offend, I sometimes say or do things that are offensive. In my quest for better understanding, better communi-

> *I think Indian people still have a hard time incorporating feminism into the conventional idea of what Indian women are supposed to be like. We worship our goddesses and confine our women to cultural straight [sic] jackets.*
> Sheethal, 23, Asian Indian, heterosexual, Ohio

cation, better partnership, I unknowingly tokenize—not because I believe that one person can speak for her group but because I want the conversation to occur.

I want there to be a place where we can all sit down and really talk it all out, where we come to the conversation with honest intentions. I want us to give one another the benefit of the doubt, understanding that fear of offending has kept us from meaningful interaction. I am not talking about truly, overt racist people who hate on the basis of skin color and think they are right in doing so—they are a whole other, more obvious, problem. I am talking about the people who care about equality, who are conscious of racism but who largely are ignorant of the implications of their own words and actions and their impact, or the people who spend so much energy searching for the right words that they say nothing. I realize that just sitting down together is not the solution, but it is an important step.

One of the greatest moments in my activist life occurred at the 1996 San Francisco "Fight the Right" March. As Californians, we were fighting two horrible propositions—Prop. 209, the "civil rights initiative" that proposed the elimination of affirmative action in the state, and Prop. 187, which proposed cutting health and social services (including public education) for immigrant populations in California. For the first time, at this march, I saw all the "groups" come together to fight discrimination. The women's movement, the civil rights movement, the labor movement, the immigration movement, the GLBT movement— six hundred different organizations were represented, and approximately fifty thousand participants were at the march. In that moment, we were powerful—instead of focusing on our differences and debating who had more at stake, we recognized that we were all oppressed by the power structure. Because we are female or gay or a person of color or an immigrant, we are denied access to full participation in society—we are denied housing, jobs, promotions, and free movement. We are disenfranchised, ignored, targeted, or denied basic rights because of characteristics inherent to who we are. We are divided and pitted against one another, fighting over a small piece of the social pie, while all the while the power structure takes the bulk of the pie. I believe that there is a conscious effort to divide our groups. But, if we can begin to recognize our commonalities rather than believe in the lines that divide us, we can share the struggle, unite forces, and emerge stronger. The power structure fears this most—fears an organizing of the oppressed who can rise up collectively and change the distribution of the proverbial pie. Unfortunately, in the end, both propositions were approved. The movements are still fractured. Today, we continue with the struggle to see the importance of our diversity and to share leadership across the board.

> As a woman, feminism obviously represents me. But as a Black American, I have goals that are much different than the goals of the feminist movement.
> Carita, 33, straight, California

I have seen racism within the women's movement. I have heard the frustrations of women of color who come to the table only to be shut out by white reality. I have seen white women negate the importance of religion and faith to women of color who often hold these as central to who they are. I have seen many well-intentioned white women make racist remarks. But I have also seen women from all ethnic backgrounds sit together in a room and discuss the challenges to women today and collectively work toward a solution. I have seen the bridging of our lives, the raising of consciousness and the commitment to band together. And it is a powerful sight.

The second wave's approach of consciousness raising is regaining momentum as young feminists are reviving the tradition and practice. And it is not just young people who need this consciousness raising, I see everyday examples of racial tensions among people of all ages and across all ethnicities. The reality is that we live in a multicultural, multiracial society. But, despite this diversity, when it comes to the debate about race, we tend to see and talk only in black and white. Certainly, historical and current tensions are significant between African Americans and whites, but these are not the only racial tensions that exist. Racism occurs between white people and every people of every other ethnicity, but it also exists among other ethnic groups. The idea of valuing one's skin color over another is not unique to white people. As JeeYeun Lee writes in her article, "Beyond Bean Counting," "Issues of exclusion are not the sole province of white feminists."[1] We categorize and discriminate in all areas of race, creating a hierarchy of value within and among varying ethnicities. At the core are issues of power—getting it, having it, and keeping it. And, indeed, historically, white people have systematically held the most power. This is, of course, still true today. However, not all white people have power. Class, age, gender, physical and mental ability, and sexual orientation all come into play when determining power. But skin color alone does afford benefits for whites. Whiteness itself provides an unearned privilege for those who carry the pigmentation. In her book *Feminism is for Everyone*, bell hooks writes:

> *I am a white person, so in large part I believe that feminism does represent me, but it is not as inclusive as it needs to be to really represent all women.*
> *Jennifer, 31, Caucasian white girl of Italian heritage, California*

> No intervention changed the face of American feminism more than the demand that feminist thinkers acknowledge the reality of race and racism. All white women in this nation know that their status is different from that of black/women of color. They know this from the time they are little girls watching television and seeing only their images, and looking at magazines and seeing only their images. They know that the only reason nonwhites are absent/invisible is because they are not white. All white women in this nation know that whiteness is a privileged category. The fact that white females may choose to repress or deny this knowledge does not mean they are ignorant: it means that they are in denial.[2]

I believe that white women must confront this denial and deconstruct our role in racism. In her writings on white privilege, Peggy McIntosh encourages looking beyond individual acts of racism to invisible systems of privilege and dominance of whites. She writes, "as a white person, I realized I had been taught about racism as something that puts others at a disadvantage, but had been taught not to see one of its corollary aspects, white privilege, which puts me at an advantage."[3] White women must begin (and continue) to deconstruct and understand this privilege if we are to be true allies in ending racism and the discrimination that accompanies it. If you are white, consider these statements when evaluating your benefits as a white person:[4]

> I live in a school district where more money is spent on schools that white children go to than on those that children of color attend.
> I went to a school where the textbooks reflected my race as heroes and builders of the United States, and there was little mention of contributions of people of color.
> I work in a job, career, or profession where there are few people of color.
> I can always vote for candidates that reflect my race.
> My race needn't be a factor in where I choose to live or where I send my children to school.
> I don't need to think about racism every day.

For a white person, examining these statements is the start to unlearning racism and beginning to look critically at the tensions we keep at arm's length—because we are certain (and often loudly proclaim) that we are not racist. In meeting after meeting of "progressive-minded" activists, I hear white women argue against concerns brought forward by women of color. Perhaps this happens because progressive white women have a lot invested in being politically correct. Perhaps it happens because there is a lot of guilt about being white among those whites who fight for equality. But fear of being accused of being racist gets in the way of *hearing* the points and views of women of color. And, instead of building a bridge, we deepen the divide.

White people need to get beyond their feelings of guilt and understand that guilt for being white (or male or straight) is self-indulgent and paralyzing. This isn't about you. It is about the structure of society and your actions within it. Feel guilty if you are not contributing to the solution, but not over something over which you have no control. Energy is much better spent working to be allies of people of color in ending racial discrimination. In his book *Uprooting Racism: How White People Can Work for Racial Justice,* Paul Kivel sets forth some important guidelines for being a white ally to people of color:

1. Assume racism is everywhere, every day.
2. Notice who is the center of attention and who is the center of power.
3. Notice how racism is denied, minimized, and justified.
4. Understand and learn from the history of whiteness and racism.
5. Understand the connections between racism, economic issues, sexism and other forms of injustice.
6. Take a stand against injustice.
7. Be strategic. Decide what is important to challenge and what's not.
8. Don't confuse a battle with the war.
9. Don't call names or be personally abusive.
10. Support the leadership of people of color.
11. Learn something about the history of white people who have worked for racial justice.
12. Don't do it alone.
13. Talk with your children and other young people about racism.[5]

As a white woman, let me add another guideline: Don't look to people of color to educate you on racism. It is not the job of people of color to take care of white folks. It is the job of white folks to raise their consciousness, to reach out and partner with people of color, to consult, include, and take the lead from people of color on the issues of racism . . . and on other issues of social justice, as well. As McIntosh asks, "having described [white privilege], what will I do to lessen or end it?" White people need to share positions of power, support and encourage the leadership of people of color in organizations and in the larger society.

RACISM AND THE FEMINIST MOVEMENT

What about the feminist movement? Does it truly represent all women? As a third waver, I have learned the history of exclusion and the politics between white women and women of color. I have heard the arguments that white women focused on issues about their lives—for example, fighting for the rights to abortion—while women of color were fighting for their rights to have children; white women have neglected to embrace and support the issues of women of color. I have seen conflict arise when white women focus solely on their gender as their oppression, putting gender above all else. All the while, women of color fight to be recognized as such and resist being forced to choose their ethnicity over their gender or vice versa. I have seen the fighting between women, and, more tragical, I have seen women give up and move further away from one another. The conflict for third wavers is in knowing this past and respecting the feelings and opinions that came from that time, while living our commitment to a more inclusive movement, doing this work every day and confronting and changing this heritage. The third wave is acutely aware of the reality of racism and the history of exclusion of women of color by so-called mainstream organizations—it has been taught to us through women's studies and is present in our day-to-day interactions, our writings, our dialogues, and our activism. The discussion of race is integral to all that the third wave does, as are gender politics, class, sexuality, and disability. And, while we certainly don't have everything figured out, we have had the benefit of learning from the women who came before us, and, as a result, we recognize and appreciate the inadequacy of valuing gender as the only oppression.

> I have mixed feelings about whether the movement represents me or not. I feel that it does represent me individually, but not some of my black sisters. There is more happening to include women (and men) of every race, but it's not there yet. Nicole, 25, heterosexual, Connecticut

White women need to recognize and respect that women of color have always been involved in social justice movements—for suffrage, women's rights, civil rights, GLBTQQI rights, disability rights, and so on. There is a misconception that women of color are not interested in the feminist movement; quite the contrary, they are leaders and visionaries working for change every day. This, of course, is not news to women of color, but it just might be news to those who know of the feminist movement only what they see on TV or read in history books. In fact, this movement is multifaceted—from nationally based mainstream organizations to local, grass-roots efforts, we all contribute to this fight for equality. We need to come together to define feminism, to define our work, and to commit to working together. Collectively, we can reclaim and redefine the image of feminism and women's rights—so that all women, all experiences, and all perspectives are represented. We are in this together, not in spite of but because of our differences and because of our commitment to justice. We must ensure that this is the foundation upon which we build and that the images of the movement reflect all women.

> Feminism is very inclusive as far as addressing the rights of women no matter their race, gender, ethnicity, income level, marital status, sexual orientation, etc. etc. etc. Christina, 22, straight, Greek, California

One of our greatest contributions as third wavers can be to close the gap across ethnicities, to build upon the failures and successes of this movement, and to live a politics that is about, and represents, all women. In order to do this, we need to be willing to join together, to be honest with one another, to build and share a dream together. And we need to tell the true story of feminism, one that is not controlled by the media, does not put forth one leader but rather reflects the contributions, the perspectives, and the lives of us all. I see today's feminists attempting to do this work everyday, choosing not to inherit this divide but to learn from our foremothers and change the course of this movement. We need to be able to call one another on our misconceptions and inaccuracies, to hold each other accountable, to listen and hear one another—each of us, across all ethnic and racial lines. It is difficult, it is confusing, it is sensitive, it is raw, but it is also vital.

WHAT CAN YOU DO?

Listen. Read. Support. Advocate. Join multicultural efforts to address issues as defined by those affected. Hold your own organizations, friends, school, and family accountable for racism, exclusion, and ignorance. Get honest with yourself and about your actions. It is not enough to believe that you are not racist; you must also deconstruct racism within our culture, your role, and how you benefit from it. We need to question the structure of society and the hierarchy of race. We must raise our racial consciousness.

We need to get honest about this, about who benefits and who does not—even when this system is not what we wish for or consciously support. We *all* need to do this. I do hold the feminist movement to a higher standard, as I do all social justice movements, but I believe that we must also recognize that racism is a challenge throughout our culture, that there is not an answer out there that the feminist movement is choosing to ignore. Which means that we—the multiracial, multicultural, multigendered, progressive masses—need to lead the way in finding the solutions.

> I identify as a feminist to a certain extent. I believe the term womanist was coined by Alice Walker to more accurately reflect the unique struggle of Black women who suffer discrimination both for being female and non-White; that term might more accurately reflect my identity. Cheria, 31, Black/African American, heterosexual, Ohio

INTERGENERATIONAL PARTNERSHIP

One of my first memories of being a leader was in first grade. Normally, story time involved a gathering on the floor around our teacher's feet. Instead, I convinced a table of fellow six-year olds that we were "close enough" to hear the story and had no need to leave our table for the cold hardness of the floor. I convinced the kids at my table to stay put, even in the face of losing recess. We sat together in quiet resolve. And, of course, after story time we spent our recess practicing how to get up from our table and sit on the floor, how to get up from the floor and sit back at our table. The point wasn't that we lost our recess; the point was that they did what I said. I was thrilled, I intuited that I had a "gift." I was a leader—or, perhaps, a little dictator!

After a few years of principal-parent conferences (don't all good activists end up in the principal's office?), I began to learn that making people follow me was not as interesting as inspiring change. Controlling people's actions wasn't as interesting as creating a dialogue about a situation and encouraging a collective solution. I realized that I still had a lot to learn from other leaders before becoming one. I could not have become who I am today without the presence of very important mentors in my life to guide me. My most successful mentor relationships were ones that not only guided me but, more important, allowed me to lead. Mentoring is an exchange, an egalitarian relationship based upon support and collaboration. As the waves of the feminist movement intersect, mentoring is crucial for the movement's growth.

One of the greatest challenges the third wave is charged with today is to continue to expand upon the movement of our foremothers, as well as to learn from their mistakes and to actively counter the misconceptions about feminism more generally. We come to this movement energetic and idealistic—

We wouldn't have the freedom that we had today if it wasn't for the women who fought for our rights. I believe this movement represents all women and men of all ages. Gabriella, 19, Hispanic, heterosexual, California

we've heard the stories of our mothers, learned our history in women's studies, and grown up expecting equality with men. We come from all races, all countries; we speak a variety of languages, practice a number of different religions and faiths; we have different economic and educational backgrounds; we have different opinions. We are active in our communities, in politics, and in organizations because we want to make a difference. Some of us identify as feminists; some us do not. We debate the word—its connotations, its meaning, its history. Wherever we enter this movement, we share the commonality of being the children of feminism, of civil rights, of lesbian and gay rights, disability rights, the fight for economic justice . . . and all the movements that occurred before us to bring true social, economic, and political equality to us all. We benefit from these movements and inherit a unique perspective on politics today. And, while we are afforded a different life from that of our mothers—through better laws, court decisions, legislation, social consciousness shifts, and the like—we are also in the unique position of being able to critique the movement without having lived through our mothers' experiences firsthand. This perspective both hinders us and provides us the objectivity with which to examine the movement constructively.

However, as third wavers, we risk offending second wavers if our opinions or views differ. As younger women who are trying to make names for ourselves, to make a difference, we may fear offending the leaders of the movement and thus being rejected or shut out by the very people we respect and with whom we dream of shared leadership. If we don't follow the party line, will we still be allowed at the table? If we question the status quo or offer a new way, what do we risk? Many of us have turned away from mainstream organizations largely because we do not see ourselves reflected within them—they don't represent our issues in the manner that we see them. We don't feel that leadership or respect is attainable in mainstream organizations that carry with them years of set history and entrenched authority. Still others of us do join these organizations, and within them we find both mentors and resistance. With mentors we find a place of encouragement and support—we find a place at the table.

Sometimes 2nd wavers seem to think they know it all, and I think they need to step back and let some of us take leadership roles. Juli, 34, white, bisexual, Massachusetts

As young women, we encounter a wide variety of resistance. Some of this resistance is intentional, and some of it is not. There is a gap in understanding between generations; in many ways, we don't speak the same language. We present new views on old ideas; we bring a new perspective and address a new reality in relation to the issues that the second wave has long been fighting. There is a great deal that third wavers can learn from the second wave. Agreed. But there is also a great deal that third wavers can teach the second wave. The dilemma is that the movement finds itself in new territory, merging voices as we continue to confront our common battles of discrimination. Whenever a new voice emerges, tension arises, sometimes out of fear and threat and other times out of ignorance. Young activists often report feeling isolated, undervalued, and unwelcome.

While veteran or older feminists have a responsibility to the movement in mentoring, supporting, and embracing young activism, young women also have an obligation to learn about and respect the work and contributions of veteran feminists. We need to appreciate that this work is ongoing. We need to recognize that this work enables us to be who we are and to have what we have today but also that the gains of the movement are not just for us. We need to recognize that we are part of a continuum and that we have an obligation, a responsibility to join with and continue the work of the first and second waves (and those who work outside or alongside those waves), contributing our perspective, our voice, and our vision. As generations merge, we struggle to find tangible ways to share leadership intergenerationally. Collectively now, we are charged with addressing these challenges and learning how to not just coexist in this movement but to learn from and support one another. Third wavers don't want to replace older women; we want to sit at the table with them. We don't want to be expected merely to show up for events but rather want to be included in the design and creation of the event. We don't want to be considered the future of the movement; we want to be a part of the movement today and help build for the future.

I was raised not to need to be a 'feminist' to believe that I am equal, to be able to KNOW without having to identify as such. Karen, 26, Aleut, heterosexual, Alaska

Earlier in the book, I spoke a bit about building bridges between generations and fostering true intergenerational leadership. At the core, it really comes down to respect—respecting that we have different experiences with similar issues, that we bring with us unique perspectives based upon our individual histories, cultures, and religions, and respecting the reality that, while we may come at a situation differently, we all want to end oppression, hate, ignorance, and discrimination. I've put together a Do's and Don'ts list to help facilitate the growth of intergenerational partnership, noting, of course, that this list is in no way exhaustive. These are my suggestions; they are based on my own experiences and on the numerous experiences shared with me—from both younger and older activists. Feel free to add to, change, alter, adapt—whatever is needed to further the conversation.

DO'S AND DON'TS FOR VETERAN FEMINISTS

Do give the benefit of the doubt, and ask questions before you make assumptions.

Do empower young activists to run with their ideas.

Do recognize that age doesn't equal experience—young feminists join this movement with a wide array of experiences and expertise. We reach our feminist consciousness at different points of our lives. In other words, just because we're young doesn't mean we don't know things.

Do ask what young activists need from you.

Do share your histories, experiences, failures, and successes, while sharing your expertise, ideas, and knowledge today.

Do recognize and respect the diversity of the third wave—in terms of our demographics, our ideas, and our approaches to activism.

Don't accuse young feminists of "not getting it"—if we're at the meeting, march, action, we do "get it."

Don't pigeonhole young feminists into specifically "young feminist" issues—we have many areas of knowledge and interests.

Don't dismiss ideas just because they "have been tried before."

Don't overlook leadership ability in young people.

Don't assume that young activists are here to take over, or that we don't value your work, past and present, or that we don't want to work with you today.

DO'S AND DON'TS FOR YOUNG FEMINISTS

Do give the benefit of the doubt, and ask questions before you make assumptions.

Do respect the energy and work—past and present—of veteran feminists.

Do recognize that you are a part of a continuum—the movement that happened before you but also the responsibility that you have to those who are coming up behind you.

Do speak your mind, bring your ideas to the table and take leadership.

Do your share of the work, but **don't** be a "gopher" to do all the trivial tasks.

Do celebrate and honor the diversity of the third wave—in terms of both our make-up and our ideas.

Don't apologize for your age.

Don't exclude older feminists from your discussions or action plans; we have a lot to learn from one another. And we have a lot to gain from working collectively.

Don't ignore the political context of our lives. This movement is not just about reclaiming knitting or wearing pink, and it is not just about our pursuits or our careers; it is about a system of oppression and the need for collective action.

Don't dismiss the ideas of veteran feminists with the assumption that "they're out of it."

DISABILITY RIGHTS

When I lived in Sweden as an exchange student in high school, I was extremely impressed with a nursing class project that required students to spend a period of time enacting a disability. They were required to go through stores, use public transportation, eat in restaurants, and go about their day with an assigned disability. They were then to evaluate these public places, meet with shop owners and city officials, and create a plan for better accessibility. People seemed receptive to these students—in terms of both their presence and their assessments. To me, it seemed that Sweden had its priorities straight, as evidenced by its commitment to make society accessible to all. Unfortunately, the United States is seriously lagging, with inadequate resources and accommodations for those who are both physically and mentally challenged.

> **Americans with Disabilities Act (ADA)—July 26, 1990**
> **101st Congress of the United States**
> *An Act: To establish a clear and comprehensive prohibition of discrimination on the basis of disability.*

Despite the passage, in 1990, of the Americans with Disabilities Act (ADA), which prohibits discrimination in employment against those with a disability, disabled people in the United States continue to experience discrimination and abuse—with women facing the greatest challenges. Women with disabilities face double discrimination—their disability and their gender. They are stereotyped and stigmatized, resulting in inequitable treatment, including barriers to equal employment and educational opportunities. According to a Center for Women Policy Studies *Briefing on Girls and Young Women with Disabilities,* young women are underrepresented in special education programs, are less likely to find images of themselves or role models in education, are less likely to receive sex education, have lower employment rates, receive lower pay, and face a greater likelihood of being employed in low-status jobs than do disabled males.[6] According to the U.S. National Institute on Disability and Rehabilitation Research's

Chart Book on Women and Disability, of children who participate in special-education programs, about two-thirds are male.[7] Additionally, women with disabilities earn between 49 and 55 percent less than their male counterparts.[8]

Clearly, the challenges faced by women with disabilities are central to the issues championed by the women's movement. Unfortunately, the women's movement has not always centralized these concerns, and women with disabilities often still feel invisible in the movement. From inaccessible meetings and conferences to the issues that they are left to battle on their own, disabled women have been marginalized both in society and within the movement. Efforts are beginning, however, with the rise of feminist disability studies, the work of the Center for Women Policy Studies, and organizational conferences such as the Disabled People's International 2004 World Summit, held in Canada, which focused on women and disabilities, and NOW's 2003 Women with Disabilities and Allies Forum. The movement must recognize its responsibility to take on the issues of women with disabilities as it would any issue that impacts women's lives—no longer can those with disabilities be seen as separate. The movement must educate itself about living with disability and advocate for equal access and respect for all women, not ignoring women with disabilities. Individually, we must educate ourselves, counter myths, advocate, make meetings and get-togethers accessible to all, incorporate, and partner between abled and disabled women.

GAY, LESBIAN, BISEXUAL, TRANSGENDER, QUEER, QUESTIONING AND INTERSEX

I remember sitting on old couches in the women's center at the heart of campus and engaging in long, detailed conversations in which we debated where we all fell on the Kinsey scale of sexuality, the spectrum of sexual orientation developed by Dr. Alfred Kinsey in the 1940s and 1950s. We spent hours debating whether or not there was truth to the idea that everyone is bisexual. We shared a collective outrage at the religious right, which argued that being gay is immoral and against God. We discussed the fluidity of gender and the influence and power of socialization. We argued the power of the media and the paucity of images of gay and lesbian characters. We discussed the misconception that all feminists are lesbians and fought against the notion that being a "dyke" is negative. We discussed the impact of these misconceptions on the public perception of feminism and their impact on the future of the movement.

TIMELINE OF LESBIAN AND GAY RIGHTS

1924—*Society for Human Rights,* the first openly gay American organization, is formed in Chicago.

1955—Del Martin and Phyllis Lyon form *Daughters of Bilitis,* the first lesbian organization in the United States, in San Francisco.

1958—The nation's first gay periodical, *One,* is allowed by Supreme Court decision to be distributed through the mail.

1961—Jose Sarria, the country's first openly gay political candidate, runs for office in San Francisco.

1961—Illinois becomes the first state to abolish laws against consensual gay sex.

1964—The New York League for Sexual Freedom protests the military's antigay policies by picketing the Whiteball Induction Center.

1967—The *Advocate* is founded.

1969—The Stonewall Riots kick off the "gay and lesbian liberation movement" in the United States.

1970—New York City hosts the first Gay and Lesbian Pride March.

1973—The American Psychiatric Association removes homosexuality from classification as a mental disorder.

1973—The Lambda Legal Defense Fund is founded.

1974—Kathy Kozachenko becomes the first openly lesbian elected official when she is elected to the Ann Arbor, Michigan, city council.

1975—Santa Cruz County becomes the first county in the United States to ban discrimination against gays and lesbians.

1976—The first Michigan Womyn's Music Festival is held.

1977—Harvey Milk is elected San Francisco City Supervisor, the first openly gay elected official in any large U.S. city.

1981—PFLAG (Parents, Families and Friends of Lesbians and Gays) is founded.

1981— Barney Frank is elected to the U.S. House of Representatives; he continues to be one of the most prominent openly gay politicians holding elected office.

1987—ACT-UP is formed.

1991—The first Black Lesbian and Gay Pride event takes place in Washington D.C.

1992—The Lesbian Avengers were founded in New York.

1994—During the 1994 Gay Games in New York, Olympic gold medalist Greg Louganis publicly comes out. This follows the much-watched 1988 Olympic Games in Seoul, South Korea, where Louganis won the gold medal for diving after hitting his head on the diving board. In 1995, he announced that his was HIV+ and addressed concerns he had during that 1988 Olympic accident.

1997—An eager public watches as character Ellen Morgan "comes out" on the TV show *Ellen,* mirroring Ellen DeGeneres's real-life "coming out."

1998—Tammy Baldwin becomes the first nonincumbent openly LGBT person to win election to Congress.

1998—Mathew Sheppard is brutally killed; his story ignites national outrage at hate crimes.

2000—Vermont becomes the first U.S. state to offer civil unions for same-sex couples.

2003—The U.S. Supreme Court case *Lawrence v. Texas* overturns a Texas law banning gay sex.

2004—San Francisco issues marriage licenses to same-sex couples.

2004—Massachusetts becomes the first U.S. state to legalize same-sex marriage.

2005—Civil unions become legal in Connecticut. Illinois adds sexual orientation and gender identity to the Illinois Human Rights Act.

2006—Washington state passes a bill to prohibit discrimination based on sexual orientation and gender identity.

As previously mentioned, the equating of feminists with lesbians or dykes has long been used as a way to discourage women from fighting for equality and claiming feminism. I've discussed how this impacts straight women and their involvement with the movement, but, additionally, how do these messages impact lesbian women and their place in the feminist movement? Certainly, lesbians and straight women, by the very nature of being women, share a mutual interest in the fight for equality.

[A key challenge that I face is] the transition from Female-to-Male and wanting all women to know that it's not that I want to have the so-called privilege of being male. It's something I need to do to bring my mind and my body closer spiritually, physically and mentally. I'm not giving up any of my roots in the women's movement. Shaun, 27, Native American and Caucasian, pansexual, Rhode Island

While issues may vary in their focus, intent, and priority, people of all sexualities have a vested interest in working together to combat the use of our sexuality against us. Like with all oppression, whether one is straight or gay, homophobia works to devalue us all. As Urvashi Vaid argues, "there is an intimate connection between homophobia and sexism: Homophobia maintains gender inequality. Labels like 'fag' or 'dyke' are deployed to police the boundaries of sexual and gender expression."[9] Unfortunately, however, like other groups within the feminist movement, lesbians have been marginalized. This marginalization can result from a heterosexist norm both within and outside the movement. Considering heterosexualism as the norm creates an "othering," much like the othering of women to men, making lesbian women second to heterosexual women. Instead, we need to recognize that, as Kristin Severson writes in "Identity Politics and Progress: Don't Fence Me In (or Out),"

as the feminist movement is learning the hard way, women's issues include homophobia, racism, classism, xenophobia, etc., because a feminist movement MUST include ALL women. It is when identity politics sells out "Others" by not being inclusive that we realize our political movements are more like that which we are fighting against than we wish to realize. But to be truly progressive, it seems we must go one step further than including all the diversity within our own identity movement, we must create a belief system that everyone can adopt as their own whatever their identity.[10]

In adopting this system, we need to also embrace all the issues faced within our community as they are our own issues: gender identity, trans issues, homophobia, sexual oppression, gender-based violence, discrimination in the workplace, and political rights such as marriage equality.

Transgender: as *an umbrella term used to describe anyone who is gender different: someone born of one gender, but having either a casual affinity for clothing and/or affectations of the opposite gender; or someone with an innate identification as the opposite gender. Transgenders can range from female impersonators, to crossdressers, to transsexuals—both male to female, and also female to male.*

Intersex: *people who are born with "sex chromosomes," external genitalia, or internal reproductive system that are not considered "standard" for either male or female.*

(Definitions come from The National Transgender Advocacy Coalition.)

RELIGION, MARRIAGE, AND
THE FIGHT FOR GAY RIGHTS

From the denial of lesbian and gay leadership within most traditional faiths to the extremist antigay organizations like GodHatesFags.org, religion is inevitably at the core of the debate surrounding the morality and legitimacy of lesbians and gays. These arguments are present among school boards, in day-care centers, within city councils and state legislatures, and in Congress. It is argued over and over that gays are a threat to American family values, to the health of our children, to our educational system, and to our political structure—it's amazing the power that lesbians and gays hold! Most recently, we have found ourselves in the midst of a battle over gay marriage. While opponents are passing so-called sanctity-of-marriage initiatives and/or legislation (somewhat ironic, given the plethora of reality TV marriages and dating shows focused on heteros!), proponents of gay marriage are pushing for city ordinances and legislation that would support civil unions and legalized gay marriage—thus affording gay couples the same rights and privileges as those in heterosexual relationships. More than one thousand specific rights are granted to heterosexual married couples, including the right to make medical decisions for the partner, the right to hospital visitation, the right to insurance benefits, social security, and inheritance among partners—hardly radical notions.

This fight for the recognition of and rights for gay couples is not new, but recent headlines have caused a resurgence in the debate. On February 12, 2004, Freedom to Marry Day, San Francisco mayor Gavin Newsom allowed City Hall to begin issuing marriage licenses to lesbian and gay couples in the city. The first to marry were Phyllis Lyon and Del Martin, long-time leaders in the feminist and lesbian rights movement, now in their late seventies and early eighties, who have been partners for more than fifty years. Following the lead of San Francisco, cities in New York and New Mexico have also begun issuing marriage licenses. Statewide legislation is key, as is fighting for federal recognition. California, Hawaii, and Vermont already grant various benefits to same-sex couples, with Vermont guaranteeing all state benefits and responsibilities equal to those for heterosexual couples. And, most notably, on November 18, 2003, the Massachusetts Supreme Judicial Court ruled, in response to an inquiry by state legislators as to whether civil unions would suffice, that only marriage can bring true equality. Indeed, civil unions are not the equivalent of marriage. But, the fight continues to support and recognize gay marriage in Massachusetts.[11] And Massachusetts is only the beginning. Federal and state-to-state recognition are not guaranteed, and, in fact, under the 1996 Defense of Marriage Act, passed by Congress and signed by President Clinton, neither the federal government nor the states are required to recognize same-gender marriages that took place in other states. If this act weren't enough, granting the federal government and states the *option* to refuse recognition, Congress is currently debating an official ban on gay marriage. In February 2004, President George W. Bush made statements endorsing a Constitutional amendment that would define marriage as legitimate only between a man and a woman. Additionally, during the 2004 elections, eleven states passed similar initiatives limiting the definition of marriage.

With the rise of gender studies and with issues of gay marriage taking political center stage, the fight for gay rights is gaining a recognition like that accorded the civil rights and women's rights movements of the 1960s and 1970s. Importantly, marriage has long been debated within feminist circles, as some have argued that the institution itself is inherently patriarchal and inequitable for women and so have questioned whether the gay community should in fact fight for marriage at all. Others argue, however, that gay marriage would both signify and afford social and political equality with heterosexuals. Many claim that marriage equality is the next big push for civil liberties as we fight to expand gender identity, domestic partnerships, employee benefits, and state and federal recognition of marriage rights. I believe that this is a fight that the feminist movement must embrace and actively participate in. We should:

> [The Massachusetts] ruling gave me a sense of equality to heterosexual couple that I never knew I wanted or needed. It truly made me feel like more of a whole person ... now that I have tasted that sense of equality there is no going back. Nothing less than marriage rights will ever create that equality and any attempt to amend the state or federal constitution to keep marriage from us will be seen as blatant discrimination and unacceptable. Nina, 30, Italian, lesbian, Massachusetts

Demand that our political representatives actively oppose the federal marriage amendment that would define marriage as existing only between men and women;

Work to have the Defense of Marriage Act (DOMA) overturned. DOMA was signed into law in 1996 and defines marriage as a heterosexual union;

Demand that federal hate-crimes legislation include hate crimes motivated by gender and sexual orientation and that conviction for such crimes carry with it serious punishment for offenders;[12]

Protect and defend the right of gay, lesbian, intersex, and transgender people to parent, whether through pregnancy, adoption, assisted reproductive technology, or surrogacy;

Support sexuality education in schools that is comprehensive, including education about sexual orientation;

Incorporate intersex in our understanding of gender and sex categories;

Support, respect ,and defend the right of people to express their gender and sexual orientation in any manner that does not harm others as we do heterosexual folks;

Require all colleges, universities, schools, and workplaces to adopt nondiscrimination policies that include gender, gender expression, and sexual orientation; and

Treat gender and sexual orientation as civil rights issues, defending them against discrimination.

We must also encourage and create a safe place for personal exploration of gender. It is the norm in a society like ours to accept, force, and/or assume the gender labels we were given at birth. But, as Kate Bornstein writes in her book, *My Gender Workbook*, "[i]t's when we begin to poke around in the piles of accumulated emotions, mannerisms, attitudes, and values, when we really let ourselves look at what we've gotten ourselves into; that's when we can begin to get some clarity on gender. That's when we can construct a gender identity for ourselves that best lets us express our needs and wants in this world."[13] In order to fight for political and social recognition, we must first understand our own gender identity and the sociopolitical constraints that inevitably follow its definition.

A WORD REGARDING MEN IN THE MOVEMENT

Men are not the enemy. They, too, are at a disadvantage in a patriarchal society. Men in the feminist movement can take a stand against gender-based oppression and speak out about the cult of masculinity that boxes them into a very narrow accepted norm. The feminist movement needs to do a better job in welcoming and incorporating men. We need to do a better job in changing the cultural interpretation of feminism that hinders male involvement. That burden is on us. But, I also believe that men need to do a better job of addressing their role in, and their experience with, gender oppression. The feminist movement should stop celebrating men's presence, but at the same time it should welcome men's involvement. It is possible to incorporate men into feminism without falling over ourselves to thank them. I find that we're either *so* happy that men have become involved that we become obnoxious or we are suspicious and/or irritated by their presence. Both of these reactions have to stop. Let's be partners—equal partners—and let's model within the feminist movement what we would like to see outside the movement.

I grapple with the notion that men can be feminists. While they can definitely identify with the movement's ideal and goals, men will never truly know what it feels like to be a woman. Milton, 23, African American, Louisiana

Similarly, men need to stop expecting that women will work it all out for them. I am asked frequently what I am going to do for men. There seems to be a rising accusation that the feminist movement left the men behind. I have two nephews whom I adore beyond words. I want them to grow up in a culture that allows them to define themselves and does not require them to be macho, über-masculine men. I embrace my role in their learning. But I am tired of being expected, as a feminist, to raise the consciousness of all men. I am sick of people demanding that I create a progressive men's movement. Women have not achieved true equality; my own movement is not yet over. Even if it were, I would still be hesitant to take responsibility for a men's movement. I am not a man, did not grow up a man, do not know what it is like to be a man. Why should I create or lead a men's movement? I shouldn't, any more than I would expect people of color to teach me how to unlearn racism. However, I would support a pro-feminist men's movement to address this cult of masculinity. I'd come to your rallies, distribute your materials, vote for your initiatives and your candidates, support your legislation; I'd work as a partner, just as I hope that you will work with me.

Besides, the reality is that there are men who are doing great work to address masculinity and feminism. Men are feminists—both within and outside the feminist movement. And feminist men, like Jackson Katz, Kevin Powell, Michael Kimmel, Allan Johnson, Greg Tate, and Scott Coltrane, to name a few, are writing, speaking, and acting to deconstruct the notions of masculinity and the intersection of race, sex, class, pop culture, and feminism. Unfortunately, however, there seems to be a notion that men, by nature of being male, cannot be feminists. Or that men who are feminist are not "real" men; they are gay or "girlie men." This is related to the culture of sexism and homophobia in which we live. And it is linked to the rampant myths about feminism. Fortunately, more and more men are breaking the stereotypes and standing up for equality. The reality is that until men recognize the importance of sharing partnership with women, honoring our differences rather than highlighting them as justification for discrimination, and begin to fight a patriarchy that hurts not just women but also men, we—women and men alike—will not achieve true equality and the endless benefits that go along with it.

Organizations such as the National Organization for Men Against Sexism (NOMAS) are working to address the challenges to masculinity and the role men have in ending sexism and discrimination. NOMAS is an activist-based organization committed to pro-feminist, gay-affirmative, antiracist ideology that is dedicated to enhancing men's lives.[14] NOMAS works to challenge the tradi-

I identify as a feminist but I feel that the word feminism pushes a lot of men away because of the labels attached to it. David, 21, black, heterosexual, New Jersey

tional stereotypes of masculinity that plague men and boys in our society. They believe in working alongside women to oppose gender discrimination, eradicate gender-based violence, and challenge social injustice, such as racism, sexism, and homophobia. Whether in organizations or individually, men are actively working to counter sexism, end discrimination, and create a new generation without gender bias.

Organizations like NOMAS, and the individual efforts of men working to end discrimination, serve as a vital resource for men who want to effectively work to end discrimination against women. And they serve as an important alternative to oppressive organizations of men that work to enforce male-dominated traditional roles, such as the Promise Keepers. Founded by the conservative Bill McCartney, the Promise Keepers are backed by Jerry Falwell (of Jerry Falwell Ministries), Bill Bright (of the Campus Crusade for Christ), and James Dobson (of Focus on the Family). The Promise Keepers, unlike pro-feminist organizations, advocates that men take back their "rightful" role as head of household by any means necessary and require that women unquestioningly follow men. Such organizations and attitudes deepen the divide between men and women, protect and advance the theory and practice of patriarchy, and continue to place women in positions of subordination to men. Fortunately, these groups represent only a minority of men. The fact is that men have always worked alongside women for justice.

MOVING FORWARD

As we continue to address the challenges both within and outside our movement, it is important to remember that collectively we are strong. Our fight is a collective one—for any to be free from oppression, we must *all* be free from oppression. Everyone deserves a seat at the table. We simply need more chairs.

MEN SPEAK OUT TO WOMEN

Sometimes, I am treated far too well simply because I am a man. Men should be feminist, and realize their male privilege, and use that to enhance sexual equality. Fareed, 18, Hispanic/West Indian, gay, Colorado

We have to lead other men by example. We have to have the presence of mind to learn from women leaders and to apply that learning to our male peers and ourselves. Zafar, 23, South Asian American, heterosexual, Texas

As a man who identifies as feminist, I feel that I have a responsibility to not only self-identify as a feminist, but to publicly identify—even to proclaim myself— as a feminist, to help other men (and women) realize that men can be feminists too, and give support to feminist women. Jesse, 21, white, straight, Arizona

I am a gay man and realized that sexism was intertwined with heterosexism, I realized that the taunts I received had to do with my not being perceived as a "real" man and that I was being seen as a sort of woman which was seen as bad, so obviously women were hated too. Chris, 33, Latino/Anglo, HIV+, Michigan

When you can see inequities it does not matter which side of the scale you are on, it is your duty as a decent human being to point out those inequities and fight for change. James, 25, white, straight, Illinois

WOMEN SPEAK OUT TO MEN

Men should actively discourage sexism in their social circles and peers . . . they should teach their children men's role in standing up for women. Emma, 21, white, heterosexual, Michigan

It is crucial to realize that women are fighting against patriarchy, not men. Lina, 21, South Korean (studying in U.S. since eighth grade), heterosexual, Massachusetts

In patriarchy, men are just as trapped as women. Amy, 22, mixed ethnicity, heterosexual, Mexico and California

I wish that men would stop being threatened and just be supportive. They should get out of the way and realize that they would be taking the same action if they were the ones being marginalized. Sara, 19, Caucasian, bisexual, California

I think that men are critical allies in the feminist movement … I do not think that we will ever achieve widespread change in sexism without partnership with men. Nicole, 32, white, heterosexual, Illinois

I think it's most important that men know that they can play a role in the feminist movement. In my experience, many men are unaware that they can be feminists. Because so many of the major decision-makers in this country are men, their involvement in the feminist movement is crucial. Erin, 23, Japanese American/Chinese American, heterosexual, California

Men should play a supportive role in the feminist movement. The leadership and the major voices should be female, because the movement is about empowering women. The movement is not about keeping men in charge and just asking a male-run society to treat its women better. Laura, 20, white, straight, New York

Men should play as much of a role as possible. They should show their support and voice their beliefs. Charrise, 19, Black, heterosexual, Maryland

I think men need to acknowledge their privilege and recognize women's specific struggles. They need to constantly challenge themselves to be anti-sexist in an environment that does not require this of them and in fact encourages sexism. They need to never stop listening to women as we articulate feminism. At the same time, they should point out ways in which gender politics and norms harm men. They need to maintain their feminist ideals even when inconvenient (as do we), and this means challenging other men's sexism. Rosalie, 22, white, straight, Maine.

SPOTLIGHT ON ACTIVISM

SisterSong: Women of Color Reproductive Health Collective

Based in Atlanta, Georgia, SisterSong is an organization dedicated to lifting "the voices of women of color to have an impact on Reproductive Justice issues that affect women of color." SisterSong is a collective of seventy-six local, regional, and national grassroots organizations representing five primary ethnic populations and indigenous nations in the United States, including Native and Indigenous Americans, Asian/Pacific Islanders, Middle Eastern/Arab Americans, Latinas, and Black/African Americans. Formed in 1997, SisterSong works on public policy and advocacy, educational programs, and community organizing and has collaborated on national political efforts such as the 2004 March for Women's Lives. It publishes a national newspaper, *Collective Voices,* which is created by and for women of color. For more information about, and to support the efforts of, Sister-Song, visit www.sistersong.net or phone the group at 404.344.9629.

TAKE ACTION

Getting Started

Listen.
Read.
Reach out.

The Next Step

Question racist, sexist, ageist, or homophobic jokes. Redefine what is funny.
Question racist, sexist, ageist, or homophobic language. Changing language can change assumptions.
Explore your own privilege—examine your status in society, what have you been able or not able to do because of your gender, race, ethnicity, religion, age, sexual identity, and so forth.
Actively unlearn racism by getting informed, challenging your own assumptions, and examining your position in society.
Go beyond tolerance. Be a model of acceptance and respectful behavior.
Celebrate and take action of the International Day of Action Against Racism, August 31.
Celebrate International Women's Day, March 8.

Getting Out There

Ask your local school board and/or schools if their curricula and textbooks are equitable and multicultural.
Examine the membership of the groups, schools, businesses, and organization that you are a part of—does everyone look like you? Is the group committed to diversity? Raise the issue if it has not been raised.

The next time you are in a public place that isn't handicapped accessible, ask the management why not.

Celebrate February 12, Freedom to Marry Day, each year. Plan special events, write editorials to your newspaper. And work every day to ensure that lesbian and gay couples are afforded the same recognition, rights, and respect as straight people.

Host an intergenerational dialogue in your community or organization or on your campus.

Pick an issue to focus on, and share perspectives from a variety of generations.

ON MY BOOKSHELF

Paula Gunn Allen, *The Sacred Hoop* (Boston: Beacon Press, 1992).

Maya Angelou, *I Know Why the Caged Bird Sings* (New York: Bantam, 1983).

Gloria Anzaldua, ed., *Making Face, Making Soul/Haciendo Caras: Creative and Critical Perspectives by Women of Color* (California: Aunt Lute Books, 1990).

Jennifer Baumgardner and Amy Richards, *Manifesta: Young Women, Feminism, and the Future* (New York: Farrar, Straus and Giroux, 2000).

Amy Bloom, *Normal* (New York: Vintage Books, 2002).

Kate Bornstein, *My Gender Workbook* (New York: Routledge, 1998).

Mary Brave Bird, *Ohitika Woman* (New York: Grove Press, 1993).

Mary Brave Bird, *Lakota Woman* (New York: Harper Collins, 1991).

Sandra Cisneros, *House on Mango Street* (New York: Vintage Books, 1991).

Patricia Hill Collins, *Black Feminist Thought* (New York: Routledge, 2000).

Parvin Darabi, *Rage Against the Veil* (New York: Prometheus Books, 1999).

Angela Davis, *Women, Race and Class* (New York: Vintage Books, 1981).

Rory Dicker and Alison Piepmeier, eds., *Catching a Wave: Reclaiming Feminism for the 21st Century* (Boston: Northeastern University Press, 2003).

Anne Fausto-Sterling, *Myths of Gender* (New York: Basic Books, 1985).

Anne Fausto-Sterling, *Sexing the Body: Gender Politics and the Construction of Sexuality* (New York: Basic Books, 2001).

Leslie Feinberg, *Transgender Warriors* (Boston: Beacon Press, 1997).

Barbara Findlen, ed., *Listen Up: Voices from the Next Generation* (Seattle: Seal Press, 2001).

Ruth Frankenberg, *White Women, Race Matters: The Social Construction of Whiteness* (Minneapolis: University of Minnesota Press, 1993).

Judith Halberstam, *In a Queer Time and Place* (New York: New York University Press, 2005).

Daisy Hernández and Bushra Rehman, eds., *Colonize This! Young Women of Color on Today's Feminism* (New York: Seal Press, 2002).

Leslie Heywood and Jennifer Drake, eds., *Third Wave Agenda: Being Feminist, Doing Feminism* (Minneapolis: University of Minnesota Press, 1997).

bell hooks, *Feminism Is for Everybody* (Cambridge, MA: South End Press, 2000).

Allan Johnson, *The Gender Knot: Unraveling Our Patriarchal Legacy* (Philadelphia: Temple University Press, 1997).

Melanie Kaye-Kantrowitz, *The Issue Is Power: Essays on Women, Jews, Violence and Resistance* (San Francisco: Aunt Lute Books, 1992).

Michael Kimmel and Thomas Mosmiller, eds., *Against the Tide: Pro-Feminist Men in the U.S., 1776–1990* (Boston: Beacon Press, 1992).

Maxine Hong Kinston, *The Woman Warrior* (New York: Vintage Books, 1989).

Paul Kivel, *Uprooting Racism: How White People Can Work for Racial Justice* (Gabriola Island, BC, Canada: New Society, 2002).

Davina Kotulski, *Why You Should Give a Damn About Gay Marriage* (Los Angeles: Advocate Books, 2004).

Audre Lorde, *Sister Outsider* (Berkeley: Crossing Press, 1984).

Rigoberta Menchú, *I, Rigoberta Menchu* (New York: Verso, 1984).

Cherríe Moraga and Gloria Anzaldúa, eds., *The Bridge Called My Back: Writings by Radical Women of Color* (New York: Kitchen Table, Women of Color Press, 1983).

Joan Morgan, *When Chicken-Heads Come Home to Roost: A Hip-Hop Feminist Breaks It Down* (New York: Touchstone, 1999).

Robin Morgan, ed., *Sisterhood Is Forever: The Women's Anthology for a New Millennium* (New York: Washington Square Press, 2003).

Vickie Nam, ed., *Yell-Oh Girls! Emerging Voices Explore Culture, Identity, and Growing Up Asian American* (New York: HarperCollins, 2001).

Kevin Powell, *Who's Gonna Take the Weight?: Manhood, Race and Power in America* (New York: Crown, 2003).

Sonia Sanchez, *Homegirls and Handgrenades* (New York: Thunder's Mouth Press, 1984).

Michele Serros, *How to Be a Chicano Role Model* (New York: Riverhead Books, 2000).

Leora Tanenbaum, *Catfight: Rivalries Among Women—From Diets to Dating, From the Boardroom to the Delivery Room* (New York: Seven Stories Press, 2002).

Alice Walker, *In Search of Our Mothers' Garden* (New York: Harcourt Brace Jovanovich, 1984).

Rebecca Walker, ed., *To Be Real* (New York: Anchor Books Doubleday, 1995).

Deborah Gray White, *Too Heavy a Load: Black Women in Defense of Themselves 1894–1994* (New York: Norton, 1999).

FABULOUS FEMINIST WEB RESOURCES

Bamboo Girl   www.bamboogirl.com
"Challenging racism, sexism, & homophobia from the Filipina/Asian Pacific Islander (API)/Asian mutt feminist point of view since 1995."

Black Women Organized for Political Action   www.bwopa.org
"The purpose of Black Women Organized for Political Action (BWOPA) is to activate, motivate, promote, support, and educate African-American women about the political process, encourage involvement, and to affirm our commitment to, and solving of, those problems affecting the African-American community."

Bitch magazine   www.bitchmagazine.com
"Bitch | Feminist Response to Pop Culture is a print magazine devoted to incisive commentary on our media-driven world. We feature critiques of TV, movies, magazines, advertising, and more—plus interviews with and profiles of cool, smart women in all areas of pop culture."

Citizen's Commission on Civil Rights   www.cccr.org
"The Citizens' Commission on Civil Rights is a bipartisan organization established in 1982 to monitor the civil rights policies and practices of the federal government."

Equality Now   www.equalitynow.org
"Equality Now was founded in 1992 to work for the protection and promotion of the human rights of women around the world."

Girls Incorporated   www.girlsinc.org
"Girls Incorporated is a national nonprofit youth organization dedicated to inspiring all girls to be strong, smart, and bold."

Grrrl Zines   www.grrrlzines.net
Resources, zines, information about the third wave, tans, queer, women in publishing, and similar topics.

Hadassah   www.hadassah.org
"HADASSAH, the Women's Zionist Organization of America, is a vol-
unteer women's organization, whose members are motivated and inspired
to strengthen their partnership with Israel, ensure Jewish continuity, and
realize their potential as a dynamic force in American society."

Lesbian Herstory Archives   www.lesbianherstoryarchives.org
Web site housing collections, exhibits, resources, and materials chroni-
cling lesbian herstory.

Mexican American Legal Defense   www.maldef.org
and Education Fund
"Founded in 1968 in San Antonio, Texas, the Mexican American Legal
Defense and Educational Fund (MALDEF) is the leading nonprofit
Latino litigation, advocacy and educational outreach institution in the
United States."

Mosaic   www.jewishmosaic.org
The National Jewish Center for Sexual and Gender Diversity—educa-
tion and advocacy. Web site dedicated to increasing the visibility of
GLBT Jews within Jewish communities.

Ms. magazine   www.msmagazine.com
The classic feminist magazine. First published in 1972, Ms. *magazine*
has been a staple in feminist households and women's studies depart-
ments.

National Asian Pacific American Legal Consortium   www.napalc.org
"Founded in 1991, the National Asian Pacific American Legal Consor-
tium works to advance the human and civil rights of Asian Americans
through advocacy, public policy, public education, and litigation."

National Association for the   www.naacp.org
Advancement of Colored People
"The NAACP insures the political, educational, social and economic
equality of minority groups and citizens."

National Congress of American Indians   www.ncai.org
"NCAI's mission is to inform the public and the federal government on
tribal self-government, treaty rights, and a broad range of federal policy
issues affecting tribal governments."

National Congress of Black Women   www.npcbw.org
"NCBW is non-partisan and is the first organization that has its pri-
mary mission the political empowerment of African American women."

National Council of Jewish Women   www.ncjw.org
"The National Council of Jewish Women is a volunteer organization
that has been at the forefront of social change for over a century. In-

spired by Jewish values, NCJW courageously takes a progressive stance on issues such as child welfare, women's rights, and reproductive freedom."

National Council of La Raza   www.nclr.org
"The National Council of La Raza—the largest national constituency-based Hispanic organization and the leading voice in Washington, DC for the Hispanic community—is a private, nonprofit, nonpartisan, tax-exempt organization established to reduce poverty and discrimination and improve life opportunities for Hispanic Americans."

National Council of   www.womensorganizations.org
Women's Organizations
"The National Council of Women's Organizations is a nonpartisan, nonprofit umbrella organization of almost 200 groups that collectively represent over ten million women across the United States."

National Transgender Advocacy Coalition   www.ntac.org
Definitions, resources, reform and advocacy for equal rights for transgender and gender diverse populations

Native American Rights Fund   www.narf.org
"The Native American Rights Fund (NARF) is a non-profit organization that provides legal representation and technical assistance to Indian tribes, organizations and individuals nationwide."

New Moon magazine   www.newmoon.org
An advertisement-free magazine for girls ages 8–14.

Older Women's League   www.owl-national.org
"As the only national grassroots membership organization to focus solely on issues unique to women as they age, OWL strives to improve the status and quality of life of midlife and older women. OWL is a nonprofit, nonpartisan organization that accomplishes its work through research, education, and advocacy activities conducted through a chapter network."

Organization of Chinese Americans   www.ocanatl.org
"Founded in 1973, the Organization of Chinese Americans, Inc. (OCA) is a national non-profit, non-partisan advocacy organization of concerned Chinese Americans. OCA is dedicated to securing the rights of Chinese American and Asian American citizens and permanent residents through legislative and policy initiatives at all levels of the government."

Southern Poverty Law Center   www.splcenter.org
Champions of civil rights, the Southern Poverty Law Center takes on pro bono cases fighting for justice. It was instrumental in implementing the Civil Rights Act of 1964. Web site provides resources and information.

Third Wave Foundation   www.thirdwavefoundation.org
> *Through grants, public education campaigns, and networking, the Third Wave Foundation "helps support the leadership of young women 15 to 30."*

Tolerance.org   www.tolerance.org
> *"Tolerance.org is a principal online destination for people interested in dismantling bigotry and creating, in hate's stead, communities that value diversity."*

Women as Allies   www.women-as-allies.org/new2.htm
> *"Women As Allies is an organization whose mission is to bring women and girls of Color and those who are our allies together to create opportunities for education, dialogue, networking, healing and action."*

4
At the Table

WOMEN AND SOCIETY

To achieve true social, political, and economic equality for all women, we must have equal representation in the institutions that shape the face of our society. We need to have a place at the table of decision making. Women's ideas, perspectives, and vision need to be considered in all social and political realms of society, and we need to have an equal role in government, education, the media, labor, religion, and the military. We must be at the tables of corporate and union workplaces, on the floor of Congress and in the Oval Office of the White House, in our churches, temples, synagogues, and mosques, in our academies and at the every level of military leadership, in our colleges and universities, in our classrooms, in administration, and on our school boards. Women's voices must be not only heard but equally counted when deciding the future of this nation—and in nations around the world.

In 1776, when this country was writing its Declaration of Independence, Abigail Adams wrote to her husband to:

> Remember the Ladies, and be more generous and favourable to them than your ancestors. Do not put such unlimited power into the hands of the Husbands. Remember, all men would be tyrants if they could. . . . Emancipating all nations, you insist upon retaining absolute power over Wives. . . . If particular care and attention is not paid to the Ladies, we are determined to foment a Rebellion, and will not hold ourselves bound by any Laws in which we have no voice or Representation.

No longer must women wait for husbands, or men, to "remember the ladies." We are now in positions of leadership and have more political and economic power than ever before in modern history. But we are still bound by laws in which we have little voice or representation, and there is still work to be done to change the consciousness about gender roles and to achieve proportional representation and true equality in all facets of society. Our history is rich with revolutionary events. We have made gains because people fought for them, and that fight continues.

Politics can help us change what is going on within our lives, if we don't agree ... CHANGE IT. Vickie, 22, Korean, California

While there is not room in this book to fully explore every key institution that shapes our society, my goal is to present an introductory look at how women are represented in society. Like all rights afforded women, the right to have a voice—politically, economically, academically, spiritually—is the result of the efforts of women who stood against individuals and a society that said no.

THE RIGHT TO VOTE AND OTHER POLITICAL ACTION

Politics and political activism are critical for our future. From the price of milk or soda pop to the rise in tuition this semester, from the pharmacist who won't fill your prescription for emergency contraceptives to the health center that can't keep its doors open, from the cuts in welfare or financial aid to tax cuts for the wealthiest few in the nation, from campaign ads to who runs for president, it is all politics. We may be frustrated with what we see as corruption and lack of representation, but if we do nothing we only contribute to the problems about which we complain. If this system of ours is supposed to be "of the people, by the people" then let's claim the system for ourselves.

I never feel alone at the polls. In fact, my booth always feels so crowded, packed with the ghosts of the suffragists who fought for me to stand there, and heavy with the thought of future generations that my vote will impact. Following her election as the Democratic whip in 2001, Nancy Pelosi, the highest-ranking woman ever in Congress, met at the White House with the president and top congressional leaders. Noting that everyone at the table but her was male, she recounts that this meeting was unique both for her and for the White House. Of the experience, she says:

[I]t sounds strange, but as I sat down, I felt that I was not alone. For an instant, I felt as though Susan B. Anthony, Lucretia Mott, Elizabeth Cady Stanton—everyone who'd fought for women's right to vote and for the empowerment of women in politics, in their professions, and in their lives—were there with me in the room. Those women were the ones who had done the heavy lifting, and it was as if they were saying, *At last we have a seat at the table.*[1]

> *I find it hard to be a feminist and not have some sort of interest in politics ... it is far too important.* Michelle, 22, female-ish, queer, Florida

Indeed, women's right to vote was fought for—not assumed, not granted or handed out. Women died fighting so that we would have the right to participate in our political system today. And, despite the conflicts within the movement, the lack of inclusion, the racial and generational politics among the suffragists, they achieved lasting change. These women were the first to ever picket the White House; they suffered violent attacks, imprisonment, even force-feeding during hunger strikes, all because they believed that women must have a voice in a political system that sets out to make decisions in their behalf. To waste that right today is an affront to their memory, a disregard of all they lost to give us this right. Wasting this right is disrespectful to ourselves and to the women around the globe who are still fighting this battle. I realize that time is tight, child care is hard to come by, candidates, issues and initiatives are confusing, poverty and lack of education stand in our way in accessing the polls, but we collectively need to ensure that everyone's voice is heard on election day. We can share resources, pool child care, demand that polling places be fair and accessible, carpool, register for absentee ballots, and initiate discussion groups on the issues. We need to support one another because we owe it to ourselves to vote.

OK, soapbox aside, I hope I have convinced you to register and to vote in every election. Now let's talk about whom to vote for and our representation in our political system. In 2006, women held 25 percent of statewide elective executive offices in the United States, with women of color accounting for only 6.3 percent of those statewide officeholders.[2] Additionally, women make up about 15 percent of the members of Congress, with women of color constituting only 3.5 percent of the members of Congress.[3] Only eight states have women governors, and no woman of color has ever served as a governor for her state.[4] Despite making up 51 percent of the

U.S. population,[5] women have never come close to achieving proportional representation in politics. Our representation is crucial, since we
cannot leave it to others to make policy that directly impacts our lives.

Fortunately, we do have notewor-
thy women who paved the way for
women in politics; we need only to follow their lead. In 1916, Jeanette Rankin,
of Montana, was the first woman
elected to the U.S. Congress. Since then,
many women have made important
contributions as members of Congress,
including Bella Abzug, Barbara Boxer,
Shirley Chisholm, Diane Feinstein,
Geraldine Ferraro, Barbara Jordan, Barbara Lee, Carolyn Maloney,
Patsy Mink, Eleanor Holmes Norton, Nancy Pelosi, Hillary Rodham
Clinton, Linda and Loretta Sanchez, Patricia Schroeder, Maxine Wa-
ters, and Diane Watson. In addition, women have served as governors
and in local and state office. Despite all that has been proven by these
women, we have yet to have a woman president. In other countries—
Finland, Iceland, Israel, Panama, India, Latvia, and Canada—women
have served as presidents and prime ministers and as leaders at all
levels of government. These women are to be honored as leaders and
as pioneers. But while these are amazing women who have
significantly contributed to their nations, overall, women currently fill
only 14.3 percent of the world's parliamentary seats.[6] The White
House Project, the National Organization for Women, Emily's List, the
Feminist Majority, the National Women's Political Caucus, and Black
Women Organized for Political Action are just a few of the organizations that are working to further women's roles in government. We
need to train women in politics, put them in the political pipeline, and
help those who run for office to raise money and win their campaigns.
Our equal representation is critical. With that said, it is also important
to note that not all women leaders support gender equity or have progressive politics. While it is important that we celebrate the gains of
any woman elected to office, it is also important to recognize that the
feminist agenda is a progressive one. We need to elect leaders, of any
gender, who support and fight for equality for all. This must be our
commitment, as it is the only way to achieve truly equal representation
in our political system.

I never saw politics relevant in my life until I started to see that the rights that I have taken for granted for my entire life can be taken away just as quickly as a vote can be taken in Congress. I am registered to vote and use my right will-ingly. Rachel, 24, Caucasian, heterosexual, California

WOMEN LEADERS

In 1960, Siramavo Bandaranaike became the first woman
prime minister in modern times when she became prime
minister of Ceylon (now Sri Lanka).

In 1966, Indira Gandhi became the first female prime minister
of India.

In 1969, Golda Meir became Israel's first female prime
minister.

In 1974, Maria Estela (Isabela) Martinez de Peron became the
first woman president of Argentina.

In 1979, Maria de Lourdes Pintasilgo became the first woman
prime minister of Portugal and Lidia Geiler became the
first woman elected president of Bolivia. Margaret
Thatcher became the first woman elected leader in Europe
when she became prime minister of the United Kingdom.

In 1980, Jeanne Sauve was the first woman appointed speaker
of the House of Commons in Canada. Eugenia Charles of
Dominica became the Caribbean's first female prime
minister. She was also Dominica's first female lawyer.

In 1981, Gro Harlem Brundtland became the first woman to
become prime minister of Norway.

In 1982, Milka Planinc of Poland and Eugenia Charles Doinica
in the Caribbean became the first woman prime ministers
for their countries, while Vigdis Finnbogadottir became
the first elected president of Iceland.

In 1985, Maria Liberia-Peters became the first woman prime
minister of Netherlands Antilles.

In 1986, Corazon Aquino became the first woman president of
the Philippines.

In 1988, Benazir Bhutto became the first woman prime
minister of Pakistan.

Elected in 1990, Mary Robison was the first woman President
of Ireland.

Elected in 1990, Ertha Pascal-Trouillot was the first woman
president of Haiti.

In 1991, Edith Cresson became the first woman prime minister
of France and Khaleda Zia Rahman become prime
minister of Bangladesh.

In 1992, Betty Boothroyd became Great Britain's first woman speaker of the House of Commons.

In 1993, Toujan Faisal became the first woman elected to Jordan's Parliament.

In 1993, Tansu Ciller of Turkey, Sylvia Kinigi of Burundi, and Agathe Uwilingiyimana of Rwanda each became their country's first prime minister.

In 1997, following her husband's death, Janet Rosenberg Jagan was elected president of Guyana. She became the first American-born woman to be president of any country.

In 1999, Vaira Vike-Freiberga not only became president of Latvia but also became the first woman president in a former Soviet state.

In 1999, Mireya Elisa Moscoso de Arias became the first woman president of Panama.

In 2000, Tarja Kaarina Halonen became Finland's first female president.

In 2005, Massouma al-Mubarak became the first female cabinet member in Kuwait.

In 2006, Chile elected Michelle Bachelet as its first female president (and only the third woman to serve as president of a Latin American country). Ellen Johnson Sirleaf was elected president of Liberia, becoming the first woman to be elected a head of state in Africa. Han Myung-Sook became the first prime minister of South Korea.

To increase our political representation, we must secure a voice for women in politics. Passing a constitutional amendment for gender equality is an important step to ensure that women, men, and GLBTQQI in the United States are afforded full equality under the law. We need to insist that the United States support CEDAW to help free the world's women from discrimination. We need to engage politically on local, state, federal, and international levels. We need to make politics integral to our daily lives. There are, and have been, great women leaders. We have proven ourselves and our capabilities beyond any question. As young women, we have role models to look up to, but we also have a responsibility to participate in our democracy. Get political if you aren't already. Get louder if you are!

WOMEN IN THE WORKPLACE—INTEGRATING WORK, FAMILY, AND CIVIC LIFE

Women have always worked.[7] Our work has not always been publicly recognized, valued, or paid. But our work has always contributed to the economic health of our families and our nations. Women's labor, both paid and unpaid, must be recognized and respected. The feminist movement has advocated for this recognition of women's labor, including the right to work outside the home, and for safe and fair working conditions for those in the paid labor force. Additionally, feminists fought for the overall economic rights and health of all women, including the right of women to own property, to keep the money they earned, to have credit in their own names (a right not afforded women until 1971!), the right to join and participate in unions, and the right to be free from sexual harassment. The efforts of the feminist movement changed the consciousness of society and in turn created a work environment that is increasingly fair.

> glass ceil·ing: *n.* an upper limit to professional advancement, esp. as imposed on women, that is not readily perceived or openly acknowledged.

There is still a ways to go to achieve full equality for working women—in both the paid and the unpaid labor forces. Most agree that there is still a glass ceiling—a barrier between women and senior levels of employment. The glass ceiling is invisible, and it is not until one tries to pass through it that its impermeable nature is discovered. For those at the top, there is a responsibility to identify who is coming up the path. We then must mentor, hire, and advocate for other women so that the glass ceiling is broken permanently.

In addition to creating networks within business, we need to address the societal factors that work to keep the glass ceiling intact. Gender socialization continues to be powerful and is often used to categorize people and determine their abilities. When we first learn of the birth of a child, often the first question is, Is it a boy or a girl? Immediately, and almost involuntarily, we begin to associate behaviors and qualities with that child. In fact, a famous study, known as the "pinks and blues,"[8] showed how society sees girls and boys differently. Using the same baby, the study evaluated how people respond to gender-specific cues. Researchers wrapped the child in a blue blanket and then asked a group of people to apply adjectives to the baby; they found that the group described the baby as strong, big, and alert. However, the same baby wrapped in a pink blanket elicited descriptive terms such as sweet, quiet, little, and weak. From birth, we are assigned gender-specific attributes that in many ways determine how we are viewed throughout our lives. Women, for example, are assigned certain qualities that can prescribe nonthreatening and disempowering roles for them in society.

> I don't necessarily feel represented by the feminist movement since I am one of the women who is viewed as rather spoiled to be able to stay at home with my children and "dabble" in my career.
> Aimee, 34, Washington

These stereotypes follow us into adulthood. Women constitute the majority of those in lower-paying careers and jobs. For example, 97 to 99 percent of childcare workers are women,[9] and 89.7 percent of maids and housekeeping workers are women.[10] According to the Bureau of Labor Statistics, maids and housekeeping cleaners make an average of $8.17 an hour, whereas janitors (a separate category and one dominated by men) make an average of $9.19 an hour.[11] Compare the salaries and status of the person who cares for children with those of someone who cares for cars—a mechanic makes an average hourly wage of $11 to $26 an hour, whereas a child daycare provider makes an average hourly wage of $7.34.[12] Women with master's degrees still make less than men with bachelor's degrees. According to the 1995 U.S. Glass Ceiling Commission report, "A Solid Investment: Making Full Use of the Nation's Human Capital,"

> While minorities and women have made strides in the last 30 years, and employers increasingly recognize the value of workforce diversity, the executive suite is still overwhelmingly a white man's world. Over half of all master's degrees are now awarded to women, yet 95 percent of senior-level managers of the top Fortune 1000 industrial and 500 service companies are men. Of them, 97 percent are white. African Americans, Hispanics, Asian and Pacific Islander Americans

and American Indians also remain woefully under-represented in the upper echelons of American business.[13]

While these statistics are daunting, the good news is that women and people of color continue to make gains and to change the demographics of the workplace. Yet, the structure of the workplace has not kept pace with these changes. We need to have flexible work hours, comprehensive paid family leave, childcare available or compensated, strict sexual harassment policies and prevention, institutionalized mentor programs, and benefits for all family members, including domestic partners.

Feminists need to concern themselves with putting feminists in positions of political, economic, and media power. By placing feminists in control of these vehicles, a diversity of perspectives may be introduced to our insular society. This has the potential for revolutionary change. Bronwyn, 26, Caucasian, heterosexual

If such changes can be put into place, not only can women begin to realize their full potential in the workplace but the workplace can become more representative and accessible to today's worker.

In addition to structural changes, we also need to change cultural attitudes and informal networks. For example, as Debra Meyerson and Joyce Fletcher write in their report, "A Modest Manifesto for Shattering the Glass Ceiling,"

> mentoring programs may help women meet key people in a company's hierarchy, but they don't change the fact that informal networks, to which few women are privy, determine who really gets resources, information, and opportunities. Launching family-friendly programs doesn't challenge the belief that balancing home and work is fundamentally a woman's problem. And adding time to a tenure clock or providing alternative career tracks does little to change the expectation that truly committed employees put work first—they need no accommodation.[14]

In order to truly support a diverse work environment, corporations, unions, employers, employees, family members, and society as a whole must participate in this shift of consciousness. While revolutionary in their goals, Meyerson and Fletcher do not advocate revolution. Rather, they encourage small, incremental changes in deeply imbedded discrimination, arguing that "gender inequity is rooted in our cultural patterns and therefore in our organizational systems."[15] Further, they argue that "existing systems can be reinvented by altering the raw materials of organizing—concrete, everyday practices in which biases are expressed."[16] Small victories are the steps to cultural change. Passing legislation and corporate policy are important steps, but we need to also include a daily practice that supports integrating work, family, and civic life.

> I don't know anything about political stuff, but I do see that politics is relevant to my life. And I do plan to [vote]. Kelly, 24, Asian

MEDIA—THE POWER OF TELLING OUR STORIES

The media impact the way we view the world around us and, more important, who we are in that world. We grow up in a media-rich society, with radio, magazines, movies, billboards, and TV readily present at every turn. Indeed, the media have a powerful influence on our idea of reality. Far too often, however, women are not in the positions of leadership that would permit them to determine and direct our stories and images in the media. Currently, women hold only 15 percent of executive positions and only 12 percent of corporate board positions with media companies[17] and only 17 percent of the jobs both behind and in front of the camera.[18] Unless women are in positions of leadership and decision making, our stories are not told and our lives are often misunderstood and misrepresented. If we turned to the media to learn about women, we would believe that men outnumber us two or three to one.[19] We would learn that 74 percent of us are white, 16 percent of women are African American, 4 percent are Asian-American, 2 percent Hispanics, and 0.2 percent Native American.[20] We would discover that 74 percent of women are under the age of forty.[21] Very few of us are lesbians, or lesbians with a sex life (with the exception of *Showtime's* L-Word), and virtually none of us have disabilities. This is hardly a true and accurate representation of women in this country.

Women's involvement in the media is critical. Not only must we hold positions of leadership, but we must also familiarize ourselves with the media well enough to become media activists—not only to get our stories in the news but to democratize the media. The third-wave writers Jennifer Baumgardner and Amy Richards have a great section about the relationship between feminism and the media in their book *Manifesta: Young Women, Feminism and the Future.* In their chapter "Feminists Want to Know: Is the Media Dead?" they write, "the media doesn't know how to deal with feminism, and feminists haven't mastered the media."[22] Pointing to the fact that we have never owned a significant portion of the media, Baumgardner and Richards use this chapter to flush out media myths about feminism. Indeed, many of the myths of feminism are rooted in the media's portrayal of feminism. The media not only have a history of ignoring and misrepresenting us, but they also have an incessant need to *soften* our image—focusing on trivial issues of make-up and clothing, rather than on the political and economic issues for which we work. For example, when I was first elected as president of NOW in California, I did a newspaper interview in which the writer spent a significant part of the article detailing what I looked like and what I was wearing, including describing me as wearing the ever-feminine color pink (which I was not), rather than using the space to discuss the agenda that California NOW was putting forth. Despite the many challenges posed by inaccurate and biased media coverage, feminists need to learn how to effectively use the media to their advantage. Women need to be media savvy—we need to know how to get our message across and our stories told. The media are a powerful vehicle in our society, and indeed in the global community.

> In general I still believe that people are wary about feminism. We have been so saturated with stereotypes about feminists that it prevents us from understanding the movement. Rebecca, 22, white, Virginia

Finally, in addition to putting women in positions of media leadership and practicing media activism, we must be knowledgeable about our pop culture. Music, television, and movies set a tone for behavior, style, sexuality, and gender. Whether we personally follow the trends or not, it is important that we be able to critique their impact on the public perception of women and our lives as women. From the lasting impact of "Leave It to Beaver" to the shows that redefine family for the twenty-first century, from the movies that reinforce a narrow stereotype of femininity to the indie films that show another image, the media create a definition of woman to which we often turn to find our own definition. We idolize our celebrities as American royalty, we are obsessed with their every move—what they eat, what they wear, how they live—they set our trends and impact how we define ourselves. Far too often, these images are unrealistic and misleading. But every once in a while we hear a song that declares our independence, a movie that shows that "real women do have curves," television that inspires our political nature and shows our intelligence, and we are proud to be women. We need to celebrate these occasions and demand that they become the norm.

GREAT MEDIA FOR WOMEN

Bitch magazine—a great third-wave, feminist magazine.
Fairness and Accuracy in Reporting: Women's Desk—a national media watch organization.
Harpo Studios (Oprah)—Oprah's multimedia enterprise.
Lifetime Television for Women—"television for women."
Media Education Foundation—a great source of films that examine social issues.
Ms. magazine—the classic feminist magazine.
Oxygen Network—cable network geared toward women.
Wolfe Video—video distributors with a focus on lesbian films and filmmakers.
Womensenews—Internet and email-based news sources for global news on women.
Women in Film—a nonprofit networking organization for women in the film industry.
Women Make Movies—a nonprofit organization that promotes media projects by and about women.

RELIGION—TO EACH HER OWN

Another key institution that shapes the face of our society and impacts the lives and status of women is religion. Indeed, women come to feminism with a great diversity of backgrounds, including religious beliefs. Many people seem to think that feminism and religion do not go together. But if feminism is to protect and support women in their pursuits, then feminism needs to do a better job of embracing women of faith. It is true that there is much to question when it comes to religion and the roles and treatment of women within it—from the reinforcement of traditional gender roles within the home to the debate about whether women should be allowed to be religious leaders—but it is a mistake of the feminist movement to assume that women within religions are not questioning these very things and working to change the structure from the inside out. Many women, particularly white women, came to feminism in the 1960s and 1970s as refugees from rigid religious doctrines. Many have wounds from these experiences. And feminism is a great place to address the gender bias in upbringing and in the houses of religion. However, we need to recognize that feminism is multifaceted, as are the people within the movement. And, for many women, faith is central to their identities and ways of life. One's religious choices are deeply personal, and one's beliefs and practice should be left to the individual. That said, religion itself can be used in ways that can discriminate against individuals, even serve as a justification for killing.

> I identify as a feminist because I think that everyone should be equal. . . . However, as a Christian I sometimes feel like feminists marginalize those that believe in the Bible because they have written it off as an oppressive text. Sarah, 23, straight, Wyoming

While the Civil Rights Act of 1964 prohibits discrimination in employment on the basis of race and gender, section 702 of the Act exempts "religious corporations, associations or societies with respect to the employment of individuals of a particular religion to perform work connected with the carrying on by such corporations, associations, or societies of their religious activities." In 1972, this Act was expanded to allow religious groups to discriminate in all employee activities, as opposed to just those within religiously oriented venues. It is on this basis that religious institutions are allowed to refuse the ordination of women as leaders within religious organizations. Despite this, women have begun to join the clergy, which is certainly a gain, but as of 1996, women still make up only one in eight members of the clergy.[23]

Throughout the world, in many cultures, there is an expectation that women are to be the keepers of the faith in their families and that they carry the responsibility to pass on these traditions to their children. It is an important role, yet women are still not permitted to join the upper-level leadership within the church itself. Indeed, around the world, religion—from Catholicism to Islam—is used as justification to treat women as second-class citizens. The Roman Catholic Church is one of the strongest opponents of women's leadership within the church and has issued strong policy statements against the ordination of women priests. However, many Catholics throughout the world disagree with the pope's position. "We Are Church" is an international organization working for equal rights for women within the Catholic Church. It believes in the admission of women to all Church ministries and argues for a positive attitude toward sexuality. It believes in making change within the Church, while working toward a "Council of all Christian churches, which will regard each other as equals in their search for peace and friendship among themselves."[24] Like the Vatican, Eastern Orthodox, Greek Orthodox, some of the Anglican Communion, the Church of Jesus Christ of Latter-day Saints, and many fundamentalist and evangelical Protestant denominations also oppose women's leadership and the ordination of women. However, many religious sects and organizations support, and are working toward, an increase in women's participation in religious leadership. Reform Judaism and the Baptist, Lutheran, Presbyterian, Methodist, and Episcopal churches, as well as the Church of Pakistan and some Anglican churches, have all allowed women to become priests, bishops, rabbis, or deacons. The Unitarian Universalist faith is founded upon tenets of equality and is the first church to have a clergy made up of a majority of women. Some women of faith have chosen traditional religions in which they maintain traditional gender roles, while others have gravitated toward reform religions, reclaiming the role and importance of women within that faith; still others have turned to a revival of Goddess, Wiccan, or Neopagan faiths, creating their own spiritual practice or rejecting religion and/or spirituality altogether. In any case, many are working to support the leadership of women in religious orders.

I realize that as a country we have never had true separation between church and state. Religion has always been influential, even foundational, to our political system. But, short of protecting one's right to voluntarily practice and participate in a religion, while not controlling or limiting the action of others, I believe that the government should stay out of religion and religion out of government. I do not look to my elected officials to represent, design, or enforce my morality, and I do not believe that they should be allowed to. Since when do those who call themselves the "moral majority," or Christian conservatives, have the market on values and morality? Who are they to decide? I believe that morality is up to the individual, and as long as someone is not harming or restricting another's right to be, believe, or act, then to each her own. But do not be mistaken; there is a strong morality among feminists and the progressive left. Great activism and social service come from religious institutions full of folks working for justice. We must stop allowing the conservative right to define faith in only evangelical Christian terms. We must stop allowing conservatives to narrowly define our nation's morality. We must remember that conservatism and religion to do not always, or even usually, go hand in hand.

JUST DO WHAT? EDUCATIONAL
AND ATHLETIC EQUITY

I'd like to end this chapter on women's roles and representation in society by focusing on Title IX. After thirty-three years of Title IX, as of this writing, how are women and girls faring in athletics? Is there educational equity? Who is most likely to be called upon in the classroom—boys or girls? How do teachers respond to girls' ideas in school? How are girls faring in math and science? How gender-specific are examples used in classes or textbooks? What sports do girls have access to? How do sports impact a girl's self-esteem and self-concept? How equitably distributed are college scholarships? These are just some of the questions that activists and academics focus on when talking about Title IX. Arguably, if there has been a significant change in women's participation in society, it can be seen in those thousands of little girls now running around on soccer fields throughout the nation—a sight that was just not seen twenty years ago.

> **Title IX, Educational Amendments of 1972: No person in the United States shall, on the basis of sex, be excluded from participation in, be denied the benefits of, or be subjected to discrimination under any educational program or activity receiving federal financial assistance.**

Although mostly associated with athletic equality, Title IX of the 1972 Education Amendments is a federal statute that prohibits sex discrimination in education. Title IX includes all educational programs and activities in federally funded schools. Title IX prohibits discrimination based on gender, marital, or parental status in:

Admissions;
Housing and facilities;
Courses and other educational activities;
Career guidance and counseling services;
Student financial aid;
Student health and insurance benefits; and
Scholastic, intercollegiate, club, or intramural athletics.[25]

Title IX also prohibits sexual harassment by employees or agents of a school. In 1981, the U.S. Department of Education's Office for Civil Rights required that schools bound by Title IX have a policy and procedure in place to address complaints of sexual harassment.[26] In 1999, in *Davis v. Monroe County Board of Education*, the U.S. Supreme Court ruled that school districts can be liable for student-to-student sexual harassment if the school district had knowledge of the harassment and did not effectively address the problem.[27]

Within coeducational schools, Title IX prohibits single-sex classes or programs unless these programs are "designed to overcome the effects of conditions that resulted in limited participation by persons of a particular sex."[28] The intent is to allow schools to address the problems of inequitable access to programs, activities, and classes that have historically disadvantaged one sex. Perhaps one day we will also work to remedy the exclusion of those who do not identify as male or female—the only two sexes currently recognized by the U.S. government. Exceptions to this single-sex rule include contact sports, sex education in elementary and secondary schools, and choral groups; these areas may remain segregated.

Numerous studies, including those done by the California Women's Law Center and the Women's Sports Foundation, show that many women and girls who participate in sports have increased self-esteem, improved academic performance, better scores on standardized tests, higher rates of high school and college graduation, and higher rates of college attendance than their nonathletic female counterparts; they have lower rates of teen pregnancy and are less likely to stay in abusive relationships.[29] Additionally, we know that girls who are involved in sports have a more positive body image and better overall health. Given these results, it is concerning that we don't do a better job at encouraging and supporting girls' athletics. Are we frightened by the prospect of girls defining themselves, feeling strong in their bodies, bench pressing 250, or running a minute mile?

In recent years we have seen a rise in women's professional sports—from the Women's National Basketball Association (WNBA) to the Women's Profes-

> It bothered me, especially in high school and college, that my peers took boys and men more seriously than girls and women. Catherine, 23, white, lesbian, California

sional Football League (WPFL)—further providing young women healthy images and models to emulate. But, despite the move into professional sports and the known positive effect that sports have in the lives of women and girls, we are still fighting for equal access, recognition, and funding. In addition to educational equity, Title IX seeks to create athletic equity. In fact, athletics is the most immediately visible part of Title IX requirements. Under Title IX, educational institutions must provide equitable athletic opportunities to all students, regardless of sex, in three specific areas: participation, treatment of athletes, and athletic scholarships. In order to evaluate a school's compliance with Title IX in athletics, the Office of Civil Rights established a three-pronged test, and schools must meet one of the three criteria in order to be compliant. The three prongs are these:

1. Proportionality: assessing whether male and female students are participating in athletics proportional in numbers to their enrollment at the school;

2. History: a school must show a history of expanding opportunities in athletics for the underrepresented sex;

3. Meeting interest and abilities: a school must fully meet the interest and abilities of the underrepresented sex.

Most schools choose proportionality to test their compliance. Unfortunately, instead of truly ensuring access to athletics, this criterion means that women and girls are often blamed for cuts to men's sports. In response to demands for Title IX compliance, schools often cut men's teams to "make room" for women's teams—thus pitting men against women. The media tell the tragic stories of the men's lacrosse team being axed because those greedy women want a softball team. But what we rarely hear are stories of hotel rooms for football players who are playing at-home games, or the practice of purchasing new uniforms and multiple practice uniforms every season; or examples such as these, found by the Women's Sports Foundation:

- One university spent $300,000 putting lights on a football practice field that has never been used for football practice. It wanted to be able to impress potential recruits.
- One college housed the whole football team in a hotel for the entire preseason football camp because dorms were not available for the last two days and the coach didn't want the interruption. The snack bill alone was $86,000.
- A university dropped its men's swimming and diving program, citing economics. That same university found the means to (1) renovate the outdoor track, (2) renovate the indoor track, including the installation of hydraulic banked turns, (3) build a multifield baseball complex with heating elements under the soil to keep the grass growing year round, (4) add a new row of skyboxes to the football stadium, and (5) install new state of the art turf in the football stadium.[30]

We also rarely hear of the challenges faced by women athletes—challenges like those faced by the women's swim team that has to share parkas between races; or the women's diving team that has to practice in the dark with flashlights after the men's water polo team has finished practicing even though they are off season; or the teams that are told that women's uniforms must to be self-funded or that the costs of travel to games are the individual responsibility of team members. We also don't hear about who is awarded the majority of athletic scholarships—"each year male athletes receive $133 million or 36 percent more than female athletes in college athletic scholarships at NCAA member institutions."[31] Scholarship awards are often a deciding factor in college attendance. The truth of the matter is that for colleges and universities the issue is about prioritizing—and it is clear that even after more than thirty years of Title IX, women are still not a priority. Despite the assertion that women's sports have caused the demise of men's sports, both women's and men's participation in athletics has increased under Title IX—women's participation in intercollegiate sports increased from 90,000 in the 1981–1982 school year to 163,000 in 1998–1999, and men's participation went from 220,000 to 232,000 in those same years.[32] It is possible to increase the number of women's teams without cutting any men's teams—as 72 percent of schools were able to do between the 1992–1993 and 1999–2000 school years.[33] If we are to believe that girls and women have as much a right to play competitive sports as boys and men, and that the word athlete is not exclusively for men, then we must continue to support Title IX.

> I realized about halfway through my undergraduate degree program that there was no representation of women in the subjects I was studying, and that the teaching methodologies were biased and patriarchal. . . . I knew something was very wrong. Sarah, 22, white, California

CHALLENGES TO TITLE IX AND WOMEN'S SPORTS

While gains have been made in women's participation in sports, we still have a way to go before we see true proportionality and representation for women athletes. And, while we have made gains in many areas, we are losing ground in coaching and leadership positions for women. Women coaches are paid less than men and face significant barriers to advancement in their fields. In college athletic programs, women account for only 9 percent of sports information directors, 25 percent of all head athletic trainers, 34 percent of athletic administrators, and a mere 2 percent of the coaches for men's teams.[34] In contrast, men now hold the majority of coaching positions for women's teams. In the 1970s, with the passage of Title IX, 90 percent of women's team were coached by women.[35] Today, only 44 percent of coaches of women's teams are women.[36] A recent study found that a whopping 80 percent of head-coaching jobs created for women's sports since 1998 were filled by men.[37]

On the professional level, we are finally seeing the emergence of women sports stars. Venus and Serena Williams, Annika Sorenstam, Laila Ali, Michelle Kwan, Mia Hamm, Sue Bird, Sheryl Swoops, Lisa Leslie, Diana Taurasi, Natalie Couglin, and the many WBNA, NCAA, and WPFL players all give us heroes to watch in sports. But as in the other arenas in which women serve as heroes, they are neither recognized nor awarded the same status as their male counterparts. The average NBA salary in 1999–2000 was 58 percent higher than the average WNBA salary; professional women tennis players make sixty-seven cents for every dollar earned by male tennis players; and in professional golf that number drops to thirty-six cents.[38] Pay inequity in sports is real. For example, based on reported prize winnings, when Venus Williams won the Wimbledon title in 2005, she received 30,000 British pounds, or about $55,000 less than Roger Federer, who won the men's singles the following day.[39] Ironically, most commentators acknowledge that women's tennis is far more exciting to watch than men's—the public seems to agree, as the television ratings for women's tennis are higher than those for men's games. When a man argues for a higher salary, we give him props, sing his praises, and never doubt his worth. When a woman does, we tell her that she is lucky to be playing a sport she loves. When a male sport star is accused of rape, domestic violence, or even murder, we usually allow him to continue playing—and often rearrange his court dates (if there are any) to avoid disrupting the season. But when a woman star poses for *Playboy*, we are outraged at her indecency. You'd think if we were going to hold women to such a higher standard, we'd pay them better!

> When I was 7 years old I wanted to play ice hockey, my hometown only had a boys' team and I was therefore not allowed to play. That day it really meant something to me, how it is different to be a girl. Just because I was a girl I couldn't play even though I was a better skater than most of the boys. Anna, 22, bisexual, Nebraska and Sweden

The French Open announced in 2005 that it would begin to pay equal prize money to female and male tennis players. This change took place in 2006. Both the Australian and U.S. Opens already have equal prize money. This leaves Wimbledon as the last holdout—perhaps with the others leading the way, we'll see equity for Wimbledon players soon.

THE STATUS OF TITLE IX

In theory, Title IX means great gains for women and girls in education. Unfortunately, theory is not the same as practice. Three decades after the passage of Title IX, women and girls still don't enjoy equal, or even adequate, access to participation in sports; they are still being barred from activities in school because of their gender; and a reported 83 percent of girls experience sexual harassment at school.[40] Girls continue to take fewer upper-level courses in mathematics and science than boys, with a significant shift between the ages of thirteen and seventeen.[41] Women represent only 27 percent of those receiving Bachelor's degrees and only about 16 percent of those receiving doctorate degrees in computer science.[42] And in terms of who is doing the teaching, women make up 38 percent of the nation's faculty members and only 23 percent of full professors.[43] The disparity in education in the representation of women and men is shameful, and yet we excel. Women's excellence in education should not be used as an argument that they don't face discrimination, and it should not be used to argue that women don't need equality of opportunity to get by. Rather, we should imagine what could be, if we truly supported and fund women and girls in all arenas of education.

I was sitting one day in my high school English class listening to my teacher lecture on Great Expectations *and the archetypes of women.... It suddenly dawned on me that in the entire four years ... not one book we had read had been by a female author. My teacher's explanation was that there were just not as many female authors to choose from. That summer I read Sylvia Plath, Virginia Woolf, Joyce Carol Oates, Jane Austen. I've been a feminist ever since.*
Lindsay, 21, Euro-mutt, California

ACHIEVING EQUALITY

Equality is our right. There can be no compromise. Our very lives depend upon it. Within the United States and throughout the globe, we must fight until all women, all people, have true social, political, and economic equality. Many came before us, and I suspect that many may need to follow us on this journey. Women have been imprisoned, harassed, threatened, brutalized, ignored, celebrated, honored, and victorious in this fight for equal rights. The question is, What will your contribution be to the lives of women you know? And to the lives of women whom you do not know but with whom you share a common plight? What will you do for justice?

SPOTLIGHT ON ACTIVISM

Class-Action Suit Against Wal-Mart

Dukes v. Wal-Mart Stores, Inc.

On June 22, 2004, in the 9th U.S. District Court, Judge Martin Jenkins ruled that that "six current and former Wal-Mart employees from California may represent all female employees of Wal-Mart who worked at its U.S. stores anytime since December 26, 1998 in a nationwide sex discrimination class action lawsuit," making *Dukes v. Wal-Mart Stores, Inc.* the "largest civil rights class action suit ever certified against a private employer."[44] The class-action suit encompasses more than 1.6 million women who have worked for Wal-Mart and who have consistently been paid less, received fewer career advancements, and suffered a wide array of discriminatory actions and comments—from being required to meet in strip clubs for office meetings to being called "bitches" and having their pay disparity justified because "God made Adam first, so women would always be second to men."[45] Richard Drogin found in his study, "Statistical Analysis of Gender Patterns in the Wal-Mart Workforce," that men's annual earnings exceeded that of women's by $5,000, despite the fact that women generally have worked longer at Wal-Mart, both in salaried and in hourly jobs. He also found that "women received 2891 fewer promotions into Support Manager ... 2952 fewer promotions into Manager Trainee ... 346 fewer promotions into Co-Manager [and] 155 fewer promotions into Store Manager than would be expected from their representation in the feeder pools."[46]

Despite representing some of the richest people in the United States, Wal-Mart, and Sam's Club, has an appalling record of discrimination—discrimination in wage and promotion, violations of the Americans with Disabilities Act, violations of child labor laws, refusal to cover contraceptives in insurance plans, refusal to dispense emergency contraceptives, and discrimination based on sexual orientation. We cannot allow Wal-Mart to continue to be the largest retailer in the United States—make a commitment to *never* shopping there, share information with friends, and join the numerous campaigns to support the class-action suit against Wal-Mart.

TAKE ACTION

Getting Started

Register to vote. Register others to vote. Remember, if you have moved or changed your name, you must re-register.

Realize that all women's work is valuable, whether paid or unpaid.

If you attend a religious institution, inquire about its policies and practices in support of women's leadership.

The Next Step

Vote. Vote in *every* election. Sign up for an absentee ballot if transportation, child care, time, or whatever has made it difficult for you to vote in the past. Coordinate group child care with your friends—watch each other's children and take turns voting. Or, better yet, take your child(ren) with you to impress on them the value of practicing democracy.

Write your U.S. senators and urge them to support the ratification of CEDAW.

Call or write the White House to encourage the administration to support CEDAW.

Support paid-family-leave benefits in your state and on the federal level; write your elected officials and ask for their support.

Getting Out There

Volunteer to work on a campaign—phone bank, precinct walk, stuff envelopes.

Get involved with media activism—write an editorial, call into a radio talk show, or write letters to television studios about their programming. See *Fabulous Feminist Web Resources* for more resources.

ON MY BOOKSHELF

Cynthia Costello and Anne Stone, eds., *The American Woman 2001–2002: Getting to the Top* (New York: Norton, 2001).

Susan Douglas, *Where the Girls Are: Growing Up Female with the Mass Media* (New York: Times Books, Random House, 1995).

Loraine Edwalds and Midge Stocker, eds., *The Women-Centered Economy* (Chicago: Third Side Press, 1995).

Berenice Malka Fisher, *No Angel in the Classroom: Teaching Through Feminist Discourse* (New York: Rowman and Littlefield, 2001).

Joline Godfrey, *No More Frogs to Kiss: 99 Ways to Give Economic Power to Girls* (New York: HarperCollins, 1995).

Arlie Hochschild, *The Second Shift: Working Parents and the Revolution at Home* (New York: Viking Penguin, 1989).

Arlie Hochschild, *Time Bind: When Work Becomes Home and Home Becomes Work* (New York: Metropolitan/Holt, 1997).

bell hooks, *Teaching to Transgress: Education as the Practice of Freedom* (New York: Routledge, 1994).

Florence Howe, ed., *The Politics of Women's Studies: Testimony from 30 Founding Mothers* (New York: Feminist Press, 2001).

Jennifer Johnson, *Getting By on the Minimum: The Lives of Working-Class Women* (New York: Routledge, 2002).

June Jordan, *Affirmative Acts: Political Essays* (New York: Doubleday, 1998).

James Loewen, *Lies My Teacher Told Me: Everything Your American History Textbook Got Wrong* (New York: Touchstone, 1995).

Frances Maher and Mary Kay Thompson Tetreault, *The Feminist Classroom: Dynamics of Gender, Race, and Privilege* (New York: Rowman and Littlefield, 2001).

Carla Washburne Rensenbrink, *All in Our Places: Feminist Challenges in Elementary School Classrooms* (New York: Rowman and Littlefield, 2000).

Myra Sadker and David Sadker, *Failing at Fairness: How America's Schools Cheat Girls* (New York: Touchstone, 1995).

Amelie Welden, *Girls Who Rocked the World: Heroines from Sacagawea to Sheryl Swoopes* (Oregon: Beyond Words, 1998).

Jean Zimmerman and Gil Reavill, *Raising Our Athletic Daughters: How Sports Can Build Self-Esteem and Save Girls' Lives* (New York: Main Street Books, 1999).

FABULOUS FEMINIST WEB RESOURCES

Air America   www.airamericaradio.com
Started by Al Franken, radio for progressives. Check Web site for local listings.

AlterNet   www.alternet.org
A great source of independent news.

American Association of University Women   www.aauw.org
With a mission of "equity for all women and girls, lifelong education,
and positive societal change," AAUW Web site provides information on
grants, educational programs, and research on educational equity.

American Civil Liberties Union   www.aclu.org
Protecting constitutional rights, the ACLU takes on legal battles to pro-
tect due process, First Amendment rights, rights of privacy, and the
many other freedoms that we hold essential to our society. ACLU Web
site includes information about legislation, the Supreme Court, and legal
activism in the United States.

American Women in Radio and Television   www.awrt.org
A national, nonprofit organization dedicated to advancing the roles and
rights of women in radio and television.

Bitch magazine   www.bitch.com
A third wave-ish Ms. *Subtitled "Feminist Response to Pop Culture."*

Center for American Progress   www.americanprogress.org
Great progressive site for current information on domestic politics, the
economy, and national security. Includes "Campaign for Women's
Lives," about medical privacy and reproductive rights.

Center for Digital Democracy   www.democraticmedia.org
Activist-based, the Center for Digital Democracy focuses on Internet and
broadband media. Web site has information about activist campaigns,
media/market watch, media ownership, and other areas of digital media.

Center for Women's Policy Studies   ww.centerwomenpolicy.org
The Center for Women's Policy Studies is our nation's first feminist pol-
icy research organization, providing a wealth of information about legis-
lation, violence against women, education and welfare reform, reproduc-
tive rights, HIV/AIDS, and workplace issues. This Web site is a great re-
source.

Code Pink   www.codepink4peace.org
More radical in nature, Code Pink is an activist organization working
for peace and social justice. It promotes creative and visually innovative
protests against war and injustice.

Common Cause   www.commoncause.org
A nonprofit, nonpartisan organization working to encourage "citizen
participation in democracy."

Disability Rights Education and Defense   www.dredf.org
Working to extend civil rights to people with disabilities, DREDF pro-
vides information on advocacy, legislation, and legal cases.

Dyke Action Machine   www.dykeactionmachine.com
Primarily focused in New York City, Dyke Action Machine "is a public art collaboration which critiques mainstream culture by inserting lesbian images into a recognizably commercial context."

Emily's List   www.emilyslist.org
Grassroots political network, providing resources to pro-choice, Democratic women running for elected office.

Equality Now   www.equalitynow.org
Promoting human rights for women around the world, Web site includes information about international campaigns to advance the status of women worldwide.

Fairness and Accuracy in Reporting   www.fair.org
A national media-watch organization. Web site includes a Women's Watch and Racism Watch Desk.

Feminist Majority   www.feminist.org
Great site for current campaigns—local and global. Also has information about the group's campus activism program.

Gay and Lesbian Alliance Against Defamation   www.glaad.org
"Dedicated to promoting and ensuring fair, accurate and inclusive representation of people and events in the media as a means of eliminating homophobia and discrimination based on gender identity and sexual orientation," GLAAD is a leader in gay and lesbian rights. Web site has a great deal of information, including information on a variety of campaigns hosted by GLAAD.

Gender Public Advocacy Coalition   www.gpac.org
Countering gender stereotypes, GPAC works to raise awareness and end discrimination and violence while expanding legal rights.

Global Exchange   www.globalexchange.org
"Global Exchange is an international human rights organization dedicated to promoting political, social and environmental justice globally." Web site includes information on international campaigns, economic and human rights, speakers bureau, and volunteer and job opportunities.

Global Fund for Women   www.globalfundforwomen.org
Grant-based organization, working to provide resources for women's groups fighting for human rights around the world.

Independent Press Association   www.indypress.org
Working toward open media, Indy Press connects more than 600 independent media sources, helping them to reach a wider audience.

International Women's Media Foundation www.iwmf.org
"The IWMF's mission is to strengthen the role of women in the news media around the world, based on the belief that no press is truly free unless women share an equal voice." Web site includes a variety of program initiatives, training, and news and research resources.

Lambda Legal Defense Fund www.lambdalegal.org
Lambda Legal works for civil rights for GLBT and HIV+ communities, through litigation, education, and public policy work.

League of Women Voters www.lwv.org
Nonpartisan organization working to bring women's voice into the political system through voter information, campaign finance reform, and election reform.

Media Education Foundation www.mediaed.org
Great source for films—including Tough Guise, Killing Us Softly III, Reviving Ophelia, *and* Dreamworlds 2.

Media Reform Information Center ww.corporations.org/media
Links and resources for media reform.

MoveOn.org www.moveon.org
Voter information and campaign organization. Hosts "meet-ups" in communities around the United States for GOTV (Get Out The Vote) activities. Great source for electoral politics.

Ms. magazine www.msmagazine.com
The classic! Many of us cut our teeth on our mother's copies. As always, a great source of feminist news.

National Committee of Pay Equity www.pay-equity.org
Great source for information on pay equity, includes statistics, research, Equal Pay Day campaign, and tips for activism.

National Gay and Lesbian Task Force Policy www.ngltf.org
Founded in 1973 as the first GLBT task force for civil rights and advocacy. Web site includes information on campaigns, research, issues, and community action.

National Low Income Housing Coalition www.nlihc.org
Dedicated to ending the affordable-housing crisis in the United States. Web site includes research, public policy, and up-to-date information on housing access.

National Organization for Women www.now.org
Check out its "Merchants of Shame" and "Women-Friendly Workplace Campaign" for information and activism on Wal-Mart. Also a good source of information on a wide array of issues pertaining to women's equality.

National Partnership for   www.nationalpartnership.org
Women and Families
"The National Partnership for Women & Families is a nonprofit, non-
partisan organization that uses public education and advocacy to pro-
mote fairness in the workplace, quality health care, and policies that help
women and men meet the dual demands of work and family."

National Public Radio   www.npr.org
Publicly controlled radio. Check its Web site for local listings.

National Women's Law Center   www.nwlc.org
Public education and advocacy promoting fairness in the workplace and
family-friendly policies in the workplace.

National Women's Political Caucus   www.nwpc.org
Multicultural, intergenerational, multi-issue organization working to
get women involved in politics. NWPC puts women in the political
pipeline through recruitment and training.

Network of Feminist 'Zines   www.feminist.org/research/zines.html
List and links to feminist magazines.

9 to 5: National Association of Working Women   www.9to5.org
Working for women's economic justice, 9 to 5 is an advocacy organiza-
tion that addresses workplace issues, including sexual harassment, pay
equity, and work/home challenges.

Pacifica Radio   www.pacifica.org
Progressive, alternative radio. Stations in Berkeley, Los Angeles, Hous-
ton, New York, and Washington, DC.

Parents, Family and Friends of Lesbians and Gays   www.pflag.org
Nonprofit, grassroots organization providing support and advocacy.

Religious Tolerance.org   www.religioustolerance.org
Web site for tolerance and acceptance of multiple religious ideologies. In-
cludes articles about women, faith, and religious leadership.

United Nations—Women Watch   www.un.org/womenwatch
A section of the United Nations Web site with a focus on women. Good
site for information about the status of women globally, particularly
with regard to CEDAW.

Voice America   www.voiceamerica.org
Progressive Internet radio.

Wages for Housework Campaign   www.payequity.net/
                                         WFHCampaign/wfhcpgn.htm
Background about the campaign, information about how to get involved,
fact sheets on pay equity, and resources.

We Are Church   www.we-are-church.org
Based in Catholicism, We Are Church is an alternative to the traditional Catholic faith, working for social justice and the acceptance of all. Web site provides an international network.

Webgrrls International   www.webgrrls.com
Webgrrls provides a network of resources for women in media—includes job and internship opportunities, business networking, and skills building.

The White House Project   www.thewhitehouseproject.org
Dedicated to advancing women's political participation with the vision of a woman president, the White House Project Web site provides research, statistics, and campaign information.

Women Enews   www.womenenews.org
Great source of feminist reporting. Sign up for daily articles via e-mail.

Women in Film   www.wif.org
Networking for women in the film industry, dedicated to mentoring and promoting women.

Women's Institute for Freedom of the Press   www.igc.org/wifp
A great source of information about women-controlled media. Includes a directory of print, Internet, film, and other sources of women-friendly media.

Women's International League   www.wilpf.org
for Peace and Freedom
Founded in 1915 with Jane Addams as its first president, WILPF is still going strong. Calling for "peaceful means world disarmament, full rights for women, racial and economic justice, an end to all forms of violence, and to establish those political, social, and psychological conditions which can assure peace, freedom, and justice for all." WILPF Web site provides issue and campaign information.

Women's Sports Foundation   www.womensportsfoundation.org
Founded by Billie Jean King, in 1974, the Women's Sports Foundation is a nonprofit charitable organization providing resources, advocacy, and education for women in sports.

Working Assets   www.workingforchange.com
Started as a phone company that donated a portion of individuals' bills to progressive causes, Working Assets now has a number of campaigns to raise awareness, fund-raise, and lobby for progressive issues, including breast cancer research, violence prevention, and the promotion of pay equity and workplace equity.

5

Good Enough

I remember reading once that "getting my head out of the toilet bowl was the most political act I ever committed"[1] and thinking—this is my life. For years I struggled with an eating disorder, bulimia, that consists of a cycle of binging and purging. I was bulimic for much of my activist life—during the grape boycott, at the same time I sat in on Bettina Aptheker's classes, and even as the president of my college NOW chapter. At my worst, I was throwing up a dozen times a day. I could throw up with no noise. I could throw up on command. I could even throw up out the car door while driving down the road. These are not braggin' rights. I was becoming more involved in the women's movement, working toward the empowerment of women and girls, and falling deeper and deeper into a pit of self-hatred.

> eat·ing disor·der: *n.* any of various disorders, as anorexia nervosa or bulimia, characterized by severe disturbances in eating habits.
>
> An·or·ex·ia ner·vo·sa: *n.* an eating disorder characterized by a fear of becoming fat, a distorted body image, and excessive dieting leading to emaciation.
>
> Bu·lim·ia: *n.* 1. Also called bu·lim·ia ner·vo·sa, a habitual disturbance in eating behavior characterized by bouts of excessive eating followed by self-induced vomiting, purging with laxatives, strenuous exercise, or fasting.

I was plagued by this question: How is it possible that someone with a growing feminist consciousness can be binging and purging while remaining a staunch feminist? I was regularly talking with young women about eating disorders and media images and their harmful effects on our self-esteem, urging them to increase their empowerment and work on their sense of self—all the while feeling like a hypocrite.

The more I encouraged others, the more I felt like a failure. Imposter phenomenon[2] is what it is called. It's the notion of hiding your true self from others while fearful that people will find out that you are not what you seem, that you've had them all fooled. Who was I to talk about empowerment? To criticize media images or advocate change? I threw up so much my voice was raspy. I lived on throat lozenges. And the barfing was only part of it—body obsession, working out, dieting, dieting, dieting. The saddest part

> *I do not think a woman's body needs to be super thin or adorned with makeup and "sexy" clothes, yet I still have lingering issues with my body and body image in general.* Heather, 22, European American, Illinois

was that I was more worried that someone would find me out, uncover the sham that I thought I was, than concerned for my health, my self-esteem, my self-definition, or even my life.

When I first became bulimic, I don't remember knowing if there was a label or an understanding for what I was doing to myself. I thought that I had discovered the perfect solution to my fat ass—I could eat in social settings, I could binge on my "forbidden foods," and then I could *just take care of it.* It seemed like the perfect solution; no one would have to know. But I also felt isolated by this secret. When I reluctantly went to a group session—because a friend needed me to go to support *her*—I was shocked that others did the things that I did. There was even a word for it. Bulimia. I began to understand but remained ashamed. I felt that I had a different standard to live up to. *I* was a feminist. I knew better. I was supposed to embrace my fat ass—hell, celebrate it!

Later, in hushed conversations with feminist friends, I began to note that I was not alone. They too confessed feelings of body hatred, acts of yo-yo dieting, binging and purging or self-starvation. I believe that there is a special type of pressure for self-proclaimed feminist women. We understand that nonfeminist-identified women struggle with self-image—look at our culture! Diet fads, personal trainers, and cosmetic surgery. Between 4 and 20 percent of college-age women are estimated to have an eating disorder,[3] and approximately 80 percent of fourth graders are dieting—they're nine years old![4] But feminists don't recognize themselves in those statistics—we're the ones who *know* the statistics; we're not supposed to be part of those statistics. And so we continue to harbor the secrecies of our betrayal. We fear betraying a movement that has spent so many years working to give us a better life, a better identity, a movement that has worked for decades to create an acknowledgement of, and resources for, those with eating disorders, a movement that was the first and loudest voice to critique the social pressures for women to fit the thin, white ideal and that countered the messages of advertising, film, television, and beauty pageants—in short, a movement that proudly said that women, in all their shapes, sizes, and colors, are beautiful.

The life event that turned me from just another Sassy reader into a committed, self-identified, and active activist was my own personal struggle with bulimia nervosa. I credit feminism for a large part of my successful recovery. Sarah, 28, Irish/English, straight but open, Oregon, originally from Tennessee

I worried about writing this in a book about third-wave feminism. I worried about being this exposed. I worried that the antifeminists would use this story as an argument to prove that feminism failed. Then I realized that these fears are the same fears that kept me silent for so long. Eating disorders and body hatred are not the fault of the feminist movement; quite the contrary. The feminist movement has struggled to provide women and girls with resources and support to fight the hidden tortures within our psyches. The fact that feminist women have eating disorders is evidence of the strength of a culture that continues to send the message to women that as we are is not good enough. The culture is what needs to change, not women and not feminism.

THE FLAPPER, ROSIE THE RIVETER, MARILYN MONROE . . . AND ME

After reading books like Mary Pipher's *Reviving Ophelia* and Laura Fraser's *Losing It* and seeing the work of documentary film makers like Jean Kilbourne, I realized that there is a correlation between the social and political power we hold as women and the projection of an ideal body size fed to us through popular culture. This emphasis is so intense that it can, and does, detract from our quest for political, economic and social representation. For example, American women won the right to vote in 1920. This was a seventy-two-year battle, one that was indeed hard fought. As a result, women had more political representation and thus more social power than ever before in our modern history. But around the 1920s, who was the major fashion idol? First the "Gibson Girl," with her tall, slender frame, and then the widely popular "flapper," who was even thinner, more boyish, and without curves. And, while the flapper fashion was a response to the corset and the desire for freedom from gowns and petticoats, it also came with a requirement of whiteness, a small body size, and an emphasis on weight control. As the fashion feminist Valerie Steele writes in her book, *The Corset: A Cultural History*, "Although the traditional boned corset gradually disappeared during the 1920s, most women still wore some kind of corset, corselette, or girdle."[5] She notes that fashion magazines and advice books continued to stress exercise and diets and reinforced the fear of fat internalized by women throughout American society. Steele further writes, "the corset did not so much disappear as become internalized through diet, exercise, and [more recently] plastic surgery."[6] Additionally, as Susan Bordo, author of *Unbearable Weight: Feminism, Western Culture and the Body*, reminds us, "the flapper's freedom, as Mary McCarthy's and Dorothy Parker's short stories brilliantly reveal, was largely an illusion—as any obsessively cultivated sexual style must inevitably be."[7] Despite freedom from the corset and a growing quest for sexual equality, women began to experience a backlash. Once again, their physical beauty and worth, rather than their independence and intelligence, became paramount,. After all, let's not forget that 1921 was the year of the first Miss America Pageant, the start of the practice of formally rewarding women for their physical appearance, as opposed to establishing a scholarship program (a common defense of beauty pageants) based upon intellect and scholarly merit.

Moving forward in history, during World War II, the strong, muscular image of Rosie the Riveter took hold. This can-do image was appropriated by the government to convince women to enter the paid labor force to support the U.S. economy, industry, and war efforts while the men were away fighting. Women were told that they could do a "man's job." I should note that this effort, like Rosie herself, was largely aimed at white women, as most women of color in the United States were already working. In her study *Creating Rosie the Riveter: Class, Gender and Propaganda During World War II*, Maureen Honey writes that "[t]he woman in a nontraditional job was portrayed as valiantly leading the nation to victory. Women were provided with positive role models for entering male occupations, and the public was given a standard-bearer of home-front solidarity and protection."[8] Like Rosie, most of

this imagery portrayed white, middle-class women and virtually ignored the contributions of women of color. Honey writes that "racial
prejudice precluded using blacks in [heroic roles] because they were
perceived by a racist culture as inferior to whites and therefore inappropriate figures of inspiration or national pride." [9] Women of color
were inaccurately and unjustly left out of images of women supporting
the war effort, and white women were sold the notion of nationalism
and valor through their war work, along with the expectation that they
would maintain their home, their family, and their femininity. After
World War II, when women were essentially kicked out of the factories
to make room for the returning soldiers, they returned home, and the
baby boom exploded. The icon of the 1950s, Marilyn Monroe, a volup-
tuous size 14 or 16 by today's standards, suggested a return to femininity and the acceptance of a larger body size. Of course, Marilyn was also
seen as a "dumb blonde" who doesn't ask too much, doesn't demand
too much, and doesn't know too much. Marilyn's image provided for a
less threatening image of white women, one that posed a smaller economic and political threat within American society.

As we moved into the 1960s, with the women's movement taking
off again and women demanding equal pay, equal representation, and
equal rights, the fashion icon was "Twiggie"—rail thin, white, boyish,
with no curves. Chris Strodder, author of *Swingin' Chicks of the '60s*,
writes that "with 31–22–32 measurements and barely 90 pounds on her
5'6" frame, Twiggy in a lime-green mini and green tights represented a
bold departure from the softer, rounder shapes on the 50's and early
60's." [10] Still referenced today, Twiggie and her waiflike appearance set
a norm for ultrathinness. [11] Women fighting for equal rights and representation were quickly confronted with an ideal that emphasized slen-
derness as an ideal—an ideal for which we were, and most of us still are,
expected to strive. However, within the Latina and African American
communities, a fuller figure is often more the norm. As Christy Haubegger put it in her essay "I'm Not Fat, I'm Latina," "Latinas in this country live in two worlds. People who don't know us may think we're fat.
At home we're called *bien cuidadas* (well cared for) . . . there is a greater
'cultural acceptance' of being overweight within Hispanic communities." [12]

Fast-forward to the twenty-first century and women have won
more elected offices and thus more recognition politically than ever

before and have begun to move up the corporate and union ladders, represent a greater proportion of enrolled students in colleges and universities, and so on—and yet we see "heroin chic" on the pages of our magazines and the much-talked-about "Lolliwood" and the shrinking actresses of Hollywood. "Lolliwood" refers to the image of the celebrity woman who has lost so much body mass that her head looks out of proportion to her body, making her look

I was seen as the odd ball. I was the only girl in my class who did not wear tight clothes, starve myself, and wear make-up. Madelon, 18, bisexual, Massachusetts

like a "lollipop." You see, your body can lose a great deal of mass, but your head, your cranium, will not shrink in size. One contrast to these images of heroin chic and Lolliwood are women in professional sports. With an emphasis on strength and ability, women athletes give girls a powerful alternative to look up to. With the increasing success of Title IX, we are beginning to see stronger, more positive images for young women through sports. Venus and Serena Williams, Brandy Chastain, Laila Ali, Danica Patrick, Annika Sorenstam, and Michelle Wei are just a few women in sports who present images of confident, powerful women who are comfortable in their bodies. Still, while it is true that the 1999 Women's World Cup win for the U.S. women's soccer team and the growing popularity of the WNBA have greatly impacted girls in the United States, the bigger message to women, particularly young women in the midst of adolescence, is that "thin is in." And at any cost.

Throughout history, when women have not possessed much political, economic, or social power—when we did not run for political office, when we did not demand equal pay for equal work, when we did not control our own reproductive lives, when we did not vote—then we did not determine our lives. If we are not involved, then we present little or no threat to the patriarchal power structure that supports and protects male dominance. But, as women and girls become more empowered, we confront a contradictory message about our value. We must begin to counter the notion that to be worthy is to look like the "ideal woman" delivered to us through television shows, movies, music videos, newscasts, magazine covers, and video games. And, in doing so, we begin to experience a shift in power; instead of being valued solely because of a physical image, we promote one that recognizes our other contributions. Here's the deal—when women are required—even informally—to meet an unattainable body size ideal, our energy is sucked away. Like the Barbie doll, usually even heavily promoted "role models," be they actresses or fashion models, do not naturally meet the image they project—airbrushing, computer alteration, piece modeling, lighting, makeup, surgery, and semistarvation are all part of the process of creating an image that can sell the average woman an unattainable ideal that often looks quite natural. When we are obsessed with this ideal, we have little time, or confidence, for anything else—including fighting for equality.

I get in seventh grade and my mother buys me makeup. I was like what do you want me to do with this then she wanted me to start wearing high heels to church. NOT. I feel bad for my mom she tried so hard to turn me into this little prim and proper lady. I am so not that. Serena, 26, Hispanic, straight, single mom, California

Recently, in some rare cases—most notably Oprah Winfrey and Jamie Lee Curtis—our celebrities have begun to speak out about this ideal, going so far as to chronicle their transformation from their normal selves to the image we see on the cover of magazines. But the more likely story to grace our magazine racks is of the weight gains and losses of our most beautiful. Played out in the public is the accusation that eating disorders are rampant among the women on popular sitcoms and in our favorite movies—and a denial that this is the case. The media industry pits one woman against the other—on the one hand publicly condemning extreme weight loss but on the other requiring extreme thinness among actresses who appear on television and on the big screen. This added pressure, in such a public position, creates an unfair demand on, and a bit of a contradiction for, famous women. Not only are they subject to this requirement, but they are in the position of projecting this unattainable ideal. Instead of endlessly targeting famous, thin women, we should recognize that they too are pressured by the media. Why condemn a woman who is also struggling with her self-concept and body size—as well as with her job? My point is not to encourage the furthering of celebrity exaltation—certainly they have enviable lives in many ways—but rather to assert that we need to change the politics of beauty, challenge the ideal, and create more room for our diversity. We must celebrate the images of larger women in the media, and we must do so unapologetically—in other words, we must end the ubiquitous notion that if she is fat, she cannot be beautiful or that if she is fat, she is unhappy.

IMAGE OBSESSED—OR "YOU CAN RUN, BUT YOU CAN'T HIDE FROM MEDIA IMAGES"

So why do we buy it, this image of an ideal woman? Oh, so many reasons. Family. Friends. High school. The media. For many of us, we begin to learn these patterns of body hatred from family and friends. We hear our mothers, or our fathers, self-criticize. Our friends are dieting. We are ridiculed at school. Our histories with body hatred, dieting, and eating disorders are as unique and as diverse as our bodies themselves. But the common denominator for American women is the media. When looking at body image, I often focus on the media because, while our family and friends are significant, they too are affected by the constant barrage of media images. In the United States, 98 percent[13] of households have a television, and it is on for an average of seven hours every day;[14] 99 percent of households have a radio; 85 percent have at least one VCR; and 68 percent have some form of cable television.[15] We are all impacted by the "ideal beauty" images, so that those images get projected back to us through our own and others' comments, pressures, and expectations.

The media are driven by advertising. According to Jean Kilbourne, a media expert and the creator of *Killing Us Softly: Advertising's Image of Women,* Americans see an average of three thousand advertisements a day.[16] Advertising is powerful and works best when we are convinced that our lives would be better with whatever product is being sold. Whether it talks to us about the cleanliness of our homes, the safety of our cars, the health of our families, or the beauty of our bodies, advertising sells self-worth through good old-fashioned American consumerism. And, with this, we transition from what we truly need to what we want to what we believe we must have, all to survive in a culture that judges and ranks us on the basis of appearances.

Every year in the United States, $180 billion is spent on advertising.[17] And where there is that much money at stake, you can bet everything is intentional—even coordinated. From the placement of a hand to the shape of the product to the race or ethnicity of the model, images are created to catch the attention of the consumer. Today's use of logos as branding has taken advertising to a whole new level. Where logos were once discreet, they now take center stage on our clothing, accessories, television screens, and products.[18] As Naomi Klein, author of *No Logo*, writes, "[t]he effect, if not always the original intent, of advanced branding is to nudge the hosting culture into the background and make the brand the star. It is not to sponsor culture but to *be* the culture."[19] It is interesting when you add to the prevalence of this branding the fact that we, as consumers, spend a tremendous amount of money paying for the privilege to advertise for these companies. In other words, we pay inflated prices for a basic t-shirt that sports a product logo and then walk around advertising that company to all with whom we come in contact. In doing so, we create a hierarchy among our peers in terms of who wears what brand—categorizing one another on first sight by the logo on our t-shirt, shoes, or handbags. The company benefits twice— once from our purchase and once from our "free advertising." But the cost for this is far greater than what we spend in the stores. This pressure to wear the right name and to mimic the image of models (although fashion models are thinner than 98 percent of American women)[20] carries with it the price of our self-esteem and our health. According to the Centers for Disease Control, about half of all women, and a quarter of all men, in the United States are dieting—and I suspect that this is a significant underestimate.

A DANGEROUS TREND

Obsessed with weight loss and a thin ideal despite the harmful effects of dieting, we continue to seek the ultimate weight loss miracle. We have spent decades dedicated to a variety of trend diets—the cabbage diet, the grapefruit diet, the Hollywood diet—not to mention the endless diet pills, programs, and promises ("lose thirty pounds in thirty days"). In fact, Americans collectively spend an estimated $34 billion to $50 billion a year on dieting.[21] But not only are we *not* attaining the unattainable; we are less and less satisfied with ourselves.

The prevalence and acceptance of prescriptive and over-the-counter diet pills and programs has gotten out of hand. Even in the face of fatalities and severe health complications, as occurred with Fen-Phen, women continue to swallow danger every day. Web-based pharmacies sell diet drugs and supplements at discount rates, chat rooms for

Atkins diet fans are popping up in Web communities across the Net, weekly weigh-ins at Weight Watchers, Jenny Craig, and L.A. Weight Loss centers nationwide have increasingly become women's social network, and the newest trend, the newest diet is surely just around the corner as Americans respond in desperation to the endless reports of America's obesity "epidemic." I say "epidemic" because this is how these issues are referred to, particularly in reference to the estimated sixty million Americans who are categorized as obese.[22] Particular attention has also been given to the rise of obesity among children, with the increase in juvenile diabetes posing the most serious health risk. While I do not want to deny that there are real concerns here, most media stories seem to use the topic of obesity as just another way to shame us about our bodies. The institutional and societal factors that contribute to obesity are often ignored; instead, we perpetuate a culture of sizeism by pointing fingers at those who are overweight and reinforcing the notion that the thinner, the better. In turn, not only do we not confront the issue of obesity, but the epidemic of Americans, primarily women, who often turn to dangerous measures to "get thin" as opposed to getting healthy also goes overlooked. We know that these diets and drugs are not achieving our goal of thinness, and we know that yo-yo dieting, chronic dieting with repeated weight losses and gains, is much more harmful than fat itself. Yet, the pressure against women to meet the ideal outweighs any concern for health. I think that it is tragic that we consistently send the message to women that their health is secondary and that their appearance is where their worth lies. Why do we, as a culture, continue to endorse and perpetuate these "requirements"—especially when women's lives are literally in jeopardy?

> I didn't realize it at the time, but I now understand that in many ways my eating disorder was a way for me to gain control and a sense of self in an environment where my selfhood as a woman was denied and devalued.
> Gayle, 32, Euro-American, lesbian, California

Young women are particularly at risk. They are targeted heavily by advertisers at a time when they are still struggling through adolescence. While diverse images of older women, women of color, and, in rare cases, women of larger body sizes are beginning to be more common on television, this diversity of size and appearance does not seem to be the case for young women. Young women are bombarded with images of thin, young and increasingly sexy female bodies on television, in movies, on the pages of magazines, and in music. In a recent internet survey of four thousand teens, the researcher Ann Kearney-Cooke found that "nearly half of the 14- to 18-year-olds said they were dissatisfied with their bodies, and a third of the teens said they were considering some type of plastic surgery."[23] Indeed, a 1999 report tells us that those under eighteen years of age made up 3 percent of the nearly two million Americans who had plastic surgery.[24] As a result of her study, Kearney-Cooke said, "what's most disturbing to me is that this is a time when their bodies aren't fully formed, yet teens feel so much pressure to be instantly perfect."[25] Perfection is a dangerous game—unfortunately, a game that too many young women play.

> **Body Dysmorphic Disorder: "A woman with this disorder sees herself as extremely ugly.... Seventy percent of the cases occur before the age of eighteen.... BDD sufferers are at elevated risk for despair and suicide.... In some cases they undergo multiple, unnecessary plastic surgeries." (Definition from the National Organization for Women *Love Your Body Campaign*)**

UNDER THE KNIFE

One of the most physically dangerous outcomes of this epidemic of body hatred is the rising popularity of plastic surgery. Plastic surgery puts women under the knife in far greater numbers than men—and more often than not for "beauty" purposes—liposuction, breast augmentation, tummy-tucks, nose jobs, and more. In fact, according to the American Society of Plastic Surgeons (ASPS), women accounted for 86 percent of the more than 7.4 million plastic surgery procedures in 2003.[26] The ASPS also found that there was a 33 percent increase in women patients between 2002 and 2003, with liposuction and breast augmentation the most common surgical procedures and botox injections the most popular "minimally invasive" procedure.[27] But is surgery the problem? I am sure that many would say that being able to afford these surgeries and take charge of our appearance—and, in a sense, our destiny—is empowering. Women today have bought into the message that their power lies in their physical bodies and, more specifically, their physical beauty. I don't think that surgery is the problem per se;

rather, the problems go back to my initial argument—the message that *as we are is not good enough*. We have set an extremely limited standard for female beauty, and, while we have begun to push back against this standard, allowing greater diversity among models and actors, the truth remains that American women are under tremendous pressure to look a certain way. Rather than emphasizing the unique beauty within us all, the media, society, and women themselves have sought to change women's bodies and appearance through increasingly extreme measures.

With the highly publicized case of the singer Carnie Wilson (who broadcast her procedure on the Web), gastric bypass surgery is growing in its popularity for weight loss, with more than 103,000 procedures performed in 2003, up from 67,000 procedures in 2002.[28] With a cost of $15,000 to $30,000 per procedure, gastric bypass surgery has become a new benchmark in the hierarchy of beauty. And, with an increasing number of stars taking this route, the message that you can never be too thin is clear. Gastric bypass is hardly a complication-free procedure, with up to three deaths for every thousand procedures and a 20 percent rate of return for second procedures;[29] the most common form of surgery is designed to block off portions of your stomach, creating a small pouch, leaving less room in the stomach and thus reducing food intake. Gastric bypass surgery is one of the most extreme acts for weight loss— and, while it is targeted at those at least one hundred pounds overweight, it is becoming increasingly common. Media showcasing of gastric bypass surgery, combined with the creation of shows such as "Extreme Make-over," "Swan," "Nip Tuck," and "Dr. 90210," make surgery increasingly favored as the ultimate quick fix to an undesirable appearance. Rather than blaming ourselves and putting our bodies under the knife, I suggest we look at the larger institutional question of how American culture promotes and reinforces an unhealthy lifestyle. Americans are inundated with fast-food commercials, with added messages that fast food is the American way. Fast food is encouraged, accessible, and convenient. Rarely is there a healthy alternative to the quick and convenient roadside stop while driving down the freeway on your way to or from work or vacation. Culturally, Americans shop for convenience, buying meals in a box or ready for the microwave. Just add water and we have instant dinner. Little emphasis is placed on nutrition in school, with many medical schools providing less than the recommended twenty-five hours of nutrition curriculum for medical degrees—and these are our health professionals![30] We live in a culture where exercise is generally not incorporated into our daily lives. Even the most basic of exercise, walking, often is replaced by driving cars; Americans drive more often than they walk. A 2001 survey by the Department of Transportation found that 90 percent of trips made by adults and 70 percent of trips made by children were in cars.[31] There is no federal law requiring physical education programs in American schools,[32] and fast-food and soda companies often contract with schools to provide their products directly to students on elementary, middle-school, and high-school campuses. What we need are healthier alternatives for food and exercise, as well as changes in our own attitudes about our bodies.

WOMEN AND THE GLOBAL MARKET— THE COST OF GLOBALIZED FASHION

In addition to having a huge impact on the media and advertising, the diet industry, and body image, the fashion industry plays a significant role in globalization, women's global labor, and the existence of sweatshops. Women throughout the world, in poor and underdeveloped nations, work in substandard and abusive conditions for below-poverty-level wages to provide rich nations affordable fashions. Women, mostly between the ages of fifteen and twenty-two, make up 90 percent of all sweatshop labor.[33] Women often are lured to sweatshops under false pretenses, having been promised jobs in wealthy countries as secretaries or waitresses. Instead, they find themselves forced to choose between factory labor and the sex trade—if we can legitimately call this choice. Women working in garment and textile factories are commonly subjected to sexual harassment, rape, and sexual assault, as well as mandatory pregnancy testing and forced abortion.[34] Factory labor wages, for example in the apparel industry, have been reported as low as four cents an hour in Burma,[35] twenty-three cents an hour in Pakistan, seventy-one cents an hour in India, $1.36 an hour in Malaysia, and $1.75 an hour in Mexico, much less than the average U.S. hourly wage of eight dollars.[36] Of course, living needs and standards differ greatly in the United States and in the lower-wage countries. The cost of living varies tremendously between developed and developing nations. But, there are some important questions to ask:

1. Should wealthy nations continue to profit from the economic situations of poorer nations, particularly if our acts of colonialism and imperialism have significantly contributed to their undeveloped or underdeveloped status?
2. Do wealthy countries' multinational corporations have an obligation to adhere to fair labor practices, safety provisions, and environmental protections?
3. Should multinational corporations serve as ambassadors from the countries in which they are headquartered—incorporating similar practices around the globe as are required at home? Or is this a violation of sovereignty and an infringement on the rights of host countries?
4. Should corporations provide a living wage to the workers they employ?

What is our obligation to our sister nations? How much profit is enough? Or too much? Even at one of the highest rates of pay cited—$1.75 an hour—laborers employed by our corporations cannot afford to purchase the products they create and cannot afford housing, clothing, or food for their families in their home countries—which often forces women and children into shanty-town dwellings and permanent states of hunger and further marginalizes them in the global economy. So, while the cost of living may be less in these countries, laborers are still not fairing well. One option women take is to go abroad looking for work, leaving children with older relatives and becoming a part of the low-wage immigrant labor pool whose members seldom see their own children, family, or homes while spending years caring for and cleaning for the homes and families of wealthy nations. In these situations, far too often, women end up with few or no rights; their passports and visas are "safeguarded" by their employers, strict house rules are enforced, prohibiting lives outside their employers' homes, and communication is monitored, keeping workers from engaging in true and honest dialogue with family or people who could help them improve their situations.

Of course, wealthy nations are not the only parties responsible. Many questions should be asked of the host country. For example, how is wealth distributed from the government to the people? Are leaders chosen by popular elections? Are elections safe and fair? What human rights (and let's remember that women's rights are also human rights) violations occur? What are the protections for the people when multi-national corporations set up shop? What protections exist and are enforced for the environment? There is certainly a two-way street between governments and corporations. As consumers, we need to ask these questions to better understand where our money goes and what it supports. We must advocate for women's voices to be heard and so that women are a part of the decision-making process—which means improving women's status so that their daily lives are about not mere survival but also quality and equality.

A campaign for livable wages has been taken up by activists in the domestic and international arenas. These activists propose a wage that allows families to live adequately and safely. A livable wage may be one of the answers to providing women with access to participate in that decision-making process. To address the issue of global labor, a Living Wage Working Summit was convened July 1998 to establish a global livable-wage equation. A coalition of organizations from around the world created the following formula to calculate livable wage rates worldwide. The coalition argued that a livable wage is one that covers a family's housing, energy, clothing, health-care, education, potable-water, child-care, and transportation costs while also providing for a savings rate of 10 percent of the household income.

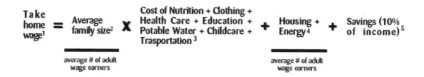

1. The take-home wage is based on the number of hours worked in a legal working week (not to exceed 48 hours in one week). The take-home wage is the worker's weekly net wage (after subtracting union dues, taxes, and other deductions).

2. The average family size is divided by the average number of adult wage earners in a family. It has not yet been agreed upon how these figures would be determined.

3. This list of "basic needs" was derived from a larger list that also included entertainment, vacation, paid family leave, retirement, life insurance, and personal liability insurance. This list is not definitive and may vary depending on regional factors.
4. The cost of housing and energy is divided by the average number of adult wage earners. Housing and energy needs are considered to expand in proportion to the number of wage earners in the household.
5. An arbitrary figure of 10 percent has been included for savings in order to permit workers to have some discretionary income and to allow workers to send money home to their families. (Sweatshop Watch, 1998)

Livable-wage campaigns advocating respect and protection for workers worldwide have taken root around the world. While the discrepancies in earnings are huge, it is important to note that workers in the United States are also not guaranteed a livable wage and that in fact, in most areas of the country, the minimum wage is not a livable one. It would be interesting, while calculating the rates of workers around the world, to use the equation to calculate the adequacy of our own wages. In fact, Barbara Ehrenreich writes in her book, *Nickel and Dimed: On (Not) Getting By in America*, "[t]he Economic Policy Institute recently reviewed dozens of studies of what constitutes a 'living wage' and came up with an average figure of $30,000 a year for a family of one adult and two children, which amounts to a wage of $14 an hour. . . . The shocking thing is that the majority of American workers, about 60 percent, earn less than $14 an hour."[37] As a result, when many of us are barely getting by, it is difficult for women making substandard wages in the United States to be concerned with the conditions of women in other countries. In other words, it is difficult to work for better wages in China when we don't have the time, resources, or energy to fight for better wages for ourselves. Additionally, making consumer choices along political lines becomes increasingly difficult when our goal is to find the least expensive product to meet our family needs. And, of course, corporations literally bank on this fact.

According to Sweatshop Watch, a sweatshop is "a workplace that violates the law and where workers are subject to:

extreme exploitation, including the absences of a living wage or
   long work hours,
poor working conditions, such as health and safety hazards,
   and
arbitrary discipline, such as verbal or physical abuse, or
fear and intimidation when they speak out, organize, or attempt to form a union.[38]

Many countries house sweatshop factories to benefit consumers in the
United States and supply merchandise to some of our most prized companies—Wal-Mart, Nike, Guess, Disney, the Gap, and Tommy Hilfiger,
to name a few. According to the National Labor Committee, women in
El Salvador are paid twenty-five cents for every $140 Nike NBA t-shirt
they sew, and they are subjected to mandatory pregnancy tests, unsafe
drinking water, and surveillance cameras in the bathrooms; Wal-Mart
factories in Bangladesh deny women legal maternity leave, often ha-
rassing them into quitting their jobs; working 60 to 90 hours a week
without overtime, workers in China assemble Disney's children's
books earning 35 to 41 cents an hour and are frequently subjected to
dangerous working conditions.[39] But foreign countries are not the only
home for sweatshop factories—the United States also reaps the benefits
of the hard labor of women. Particularly in states that are major points
of entry—California and New York are two key examples—the fashion
or apparel industry has factories that employ low-wage immigrant
labor. California, for example, is home to more than 140,000 garment
workers—mostly Latina and Asian women—who work ten to twelve
hours a day without overtime or a guaranteed minimum wage (not to
mention a livable wage) in dangerous and unsanitary conditions.[40] This
occurs in a state and a country that are supposed to have safety and
wage protections for workers.

   The issues of sweatshop labor are pervasive and challenging. On
the one hand, there are the extensive problems outlined earlier. But, on
the other hand, there is the argument that some work (even poorly
paid work in abusive settings) is better than no work. Many argue that
multinational corporations provide a source of income for untrained
and uneducated, low-wage workers that would not exist should
multinationals disappear. Some argue the tenets of capitalism and the
"right" to profit at any cost—and assert that in business the bottom
line must be the primary focus. Of course, I question how much profit

is enough. There's no surprise that governments and corporations are motivated by money. But what we must remember is that both governments and corporations are made up of, and rely upon, people. Their greatest success is not their money, or their prestige and recognition. Their greatest success is their ability to convince people that they exist in a vacuum and that their power lies within their structure and not with people.

Corporations and governments are not the only entities that carry responsibility for the existence of sweatshops and the exploitation of workers. As we buy the message sold to us through advertising, we harm not only ourselves but the lives of women worldwide. It is a vicious cycle that isolates us from one another globally. We deal daily with the struggles of fitting in and looking cool without knowledge or understanding of the lives of women who make our coveted designs. These struggles are so powerful—the desire to follow the current fad is so overwhelming—that we spend beyond our means, we endanger our bodies to meet a physical ideal, and we play into a globalized system that profits off the desperate struggle for survival of women in one region and the desperate need for popularity of women in another region. The connection among sweatshops, capitalism, and globalization and their relation to body image, self-esteem, advertising, and the beauty industry is that the entire cycle—from production lines to the donning of clothing—profits from the exploitation of women.

But we can stop this pattern and create a new reality. Companies cannot profit if people do not buy their products. Our consumer choices have power. If we make wise choices collectively, we can change the practices of the beauty and garment industries. If we could create a movement where it is "cool" to be socially and globally aware, where we care about where our products come from, and where we look not just at the economic price tag but also at the human price tag, then we could redesign the system. I believe that if enough of us contact our favorite companies and say that we will stop buying from them until they pay a livable wage to their workers worldwide, then companies will eventually begin to do so—not necessarily because of altruism but because their economic bottom lines will decrease—remember, their success is dependent on our support. In the meantime, we must also support those companies that support unions, fair pay, livable wages, and the advancement of women. Look for union labels on clothing and products. Reference organizations like Sweatshop Watch and the Coalition for Labor Union Women for their recommendations of union and woman-friendly companies. Consider the health, safety, and equality of women as you spend your consumer dollars.

There is a fine line between boycott and consumer power. I am reminded of an interview with Naomi Klein, author of *No Logo*, who recounts her travels through Asia researching sweatshop labor issues. She tells of interviews with Filipino women who want their stories told about working in the factories but also share a concern about a boycott of the product line. They fear the loss of jobs if production declines and ask that Naomi bring their plea for improved working conditions and a hope for job protection to the consumers of wealthy nations, whom they see as having the power to change corporate practices.[41] Klein says in her interview, "I felt a tremendous sense of responsibility from the workers because they shared their stories with me . . . they said to me over and over again, 'please tell people what it is like for us' and at the same time their greatest fear was that I was going to go home and tell people to boycott these companies and that they were all going to lose their jobs. So there is a tremendous uncertainty and confusion about what to do."[42] In response to the World Trade Organization protests in Seattle, in 1999, Klein gives us some advice. She says we must "fight genuinely to raise labor standards around the world . . . stop just opposing the World Trade Organization and start proposing an alternate vision for globalization which answers these problems, which does propose minimum labor standards."[43] As consumers, we need to contact companies and tell them what we want—we want to buy products that are the result of fair labor practices. We need to tell them that company revenues must be better allocated to provide livable wages for their workers—while still allowing for significant gains for the company's bottom line. We must increase awareness among corporations and consumers and empower people to make a difference.

CHANGING THE IMAGE

As Laura Fraser writes, in *Losing It: America's Obsession with Weight and the Industry that Feeds On It*, "we need to resist and change the diet culture for ourselves."[44] Perhaps the largest change we must make is to begin to raise girls to believe in themselves regardless of the images on television, in the movies, and on the pages of magazines. As a culture, we must demand an end to advertising that objectifies women and girls or articles that encourage girls and women to ignore their own needs, dreams, and desires in favor of those of men. Instead of bombarding our girls with their own teen versions of *Cosmo,* we should create more magazines like *New Moon,* which focuses its attention on the empowerment of girls rather than drawing them into a cycle of diet trends and fashion fads. We need to promote the message that women and girls' value lies in themselves, in their capabilities, in their thoughts, in their health, and in their strength. For our girls' and women's health, we must change our messages, teach them to be proud of who they are, help them to find their own strength and beauty, and respect women and girls as they are—because as they are is more than good enough.

SPOTLIGHT ON ACTIVISM

New Moon Magazine for Girls

Founded in 1992 by Nancy Gruver, mother of twin daughters, *New Moon* magazine provides a radical alternative to most magazines geared toward young women. *New Moon* emphasizes self-exploration and discovery in an ad-free environment. With a true commitment to girls' voices, *New Moon* worked with twenty girls, ages 8–14, to initially develop the focus and content of the magazine. Today, a fifteen-member Girls Editorial Board continues to advise *New Moon.* Full of fiction, poetry, artwork, science experiments, and cartoons, *New Moon* is a great resource for girls. *New Moon* provides a critical source of information about coming-of-age issues for girls, including a comprehensive look at girls' lives—their hopes, fears, and dreams. Not stopping there, the education within *New Moon* extends beyond our borders, often including stories of girls from around the globe.

In addition to this fabulous magazine, *New Moon* provides curricula, a speakers' bureau, workshops, a book club, a pen-pal program, and Adventure trips (dolphin camp in Florida and dog sledding in Minnesota). For more information about New Moon, visit the magazine's Web site at www.newmoon.org.

TAKE ACTION

Getting Started

Read up! Great books are out there to educate, empower, and change the way we view ourselves. See the suggested book list at the end of this chapter for a few of my favorites.

Listen to self-affirming music, poetry, and comedy! Check out Margaret Cho, Ani DiFranco, Alix Olson, Dre, Pink, India Arie, Maya Angelou, Lucille Clifton—just to name a few.

Move your body in ways that feel good—dance, run, swim, stretch, do yoga or tai chi.

Eat! Remember that food is not the enemy; it is our fuel. And we need fuel to take care of ourselves and to change the world!

The Next Step

Try subscription card activism; using the abundance of subscription cards in magazines, write a brief message to the magazine. It foots the bill (postage paid!). A couple of my favorite messages—"Stop starvation imagery" and "Feed the models."

Create collage projects—using the advertisements in magazines, cut and paste new messages that are empowering and counter the messages of fashion/beauty advertising.

Be an active and informed consumer—find out the politics of the company behind the product—how much do they pay their workers, is there fair trade involved, do they reinvest into host countries, where are products made, and what are the human rights records of those countries?

Celebrate Buy-Nothing Day the day after Thanksgiving every year—commit to not shopping on the most popular shopping day of the year. Visit www.adbusters.org for more information.

Getting Out There

Shop alternatively. Shop at locally owned, thrift, or secondhand stores. See the appendix for woman-friendly shops.

Take action—write companies to tell them how their advertising is affecting the health of women and girls. Tell them that you won't buy their product(s) until their advertising features healthy women and girls.

Host groups, house parties, and meetings to discuss body image with other women. Show a film, discuss a book, share your stories.

Cover the mirrors in your home/office/school for twenty-four hours and become conscious of the role a mirror plays in your life—how often do
you try to look? What is the response of others who come to your
house or are in your school or office? Journal or start a dialogue about
your reactions.

Make a celebration out of International No-Diet Day—May 6.

Contact the National Organization for Women Foundation (www.nowfoun-
dation.org) and request "Love Your Body Day" campaign materials for
more facts, actions, and resources.

Host a No-Logo Day on your campus, at your community center, or with
your friends or family—commit to wearing logo-free clothing. Set up a
table with sweatshop information.

Encourage your campus to use sweatshop-free manufacturers for all university or college clothing. Visit the Web site of Students Against Sweatshops, www.studentsagainstsweatshops.org, for more information.

ON MY BOOKSHELF

Susan Bordo, *Unbearable Weight: Feminism, Western Culture, and the
Body* (Berkeley: University of California Press, 1993).

Joan Jacobs Brumberg, *The Body Project: An Intimate History of American
Girls* (New York: Random House, 1997).

Kim Cherin, *Reinventing Eve* (New York: Times Books/Random
House, 1987).

Margaret Cho, *I'm the One That I Want* (New York: Ballantine Books,
2002).

Ophira Edut, ed., *Body Outlaws: Rewriting the Rules of Beauty and Body
Image* (Emeryvill, CA: Seal Press, 2003).

Eve Ensler, *The Good Body* (New York: Villard Books, 2004).

Laura Fraser, *Losing It: America's Obsession with Weight and the Industry
That Feeds on It* (New York: Dutton/Penguin Group, 1997).

Sharlene Hesse-Biber, *Am I Thin Enough Yet? The Cult of Thinness and
the Commercialization of Identity* (New York: Oxford University
Press, 1996).

Jane Hirschmann and Carol Munter, *When Women Stop Hating Their
Bodies: Freeing Yourself from Food and Weight Obsession* (New York:
Fawcett Columbine, 1995).

Jean Kilbourne, *Can't Buy My Love: How Advertising Changes the Way
We Think and Feel* (New York: Touchstone, 1999).

Naomi Klein, *No Logo* (New York: Picador USA, 2002).

Miriam Ching Yoon Louie, *Sweatshop Warriors: Immigrant Women*

Workers Take on the Global Factory (Cambridge, MA: South End Press, 2001).

Margo Maine, *Body Wars: Making Peace with Women's Bodies* (Carlsbad: Gürzw Books, 2000).

Camryn Manheim, *Wake Up, I'm Fat* (New York: Broadway Books, 1999).

Judy Mann, *The Difference: Discovering the Hidden Ways We Silence Girls: Finding Alternatives That Can Give Them a Voice* (New York: Warner Books, 1994).

Susie Orbach, *Fat Is a Feminist Issue* (New York: Galahad Books, 1982).

Mary Pipher, *Reviving Ophelia: Saving the Selves of Adolescent Girls* (New York: Ballantine Books, 1995).

Geneen Roth, *When Food Is Love* (New York: Plume, 1991).

Marilynn Wann, *Fat! So? Because You Don't Have to Apologize for Your Size* (Berkeley: Ten Speed Press, 1998).

Jane Wegscheider and Esther Rose (with Boston Women's Health Collective), *Sacrificing Ourselves: Why Women Compromise Health and Self Esteem . . . and How to Stop* (Freedom, CA: Crossing Press, 1996).

FABULOUS FEMINIST WEB RESOURCES

About Face   www.about-face.org
A San Francisco–based nonprofit promoting positive self-esteem through education, outreach, and activism. Web site has great information and resources.

Adbusters   www.adbusters.org
A magazine and a Web site, Adbusters is dedicated to looking critically at the role of advertising, consumerism, and media in our lives. A host of a number of campaigns including "Buy Nothing Day"; check 'em out.

Anorexia Nervosa and Related Disorders, Inc.   www.anred.com
Provides comprehensive information about eating disorders, including statistics, as well as warning signs and information on treatment, and recovery.

Body Positive   www.bodypositive.com
A fabulous Web site dedicated to helping women change the way they see and relate to their bodies. Web site include resources, message boards, Q & As for body size acceptance, and other great resources for combating negative attitudes about our bodies.

Coalition of Labor Union Women   www.cluw.org
The only organization for union women in the United States, CLUW provides resources and networking for union-based issues.

Coalition to Abolish Slavery and Trafficking (CAST)   www.castla.org
Resources, services, and information about forced labor and slavery. Provides information on case management, advocacy, public education, and training.

Coalition Against Trafficking in Women   www.catwinternational.org
A nongovernmental organization promoting women's human rights. Web site includes information about countries throughout the world, with facts and campaign information.

Corporate Watch   www.corpwatch.org
Critical of corporate-led globalization, Corporate Watch provides issue information, activism, and networking.

Eating Disorders Referral and   www.edreferral.com
Information Center
Resources and referrals for eating disorders. Web site has a national and international database for therapists focused on eating disorders. While primarily covering Canada and the United States, site does have referrals for the United Kingdom, Germany, and Australia. Site also includes a wide range of information, from definitions of specific eating disorders to information on research and advocacy.

Fat and Feminist: Large   www.fwhc.org/health/fatfem.htm
Women's Health Experience
A part of the Feminist Women's Health Center Web site, Fat and Feminist provides first-person accounts, research information, discussion on size prejudice, and additional resources.

International Size Acceptance Association   www.size-acceptance.org
An international organization working to end size discrimination. Web site includes resources, chapter affiliate information, discussion board, and ideas for activism.

Largesse   www.largesse.net
A network for "size esteem," Largesse provides size-positive education, publication, organizations, and Web links. Also includes weight discrimination legal referrals and media information.

National Eating   www.nationaleatingdisorders.org
Disorders Association
Information for professionals as well as general public—education, resources, and treatment referrals. In the United States, call 1.800.931.2237 for more information.

National Organization for Lesbians of Size   www.nolose.org
> *Size-acceptance resources specifically for the lesbian and queer community. Web site includes information about events, conferences, speakers, and links to supporting organizations.*

NOW Foundation—   www.nowfoundation.org
Love Your Body Campaign
> *A project of NOW, Love Your Body Campaign is a nationwide effort to raise awareness about body image, eating disorders, and women's health issues. A great source of information as well as a connection to activism.*

The Real Women Project   www.realwomenproject.com
> *Funded through the Athena Charitable Foundation, the Real Women Project features images of women through art, music, and poetry. The intent of the project is to educate women about their health and self-worth.*

Size Wise   www.sizewise.com
> *A size-acceptance Web site with resources including related books, articles, and links to size-acceptance shopping.*

Sweatshop Watch   www.sweatshopwatch.org
> *Great site for information about global labor issues, including up-to-date information about sweatshop campaigns.*

UNITE! HERE   www.unitehere.org
> *Web site dedicated to union workers, primarily women. Information about union activity within textile, hotel, and restaurant industries.*

6

Knock 'em Up . . .
Knock 'em Down

"Monica" gave birth at seventeen. The pregnancy was wanted, celebrated, and shared with her partner. She knew about the politics of abortion, pregnancy, and women's health. She had been paying attention. So when Monica got pregnant she decided to activate her choice by choosing to become a parent. She thought that by making the decision to have a baby, she was making the decision most supported in our culture. However, from the moment of her first prenatal care appointment, she felt ignored and mistreated. Monica had done the research, had come prepared with questions, and attempted to be an advocate for herself. But, throughout what proved to be a difficult pregnancy and birth, her questions and needs went unmet. Monica looks back at this time with a certainty that she received this treatment solely because of her age; being a "teen mom" carried with it a stigma of mistake and irresponsibility. Monica was one of my students, and, unfortunately, her story is all too common.

This chapter looks at the health of girls and women. As women, we face different issues about our bodies than men—menstruation, birth control, pregnancy, breast cancer, menopause. Simply put, our bodies do things that male bodies don't do, and we need to make sure that the health care we receive is designed with our bodies in mind. What I'm talking about is women-centered health care. Women-centered health care puts the needs of women's bodies at the center of treatment. Such a system values the legitimacy of our experiences, provides full disclosure of medical risks, and respects the choices that we make. Indeed, today's health care for most Americans, certainly those who have health insurance, is arguably better than it's ever been. Technology has allowed us to extend our lives, to cure diseases, and to greatly improve our chances when we do get sick. As women, we are beneficiaries of this improved system; however, there are still advances to be made, and there are still obstacles to receiving the best care.

PUTTING WOMEN AT THE CENTER

What would a health care system that had women at the center look like? It seems common sense that the more information we have, the more likely we are to make decisions that benefit our lives, and the less fearful, disengaged, and dependent we are. The principles of women-centered health care are these: put women at the center of their experiences; re-claim the knowledge that used to be passed down between generations of women; believe in our experiences and their legitimacy; demand full disclosure of information to clients; respect the choices we make.

I remember my first gynecological exam. I was fifteen, and the gynecologist told me that I had a tipped uterus. I was too afraid to ask what this meant. I thought that I had been born wrong and that I would never be able to have babies—or at least, bizarrely, somehow develop a limp. For years, I walked around feeling deficient and scared. Not until I went to a Feminist Women's Health Center, one that provides women-centered health care, did I learn how misguided I was. I thank them because they changed the relationship I have with my body. A tipped uterus is common, no biggie: the uterus is just tipped back toward the back of the pelvis, away from the belly; it is usually not painful, and it doesn't mean you can't conceive or give birth.[1]

This is one example, and a fairly innocuous one at that, of what many other girls and women often face in the doctor's office or in the hospital operating room. A more disturbing story might involve the unnecessary hysterectomies that many women still have each year—90 percent of which many reports show to be medically unnecessary. Yet, hundreds of thousands are performed in the United States annually.[2] Another example is the continued and systematic gender bias in medical research and funding.[3]

What we need is a women's health agenda. While there certainly are some groups working toward this goal—some of which I will highlight later—we need a broad approach to women's health that is women-centered. A women's health agenda, for example, questions why men who have health insurance can get prescription coverage for Viagra (and Levitra, Cialis, and the other "male enhancement" products on the market), but women who have health insurance usually have to pay-out-of pocket expenses for their birth control. A women-centered health movement might also question why women's health concerns are consistently unfunded or underfunded or why women are less likely to appear in medical trials. A women-centered health movement might also see the wisdom in midwifery, a tradition of women helping women to birth babies that dates back centuries. And, even for those who choose to have their babies delivered in modern hospitals, as many of us do, this movement would still recognize and value our right to make that choice. A women-centered health movement is about allowing women to be in control of the choices that affect our bodies.

This chapter focuses on women's health and women's bodies. I want to make it clear that this women's health agenda contains a number of issues we've got to learn about and fight for. At the same time, there is perhaps no issue more essential to women's bodies than the right to control our reproduction—from birth control to abortion to adoption and pregnancy. Central to much of this debate is the *Roe v. Wade* decision, since it guarantees women the right to privacy, essentially allowing them to decide for themselves what to do if they become pregnant. Since so much of the past thirty years has been spent fighting for and against this decision, and since the decision still seems imperiled as the Supreme Court balance is always in flux, I will spend a good deal of this chapter discussing "the politics of choice." But, as essential as this issue is to the feminist movement, it's important to stress that the concerns of women's health encompass more than just this issue. So for those women (and men) who do not consider themselves pro-choice, there is still much here to fight for.

Roe v. Wade, 410 U.S. 113 (1973)—a landmark U.S. Supreme Court decision in which the Court ruled that established laws against abortion violated a constitutional right to privacy. This ruling established legality for abortion, overturning more than one hundred years of judicial precedent and state laws in all fifty states that restricted abortion.

TAKE A GOOD LOOK

We don't have to go very far back to find the origins of the modern feminist health movement. In 1971, the Feminist Women's Health Centers were founded by a group of Los Angeles women who wanted to know more about their bodies and their reproductive selves. At a time when pregnancy tests and yeast infection treatments were available only at physicians' offices and when libraries and bookstores were void of women's health books, the Feminist Women's Health Center provided a source of information and a place for women to gather to share experiences about their bodies, health, and lives.[4] They helped women across the country and around the world set up "self-help groups," where women came together to share information, learn from one another, and practice cervical self-exam. Yes, basically a group of women hangin' out and looking at their vaginas—despite the efforts of Eve Ensler to bring vaginas into fashion today, this still may sound a bit weird to people of my generation—but it was a real revelation to women then (and still is today!). The cervical self-exam was a way to gain control of one's body at a time when this domain belonged more to women's doctors and sexual partners. The practice continues to put women in touch with themselves and to assist in their awareness of their bodies—which returns our power to us. The Feminist Women's Health Centers' self-help is about understanding how our bodies work through our eyes; it is about making our bodily knowledge available and legitimate. Perhaps this is the first step in freeing ourselves from dependence on a medical system that does not value us. So, if you haven't done so, grab a mirror, and take a good look.

Vaginal and Cervical Self-Examination

Vaginal and cervical self-examination is one of the most useful health tools a woman can have. It enables us to see a vital part of our anatomy that is hidden from plain view—the vagina and cervix (the neck of the womb). By using a speculum, you can observe changes in your cervix and its secretions, the menstrual cycle, and indications of fertility; you can identify and treat common vaginal conditions such as yeast, trichomonas, or bacterial infections (which often cause itching or discharge); and you can learn what your cervix looks like day by day, rather than depending on a physician to look once a year to pronounce what is normal for you.

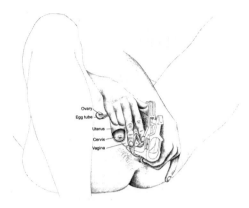

To insert a plastic speculum, spread the inner lips of the clitoris with two fingers of one hand, hold the bills of the speculum tightly together with the thumb and index finger of the other, and guide it into the vaginal canal. You can use a water-soluble jelly or just plain water to make insertion smoother. This woman is inserting her speculum with the handles upright, but some women prefer to insert it sideways initially. Inserting the speculum with the handles down is strictly for the doctor's convenience, and it requires that a woman put her feet into stirrups at the end of an exam table.

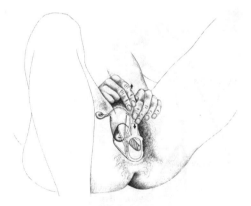

When the handles of the speculum are pinched together, they force the bills open, stretching the vaginal walls and revealing the cervix. With the handles held tightly together, the short handle slides down and the long handle slides up. When there is a sharp click the speculum is locked into place.

With the speculum locked, both hands are free to hold a mirror and a flashlight or gooseneck lamp. If a flashlight is used, shine the beam *into the mirror,* and it will, in turn, be reflected into the vagina, illuminating the vaginal walls and the cervix. The cervix won't always pop instantly into view. Sometimes you have to try several times. If it stubbornly refuses to appear, you can move around or jump up and down a few times. Sometimes it is also helpful to move to a firmer surface, like the floor or a tabletop. When the cervix is visible, you can see a rounded or flattened knob, between the size of a quarter and a fifty-cent piece, like a fat doughnut with a hole or slit in it. The hole, called the cervical os, is where the menstrual blood, other uterine secretions, and babies come out. Your cervix might be pink and smooth, or it might have a few reddish blemishes. It can also be uneven, rough, or splotchy. In any case, the only time to worry is when abnormal cells are found in a Pap smear.

* Material adapted from *A New View of A Woman's Body,* Federation of Feminist Women's Health Centers, Feminist Health Press, Los Angeles, CA. Suzann Gage created these beautiful illustrations, pp. 22–24. Reprinted with permission.

Beyond getting to know one's own vagina, a women-centered health agenda might also start at the beginning of our young lives and recognize the different ways that we are treated and taught to understand our own bodies. Little boys are often encouraged to be baseball players; little girls are encouraged to be fairy princesses. Little boys are encouraged to use their bodies in physical ways, whereas little girls are encouraged to dress their bodies in different clothes. When a little boy gets dirty, some say, "that's just a boy being a boy," but when a little girl does the same, she is a "tomboy" or "not acting like a nice little girl." While some of these tendencies may be biological, there is no doubting that society encourages these stereotypes. (Some might even say that this is how patriarchy continues itself.) Thankfully, there are now soccer leagues for both boys and girls, but there is still no doubting that there are many more athletic opportunities for boys than for girls and that, overall, boys are encouraged to be more physical and athletic than girls.

These bodily differences all but erupt at puberty. From the start, we are divided in gender-specific groups to see separate films about our changing bodies. Many of us struggle to pay attention during the coming-of-age video that highlights young girls that we barely recognize, while our curiosity wonders what the boys are learning about us—from someone else. We are both envious and fearful of the girls who begin menstruation before us—wanting to both be them and avoid the situation altogether. Very little if anything is shared ahead of time—as with most of our "education," we swap stories with our friends, trying to sort out this mess called *womanhood*. And then . . . the day—the day we see blood. We are indoctrinated into this new club, but usually with very little celebration. And our modern ritual begins—pads versus tampons, Midol versus heating pad—we learn the tortures of "the curse." We are bombarded with messages of fear—fear of someone knowing, fear of odor, fear of bloating, fear of leakage, fear of staining, fear of pain, fear, fear, fear. We are told that we need protection—but from what? Ourselves, our menstruating selves. The Solution: Deodorize, minimize, and hide the fact that we are women. Though this "secret" of womanhood is something that only women share as a rite of passage and though it may give us a certain sense of bonding (though the bonding over an "emergency" tampon gets you only so far), ultimately, this is a shameful secret to be kept, even from other women, in public. Even if we may want to, it is no wonder that we don't embrace and celebrate our femaleness; the messages that we should be ashamed are too strong.

We usually learn that menstruation and our cyclic bodily functions are disgusting. Just as quickly, we learn to judge these bodies harshly, and from another's point of view. As Emily Martin writes in *The Woman in the Body: A Cultural Analysis of Reproduction,*

> [b]ut because women are aware that in our general cultural view menstruation is dirty, they are still stuck with the "hassle": most centrally

no one must ever see you dealing with the mechanics of keeping up with the disgusting mess, and you must never fail to keep the disgusting mess from showing on your clothes, furniture, or the floor.[5]

As a result, I argue that we gradually become disconnected from our bodies, particularly female bodies. And it is also no wonder that we are so disconnected—between the lack of adequate education and the widely endorsed negative attitudes about our bodies, our menstruation, and our sexuality—women learn early on to ignore, underemphasize, or keep quiet about the functions of our bodies. As Martin writes, ultimately, women are taught to see bodily functions such as menstruation, birth, and menopause as happening to them; they become an object to be dealt with and manipulated by the medical field.[6]

If we are to create a women-centered health agenda, we must recognize and appreciate the differentness of our bodies, perhaps even celebrate our female bodies. In addition to the Feminist Women's Health Centers, organizations like the Boston Women's Health Collective and the National Women's Health Network advocate for women's health so that we may have research that represents us and information that is accessible and comprehensible. Organizations like Good Vibrations and Babes in Toyland offer women a positive image and support for our sexuality. Authors like Christiane Northrup, Inga Muscio, Laura Owen, Geneen Roth, Eve Ensler, Laura Fraser, and Marilyn Wann encourage us to embrace and celebrate our bodies. It is from each of these that we find resources and support for a women-centered approach to our health and wellness. Or, as Eve Ensler has said, "I love the word *vagina*."

SUGAR AND SPICE AND EVERYTHING NICE

In a sea of glamorized sexuality, young women today are left with conflicting messages about themselves—to be sexy but not too sexy, to be available but not too available. Good girl vs. slut. Short skirts. High heels. Sweet talk. Naughty whispers. He wants me. He wants me not. He loves me. He loves me not.

Tremendous pressure is placed on young women around sexuality and sexual activity. We see heterosexual sex everywhere—in movies, television shows, commercials, billboards, and magazines. We're even starting to see some "sex-positive" images of gay men and lesbians, though they're often seen less as sexual and more as just funny (think *Will & Grace, Queer Eye for the Straight Guy,* or *Ellen*). And, yet, we often leave young people without adequate knowledge or resources to empower themselves to make decisions that are best for them or to protect themselves from possible negative results of uneducated actions. We are in the midst of a long battle surrounding sex education in our schools. The way young people actually live their lives often gets lost in this debate. Sex education is inconsistent; we leave individual school districts to decide what is to be taught. Our federal government is in the midst of a national crusade to limit sex education to abstinence-only-until-heterosexual-marriage programs, even while denying a true conversation about abstinence. To say "just don't have sex" without explaining the true definition of abstinence or teaching negotiation skills or providing a "back-up" plan (if abstinence does not remain the choice) is, in my not-so-humble opinion, a crime. Those who force this approach are responsible for unintended pregnancies, HIV infections, the spread of sexually transmitted infections (STIs), and the sexual disempowerment of young people.

> **Abstinence means forgoing, or limiting, sexual activity to prevent the sharing of bodily fluids (i.e. semen, vaginal secretions, and blood) that can cause pregnancy or spread sexually transmitted diseases.**

IGNORANCE IS BLISS?

There is no uniform approach to teaching about sex and sexuality in our public schools. Thirty-nine U.S. states do require some sort of education—either sex education or education on HIV/AIDS and STIs—and "two out of three public school districts have a policy of teaching sex education."[7] What does exist is almost always decided upon at the local level, allowing community politics to dictate the depth of education and creating a lack of consistent education nationwide. More and more, however, we see school districts gravitating toward abstinence education, with 86 percent enforcing a sex education policy that requires "that abstinence be promoted over other options for teenagers."[8] Alarmingly, "one in four sex education teachers are prohibited from teaching about contraception."[9] Further, the Alan Guttmacher Institute found that there was a significant gap between what is taught and what teachers believe should be taught. "As a result," AGI writes in its report "Sex Education: Needs, Programs and Policies," "one in four teachers believes they are not meeting their students' needs for information."[10] Ironically, the majority of parents—some 75 percent—do want their children to receive comprehensive sex education, on topics including contraceptive and condom use, sexually transmitted infections, safer sex practices, and even abortion and sexuality education.[11]

Yet, the Bush administration actively promotes abstinence-only programs, requesting $273 million for "abstinence grants" in 2005. But if you take a closer look at these abstinence-only programs, you see that they are inherently flawed. In 2004, Representative Henry Waxman and the U.S. House of Representatives Committee on Government Reform, Special Investigations Division, found that "the curricula used in SPRANS [the Special Programs of Regional and National Significance Community-Based Abstinence Education] and other federally funded programs are not reviewed for accuracy by the federal government."[12] SPRANS is the key vehicle through which the Department of Health and Human Services provides grants to teach abstinence-only education geared toward youth. Further, the Waxman report found that more than 80 percent of the abstinence-only curricula contained "false, misleading, or distorted information about health."[13] Such misinformation includes false statements regarding the effectiveness of birth control methods ("condoms fail to prevent HIV approximately 31% of the time" and "pregnancy occurs one out of every seven times that couples use condoms") and false information about abortion ("5% to 10% of women who have legal abortions will become sterile" and "tubal and cervical pregnancies are increased following abortions"). In addition, in these curricula, science and religion are blurred ("Conception, also known as fertilization, occurs when one sperm unites with one egg in the upper third of the fallopian tube. This is when life begins."); gender stereotypes are referenced as fact ("women need 'financial support' while men need 'admiration'"; "Women gauge their happiness and judge their success on their relationships. Men's happiness and success hinge on their accomplishments"); and scientific errors are presented as fact (they list sweat and tears as risk factors for HIV; some curricula state that we have twenty-four chromosomes, instead of the correct number, twenty-three).[14] This false information has the potential to deeply impact the health, wellness, and safety of our youth.

Despite having patterns of sexual activity like their counterparts in other developed countries, U.S. teens have higher pregnancy, birth, and abortion rates and higher rates of sexually transmitted infections.[15] The Alan Guttmacher Institute found this to be largely a result of the fact that U.S. teens are less likely to use contraceptives and more likely to have shorter relationships and more partners.[16] Additionally, teens in other developed countries receive more social support and have better access to contraceptive services and comprehensive sex education.

Social attitudes in the United States regarding teen sexuality differ significantly from those prevalent in other developed countries. In its report "Sex Education: Needs, Programs and Policies," the Alan Guttmacher Institute writes:

> There is evidence that in many developed countries with low levels of teenage pregnancy, childbearing and STDs, adults tend to be more accepting of sexual activity among teenagers than are adults in the United States. However, adults in these countries also give clear and unambiguous messages that sex should occur within committed relationships and that sexually active teenagers are expected to take steps to protect themselves and their partners from pregnancy and STDs.

> Moreover, while these societies may be more accepting of teenage sex than the United States, they are, in fact, less accepting of teenage parenthood. Strong societal messages convey that childbearing should occur only in adulthood, which is considered to be when young people have completed their education, are employed and are living in stable relationships. Societal supports exist to help young people with the transition to adulthood, through vocational training, education and job placement services, and childcare. As a result, teenagers have positive incentives to delay childbearing.[17]

Better information, better resources, and better attitudes from adults—sounds about right. Not only have we created a culture that refuses to drop antiquated attitudes about sex, but we have so politicized sex that our teens lack resources that could literally save their lives.

In the meantime, our culture demonizes young women who become pregnant. Recent high-profile cases of teens hiding pregnancies or giving birth silently in basements or public bathroom stalls and the highly dramatized images of these girls being hauled off to jail are indicative of the contradiction in which young women live their lives in this culture. Young women often have sex to find love and approval, but this comes with very little if any self-definition and little understanding of how their reproductive bodies work. Young women often have few places to turn for this information, with marginal access to birth control to prevent pregnancy and little or no access to abortion once they are pregnant. And let's be clear: the burden falls on the young woman— very little attention is given to the young man who helped to create this situation.

We need to provide adequate information and resources, to teach girls to embrace and honor their bodies, to empower them to discover their sexuality on their own terms and not through peer and social pressure (and we must not discourage or penalize girls who do embrace their sexuality). We need also to create a dialogue and a reality where girls can get their questions answered and get the support they need in any situation without shame and blame. Providing this information, resources, and dialogue is what a feminist health agenda is all about.

STICKS AND STONES

Murderer! Baby Killer! Sinner! shouted a group of white men crowding the sidewalk across the street from the clinic. Rocks were hurled through the air toward my head, coming from behind the oversized signs of bloody miscarriages claiming to be the results of abortion. I heard women's voices close to my ear, fervently thanking me for putting my body between them and these crazy men who did not know them. They did not know me, either. They did not know that I babysat through my teen years, that I love children and may have my own one day. They did not know that I fight as hard for women to get birth control services, adoption services, and prenatal care as I do for abortion care. They also did not know, or did not care, that women from all walks of life come to this health center for care that is woman-centered, so that they might better understand their bodies and make choices in a supportive environment that is free from blame and shame. They did not care about women who were denied services in other health facilities because they did not have insurance or enough money, or because they were drug addicted but trying to care for themselves when no one else would, and came here to this amazing nonprofit women's health center.

They did not care as they yelled, chanted, and threw sticks and stones at the women entering the health center.

My first day escorting at the Chico Feminist Women's Health Center, in 1992, was eye opening, to say the least. I volunteered to be there because I believe that women should be safe when accessing a legal option. I volunteered because the stories of women dying in back-alley abortions haunted me. I volunteered because I believe in women and I trust them to make choices that are best for them in their lives. And I volunteered because the Feminist Women's Health Center changed my life, and I wanted to make sure that other women had access to the same care.

> The thought that anyone else could interfere in decisions I make about my body both infuriates and frightens me. If I don't have the right to choose over my own body, then I do not belong to myself. Shawna, 30, white, heterosexual, California

The attack on abortion is so great that we are constantly reminded about the importance of protecting a woman's right to choose. From the lack of education women receive about their bodies to the lack of funding and access to needed services to the dangerous and debilitating acts aimed at those who provide services and staff the health centers to which women turn—we face the reality that legal abortion and health information are not readily available to women. Currently, 87 percent of counties across the United States do not have an abortion provider.[18] Religious hospitals and health service organizations are quickly buying out medical practices, health plans, and hospitals, making abortion and contraceptive care even more difficult to obtain. Unfortunately, recent attempts to win legislative protection have failed, to be replaced with legislation targeted at reducing women's right to choose. Additionally, conservatives are determined to appoint circuit judges and Supreme Court Justices who do not support abortion rights.

Acts of violence continue to plague our reproductive health care— threats, harassment, bombings, and murders are a reality for many providers. The Nuremberg Files—a Web site that spews false accusations about abortion, posts personal information about anyone connected to abortion care (i.e., advocates, providers, activists, escorts, health workers), and runs video of clinic entrances—has repeatedly been supported by the Ninth Circuit Court, particularly under Carolyn Kuhl (whose nomination by George W. Bush to the Federal Court of Appeals was successfully defeated). And in the White House, the anti-choice activists have a great supporter in George W. Bush, who has appointed anti-choice zealots to key political offices, supported religion-based (actually, Christian-based, despite the multitude of religious beliefs in the United States) programs for health education and services, and pledged support for all legislation that further hinders women's right to abortion. Since taking office, this administration has delivered devastating blows to the reproductive rights of women in this country and well beyond our borders. Under George W. Bush, we have seen the loss of contraceptive insurance coverage for federal employees, the reinstatement of the global gag rule, the appointment of extreme anti-choice individuals to critical political positions, and a serious threat to the Supreme Court—and *Roe v. Wade* hangs in the balance.

> *Being from a third world country, Peru, I know what other women are living. I have a good idea what it was like before* Roe v. Wade *because it's still like that in my country. I know how Bush's global gag rule affected women, because it's happening in my country.*
> Deborah, 25, Peruvian-Hispanic, Massachusetts

Officially titled the Mexico City Policy, the global gag rule mandates that "no U.S. family planning assistance can be provided to foreign NGOs that use funding from any other source to: perform abortions in cases other than a threat to the woman's life, rape, or incest; provide counseling and referral for abortion; or lobby to make abortion legal or more available in their country" (The Global Gag Rule Impact Project, www.globalgagrule.org). This policy affects countries even where abortion is legal. There is no evidence that the gag rule has reduced the number of abortions worldwide, but research has shown that, in addition to limiting free speech, it has negatively and with devastating effect impacted family planning and reproductive health services in developing countries.

Today, we have a generation that came of age knowing some degree of reproductive freedom. This is a blessing and a curse; on the one hand, we have freedom of choice, but, on the other hand, we have the luxury of believing that abortion is not an issue that we need to fight for. The result is a generation that largely takes legality, and the availability, of abortion for granted. Fortunately, among this generation there are also numerous activists who do understand the fragility of choice in today's politics. And their activism is palpable in local communities, as well as on the national scene—as evidenced by the 1.15 million who marched in Washington, DC, in April 2004.

Whether we are disengaged from the politics of abortion or on the front lines of the abortion battle, whether we have adequate access to abortion care or are without the money, the transportation, the legal right, or a provider within reach, whether we are fighting for the

I believe that being an abortion provider and working toward safe, effective contraception for any and every woman is how I can be the most help for today.
Sherry, 34, medical student, California

right to have children while on welfare or in prison or fighting the abuse of sterilization, the fight to make choices for ourselves and about our bodies belongs to each of us.

THE POLITICS OF ABORTION

Abortion is a hugely controversial issue in our society. Who should decide? What should be legal? Who should have access? Is abortion murder? When does life begin? All very important questions to sort out—personally but also politically. On a personal level, it is essential to explore these issues because it comes down to choice—and the right for you to make yours. Finding out where you stand on these issues is the pathway to deciding what you might choose when facing an unintended pregnancy. This is also true for men; while I believe that women should have the final decision in these cases, men can more effectively volunteer their voices regarding pregnancy if they know where they stand before having sex and if they communicate with their sexual partners. Given the political environment of the day, it is also important to address these questions on the public front as we have seen a decades-long battle to secure a woman's right to choose—a battle that is far from over. While I would argue that abortion is a personal decision and one that should belong to women and whomever they choose to include in their decision-making process, there is no argument about the reality that abortion is a significant political matter in our society today. We'll come back to the political challenges facing abortion rights in the United States—truly unique in the world—and I will also detail the history of abortion. But first I think that it is important to understand the context of abortion in women's lives today in order to fully understand what is at stake.

WHY DO WOMEN HAVE ABORTIONS?

I have worked with the Feminist Women's Health Centers in Northern California (now the Women's Health Specialists)[19] since 1992. I have escorted; I have been an advocate, a health worker, a health educator, and a manager. I now serve on the board of directors. I have talked with many women who volunteered to share their stories with me—stories about how they got pregnant, the role of the guy in their decision to have an abortion, their religion, family, work, school, and futures. They shared the many reasons behind their decision for abortion—from being too young to being too old; from financial concerns to health concerns; from fear to freedom. The reality is that the reasons why women choose abortion are as diverse and unique as the women themselves.

Some studies, however, have given us a framework for exploring the general reasons behind a woman's choice for abortion. The Alan Guttmacher Institute found that "on average, women give at least four reasons for choosing abortion: three-fourths of women cite concern for or responsibility to other individuals; three-fourths say they cannot afford a child; three-fourths say that having a baby would interfere with work, school or the ability to care for dependents; and half say they do not want to be a single parent or are having problems with their husband or partner."[20] Indeed, these are common reasons behind a woman's choice of abortion. Other reasons include fear of disappointing a parent, physical or sexual abuse at home or in an intimate relationship, and rape and sexual assault. These are important reasons to recognize; not only are they issues that we must address in order to ensure safety to women and girls, but we must also appreciate the realities in which we live. Should we compound the tragic reality of abuse with a pregnancy that results from this abuse? Should women be forced to give birth to the biological offspring of a family member? A rapist? It is important to note that some women do continue with pregnancies that come from abuse and rape. It is important to support and respect that choice. But it is also important to respect and protect a woman's right to choose not to continue that pregnancy. Only the individual knows what she can handle, and my point is that we need to respect her choice and not force her to make one that fulfills someone else's agenda. These are appalling but real situations that must be remembered when exploring legal and physical access to abortion.

WHO ARE THE WOMEN WHO HAVE ABORTIONS?

The anti-choice movement would like to paint a picture of women who have abortions as irresponsible, lazy, and promiscuous. But the reality is that all "types" of woman is equally likely to have an abortion: women with one partner, women with multiple partners, religious women, women of all ethnicities, women of different ages, married women, single women, straight women, bisexual women, lesbian women—and even women who argue against abortion rights. In my work with a woman's health center, I helped to provide abortion services to a woman who frequently stood on our sidewalks in protest of abortion. She returned to the sidewalk the following week, signs of protest in her hand, after her safe, legal, nonjudgmental procedure. Additionally, I have had friends who have argued vehemently against abortion, but who, upon discovering they were pregnant, chose abortion as the only option for them. One friend told me, on the drive home from her safe and legal abortion, that she was glad that it had been there for her but didn't think abortion should be legal.

I don't tell these stories to judge these women, but rather as a wake-up call. Situations that we never dreamed of can occur that ultimately lead us to abortion. Almost half of all pregnancies among American women are unintended—and half of those unintended pregnancies are terminated by abortion.[21] Contrary to popular myth, very few women use abortion as a method of birth control—in fact, the National Abortion Federation, a group of providers and researchers, found that "half of all women getting abortions report that contraception was used during the month they became pregnant."[22] Further, the Alan Guttmacher Institute found that "fifty-four percent of women having abortions used a contraceptive method during the month they became pregnant" and only "8% of women having abortions have never used a method of birth control."[23] Abortion is not the enemy, nor are the women who have them. Abortion is a health issue and a reality.

One of the things that I have learned in the years of working in reproductive health care is that women will always need access to abortion. We know this from our history, and our current reality is our confirmation. Let's be clear—not all women will have abortions, but those who do not want to be pregnant—for whatever their reasons—will find a way not to be. Women's stories from around the world prove that, regardless of legality, safety, resources, culture, religion, fear, and risk, women who want an abortion will find a way. The question is not whether women will have abortions but whether they will be safe in doing so. I believe that when we have the capability, the know-how, and the resources for abortion services, we have an obligation to make sure that women are safe. Abortion is about life and death—but not in the sense the opposition would like us to believe. The difference between illegal abortion and safe, legal, accessible abortion is whether women survive. Abortion, despite its controversy, is a medically safe and simple procedure. Unfortunately, the politics surrounding abortion—particularly the goal of making abortion illegal—is what makes abortion unsafe.

THE SAFETY OF ABORTION

Abortion in the first trimester (less than twelve weeks' gestation) is safer than a tonsillectomy, an appendectomy, or a shot of penicillin.[24] The risk of death associated with childbirth is eleven times greater than the risk of death from an abortion, and fewer than 0.3 percent of all women who have an abortion experience a major complication requiring hospitalization.[25] The risk of abortion lies less within the practice of abortion than within the politics of abortion. From the declining number of providers (we saw an 11 percent decline in the number of providers between 1996 and 2000)[26] to the political environment in this country, access has become a key issue impacting the safety of abortion. In 2000, 87 percent of counties in the United States had no abortion provider, and one-third of American women lived in these counties.[27] And of all women who obtained abortions in 2000, "25% traveled at least 25 miles, and 8% traveled more than 100 miles."[28] Anti-choice activists have hindered medical research as well as access to clinic services. They fought the release of RU-486, or medical/nonsurgical abortion, even though the medication has been used successfully for years in Europe. They continue to fight for legislation that would limit and restrict a woman's right to choose—and now have one of their greatest allies in George W. Bush. They picket clinic entrances and badger staff and clients. And some within the anti-choice movement are violent terrorists who stalk, harass, and even murder doctors and clinic staff. They harass the children and family members of providers and have even been known to poison pets. What makes abortion unsafe is the fact that women have to travel extended distances, cross violent protest lines, and confront a culture of shame that far too often silences them.

THE FIGHT FOR YOUNG WOMEN

The debate around teen access to abortion is brutal; in most cases, it is conducted in the absence of teens themselves, who are rarely included in decision-making or policymaking positions about reproductive health care, who are generally not included in the dialogue about teen sexuality and pregnancy, and who are not able to cast a vote regarding initiatives or propositions or for the officials who are charged with representing them. And yet, they are directly impacted by the laws and regulations that are put in place without their voice.

Minors' access is perhaps one of the most politically and socially controversial aspects of the abortion debate. Most voters support the inclusion of some parental-involvement provisions in the law—I think because they believe that it will *guarantee* that their teen will talk to them when faced with an unintended pregnancy. Honestly, emotion aside for a moment, is it possible to enforce legislation that demands that teens talk to parents? Think about it for a minute. My reaction is that it's impossible to demand this. (Fortunately, however, 61 percent of teens report that they would willingly discuss an unintended pregnancy with their parent(s).)[29] When looking at this debate, I believe that we are obligated to see the bigger picture and not focus just upon our own family. We must think of those teens who do not believe that they can turn to their parent(s). Whether abuse is involved or fear of disappointing a parent, if she does not believe that she is safe in confiding in a parent, a teen will not. Like women who sought illegal abortions in the years prior to *Roe v. Wade,* these young women will also seek the termination of a pregnancy in any way they can. And in states where there is a parental-notification or parental-consent requirement, young women will be forced into self-inducement or "back-alley" abortions. Despite the availability of legal and safe abortion in this country, young women are dying, or seriously harming themselves. Most notable to this reality was the death of Becky Bell, in 1988. Becky died, at age seventeen, from complications following an illegal abortion. She was a teen who lived in a parental-consent state. Her parents, who prior to her death supported parental-consent laws, bravely traveled the country to tell their daughter's story and to encourage other parents to oppose laws restricting minors' access to abortion. In many ways, Becky has become the symbol of the fight for minors' access. But Becky is not the only teen who turned to desperate measures when confronted with an unintended pregnancy. I have spoken with young women who have thrown themselves down stairs, taken baseball bats to their abdomens, intentionally gotten into car accidents—all with the desperate hope of inducing a miscarriage. Is this the reality that we want for our youth? As long as we continue to allow restrictions to minors' access to abortion (and contraceptive) care, this is the reality they will live with.

> *Many of my peers are not aware of the political climate and threats that are being made to women's rights, particularly with reproductive freedom.* Diane, 23, Caucasian, heterosexual, Michigan

> **Generally, parental-notification laws require a health provider to notify a young woman's parent of her intent to have an abortion, and parental-consent laws require permission from a parent before a teen can access abortion services. In most cases, a "judicial bypass" option is available that allows a teen can go before a judge to request permission for access to abortion services. But this option hardly seems an *option* when courts are difficult and intimating to traverse, judges are biased, teens have to leave school to go to court, leaving them subject to calls home for absenteeism, and when confidentiality is compromised.**

A BRIEF HISTORY OF ABORTION IN THE UNITED STATES

Abortion in the United States was not always the political firecracker that it is today. Not to romanticize the past, but there was once a time when women's health was in women's hands—including all aspects of repro-

ductive care, from abortion to prenatal care, pregnancy to birth, infertility to birth control. Prior to the mid-1800s, women worked in community
with one another, familiar with the use of herbs and massage and knowledgeable in the cycles of the female body. Women would visit women
healers, including midwives, to receive assistance with infertility, the
prevention of pregnancy, support during a pregnancy and/or a birth or
for assistance in terminating a pregnancy when needed. To the general
public, abortion was really a nonissue. Throughout history, abortion was
not controversial; for example, abortion was readily available and used
in the Roman Empire; there are no references to, or provisions against, induced abortion in the Christian Bible or the Jewish Talmud; and Catholic
canon law found early abortion legally unimportant.[30] Initially, American legal opinion followed suit, but, as women's health moved more into
the realm of male-controlled science, knowledge and control were taken
away from women. The science of women's health, or obstetrics and gy-
necology, emerged, replacing women healers with male "experts." In
order to become these self-proclaimed experts, male doctors practiced
surgical procedures on slave and immigrant women without consent or
anesthesia.[31] They also created a campaign—the witch trials—to exter-
minate women healers and thereby eliminate their abilities and to scare
other women away from woman-controlled knowledge and health
care.[32] With the eradication of women healers, men began to takeover
healing and medicine—first in Europe and then in the United States. As
Barbara Ehrenreich and Deirdre English, authors of *Witches, Midwives
and Nurses: A History of Women Healers*, ask,

> The question is not so much how women got "left out" of medicine
> and left with nursing, but how did these categories arise at all? To put
> it another way: How did one particular set of healers, who happened
> to be male, white and middle class, manage to oust all the competing
> folk healers, midwives and other practitioners who had dominated
> the American medical scene in the early 1800s?[33]

The answer, according to Ehrenreich and English, are the class and sex
struggles of the nineteenth century. These struggles led to the rise of a
medical profession that considered women, and women's health, sub-
servient to men. And, as G. J. Barker-Benfield writes in *The Horrors of the
Half-Known Life*, "one of the casualties of the male drive to take control
of women was the midwife."[34] With the loss of the midwife came the

loss of woman-centered health care and knowledge, the loss of woman's control over her body, and the politicizing of women's bodies, which served as a means to control women and to maintain male— specifically white male—power.

Nowhere do we see greater evidence of this than in the drive to control women's reproductive lives. Men's takeover of medicine in the 1800s gave rise to a growing "right to life," or antiabortion movement, in the 1900s.[35] Despite the fact that early-nineteenth-century America had "no statute laws governing abortion" and only minimal regulation of abortion after "quickening" (that is, when a pregnant woman begins to feel fetal movement), by 1900, every state had passed some sort of law restricting abortion at all stages of pregnancy.[36] Although provisions existed for the preservation of the woman's life, these restrictions were the beginning of a far-reaching and contemptible politic regarding abortion, which we continue to combat today.

Kristen Luker, author of *Abortion and the Politics of Motherhood,* writes that "[m]any cultural themes and social struggles lie behind the transition from an abortion climate that was remarkably open and unrestricted to one that restricted abortions (at least in principle) to those necessary to save the life of the mother."[37] As the United States shifted from an agriculture-based society to an urban one and with the rise of immigration, abortion became a central theme in women's health and politics. Change in the status of women that paralleled the demographic shift from rural to urban life, along with changing social values and "strains between rural and urban dwellers; between native-born 'Yankees' and immigrants; between the masses and the elites; and possibly between men and women"[38] all contributed to the growing politic of prohibiting abortion. Like Ehrenreich and English, Luker cites the rise of male physicians as a main influence leading to restrictive abortion laws. She writes,

> The most visible interest group agitating for more restrictive abortion laws was composed of elite or "regular" physicians, who actively petitioned state legislatures to pass anti-abortion laws and undertook through popular writings a campaign to change public opinion on abortion. The efforts of these physicians were probably the single most important influence in bringing about nineteenth-century anti-abortion laws.[39]

She goes on to argue that these same physicians viewed the issue of abortion through a political and social lens that continues to influence the debate today. Abortion became increasingly difficult to obtain throughout the early and mid-1900s, further impacting the political debate about women's lives while simultaneously endangering women as back-alley butchers, who posed as doctors, took advantage of the situation.

It is impossible to know how many abortions occurred prior to legalization, or to fully understand the impact of illegal abortion on the lives of women prior to *Roe v. Wade*, the landmark 1973 U.S. Supreme Court decision that legalized abortion in the first trimester. Statistics were not often tracked, and fear of prosecution kept many women and practitioners from reporting abortion. Additionally, the cause of death for women who had had botched abortions was often misreported. Poor and low-income women suffered the most during these times, since they lacked the financial resources to obtain private and less dangerous (albeit illegal) abortions in the United States or to travel to other countries for safer abortion procedures. For poor women, the price of abortion often included danger, disease, unsanitary conditions, rape and sexual assault, and death. Patricia Miller's book *The Worst of Times* details accounts of such illegal abortion. In one story, a woman tells of her abortion in 1952. She recalls, "he made me have sex with him before he would do the abortion. My husband never knew that. He would have been wild if he had known. This abortion was expensive in lots of ways."[40] One Pennsylvania coroner, in comparing abortion death rates before and after *Roe v. Wade,* said, "in the coroner's office we would see three or four deaths a year from illegal abortions . . . the deaths stopped overnight in 1973, and I never saw another abortion death in all the eighteen years after that until I retired. That ought to tell people something about keeping abortion legal."[41]

The *Roe* decision is fundamental to abortion rights in this country, and a decision that we must protect. But legalization did not end the attack on abortion. Today, we continue to fight a daily battle against the chipping away of abortion rights and reproductive rights in general—from the debate about when life begins to the battles over judicial nominees and the court system to the language we use and the fight for a greater recognition and protection of all women's reproductive health care needs.

WOMANHOOD VS. "FETUSHOOD"

While the debate between which to value—woman or fetus—is long in our history of abortion rights in this country, today we are seeing an interesting shift in the language used to frame the debate. Where once the term "unborn children" was central among anti-choice Republicans and zealots and was frequently used in debates, campaigns, and propaganda, we now see this phrase commonly used as well on soap operas and television shows and during news reports. Not only does such language reframe the debate so that the pregnancy is valued over the rights of the woman; it is also now influencing policy. Nowhere do we see this more than in the public pronouncements of the G. W. Bush administration, which has put forth and supported a number of policy proposals that define fetuses as people—from the Unborn Victims of Violence Act to medical coverage for the "unborn" to the so-called Partial Birth Abortion Ban Act, which equates late-term abortion with "infanticide." What is important to know about the so-called partial-birth procedure is that, medically speaking, it does not exist. Rather, the terminology is central to the anti-choice movement's goal of fooling people into envisioning a baby that is brutally murdered by heartless women and abortion providers. This personification of the fetus shifts the focus away from women and their experience, thus allowing the political debate about abortion to exist in the absence of women. As a result, anti-choice advocates have a powerful tool in arguing against abortion rights for women. Unfortunately, theirs has been a very successful campaign; the House of Representatives passed the Unborn Victims of Violence Act in 1999 and 2001, and "partial-birth abortion ban" acts have passed in approximately thirty states; while similar federal legislation was vetoed twice by President Bill Clinton, President Bush signed a federal version in October 2003, making it the first federal ban on abortion in the United States.

Make no mistake: the ultimate goal of the political right is to overturn *Roe v. Wade*. The right's tactics include opposition to sex education in public schools, opposition to comprehensive reproductive-health-care options, opposition to state or federal funding for reproductive-health services, and a complete ban on abortion services. They conjure false images in the minds of the American public and gain support for banning abortion in all circumstances by slowly chipping away at reproductive-heathcare rights, access, and education. The intent of the right has always been a source of concern, but the movement's infiltration into popular culture is even more worrisome. As our media adopt the language of the right and projects this politic onto the American public, women face a greater challenge in remaining central to the discussion about abortion. Increasingly lost are our voices and our stories, since claiming to have had an abortion is seen as shameful—a dirty secret—replaced now with images and discussions of the "unborn." The result is greater shame and blame targeted at women, the eventual loss of abortion rights, and the devastating return to back-alley butchers.

THE ROLE OF THE COURTS

Another critical area of concern related to women's reproductive rights is the courts. Between 2001 and 2006, we witnessed an intense fight over judicial nominees, one whose outcome will continue to impact us for many generations to come. With a Republican-controlled Congress and White House, we saw a pattern of nominating extreme ideologues to high appointive positions, particularly to the federal Court of Appeals (district courts or circuit courts) and to the U.S. Supreme Court. These court appointments are lifetime positions, and it doesn't take much to imagine the impact that this pattern will have on women's rights, reproductive rights, civil rights, and GLBTQQI rights.

The Supreme Court is critically important, because Supreme Court justices have the power to influence every aspect of our lives with their decisions, from the right to privacy (including abortion) to the right to free speech. Much focus has been on the Supreme Court in recent years—and rightly so, as the Court is becoming more slanted toward an anti-choice position with the appointment, in 2005, of John Roberts as Chief Justice and the confirmation, in 2006, of Samuel Alito as an associate justice of the Court. Additionally, it is important that we not ignore the significance of the U.S. Court of Appeals, which, at the bare minimum, decides which cases go on to the Supreme Court. Carolyn Kuhl, Charles Pickering, Priscilla Owen, D. Brooks Smith, and Miguel Estrada are just a few in a long line of Bush nominees who are disconcerting to women's rights activists. These nominees have opposed the use of buffer zones to protect health centers, limited minors' access to abortion, and supported bans on abortion practices. These nominees are evidence of the agenda among conservatives to pack the courts with judges who do not support women's reproductive rights. In contrast, the feminist movement is fighting for judges who uphold the Constitution and continue to protect women's right to privacy and their right to safe abortion. We must have courts that represent and protect the people, not courts that carry out the will of a few powerful politicians.

NOW v. Scheidler[42]

Since 1986, the National Organization for Women has been fighting to charge anti-choice terrorists like Joseph Scheidler with a "nationwide criminal conspiracy to close women's health clinics."[43] Under antitrust laws, NOW was able to win the first nationwide injunction against violence directed at abortion clinics. As a result, the violence (but not the harassment of) against clinics did stop—for a while. In 1989, by using the RICO (Racketeer-Influenced and Corrupt Organizations) Act, NOW was able to add charges of extortion and violation of federal racketeering laws to strengthen its case against Scheidler, PLAN (Pro-Life Action League), and, more recently, Randall Terry and Operation Rescue. The use of RICO is particularly vital in this case, as NOW states:

[RICO] laws were originally designed to address mafia-type crimes. RICO imposes liability on those who operate a criminal enterprise. The RICO Act requires a pattern of racketeering and at least two serious criminal acts. RICO allows for triple damages to be awarded if a group is found guilty, making it a powerful tool to fight anti-abortion extremists who use fear, force and violence to close clinics.[44]

There has been great opposition to the use of the RICO statute in this case, and such pro-choice notables as Martin Sheen have spoken against the case. But what is important to note is that RICO cannot be used against peaceful protests and would not interfere with an individual's or group's right to freedom to speech or to protest. In 1998, NOW won a unanimous verdict in its favor, "finding that the defendants engaged in a nationwide conspiracy to deny women access to medical facilities ... [and holding defendants] liable for triple damages for the harm their violent acts caused to women's health clinics."[45] Unfortunately, on February 26, 2003, by a vote of eight to one, the Supreme Court overturned the verdict, relieving

Scheidler of any wrongdoing. The recent ruling serves as a green light to additional antiabortion clinic violence. In a country with increasingly high rates of clinic violence, it is realistic to fear that harassment, arson, and property damage will continue to escalate, given this decision. NOW went back to court. Arguments were heard again by the Supreme Court, on November 30, 2005, to determine support for an injunction under RICO. The U.S. Department of Justice, as directed by the Bush administration, stood in support of Joseph Scheidler and against NOW.

It is critical to protect and respect women's right to choose—and it is particularly urgent that we put a stop to the attack on abortion rights, abortion providers, and the women who choose and need abortion. But abortion is only one part of women's health. It is not the whole story.

PRO-CHOICE IS ABOUT YOUR CHOICE

Let's look at language—"pro-choice" versus so-called "pro-life." Since entering the movement to protect safe, legal, and accessible abortion for women, I have been on a campaign to change the way we talk about abortion politics in the United States. "Pro-choice" is exactly that—making a personal choice about abortion. Pro-choice encompasses both those who choose abortion and those who do not. Pro-choice is about exercising your ability to evaluate options in the context of your individual life—after all, who better to make decisions in your life, to know the intimate details of your life, than you? But "pro-life" does not accurately reflect the politics of that side of the debate. The "pro-life" movement argues against abortion—often under any circumstances, including rape and incest. They place value on a potential life as opposed to a woman's life.

Particularly saddening about the politicization of these terms is the polarization that can occur among women themselves. Through the misrepresentation and manipulation of the "pro-choice" position as one that does not support having children, some women who have, or desire to have, children of their own may feel that they cannot be "pro-choice." The politics of this debate has mistakenly pitted women against one another, when we ought to be standing together in support of healthy, wanted, funded pregnancies and children. And, indeed, you can be pro-choice and be committed to the health, safety, and rights of children.

Additionally, the tactics used by the "pro-life" movement often contradict the movement's name—with clinic violence, doctor and clinic worker murders, harassment, stalking, fire bombing, and butyric acid attacks among the tactics its adherents have used. In fact, there have been more than four thousand acts of violence since 1997, including 7 murders, 17 attempted murders, 41 bombings, 100 butyric acid attacks, 125 assaults and battery, and 355 death threats.[46] There have also been nearly seventy-eight thousand reported incidences of harassment, hoaxes, picketing, and bomb threats.[47] To be fair, this violence represents only a fraction of this movement's activities, but, nonetheless, the statistics are staggering and affect the lives of women every day.

Noting all of this, I think that it is critical to revisit the language of this abortion movement. This movement is about choice, having one and not having one. Consequently, I refer to the "pro-life" movement as the "anti-choice" movement. They believe that women are not capable of making a difficult and complicated choice. Ironically, many anti-choice activists are men who will never become pregnant and who therefore will never have to make this choice.

Additionally, the language of "choice" does not always represent the greater concerns of reproductive health. I see abortion as one part of women's health care—and I think that it should be treated as such and destigmatized. Unfortunately, the politics of abortion have created a steady threat to abortion rights, causing activists to focus their attention on this single issue. Whether or not this result was intentional, I believe that it might be one of the most effective tactics of the anti-choice movement, in that other, equally important health issues have taken a back seat to abortion and the issue has divided women within the movement. And whenever we are divided, we lose strength. While we must continue to fight for the safety, accessibility, and legality of abortion services, we must also fight for the overall reproductive health of all women.

MORE THAN ABORTION

One of my greatest frustrations about the abortion rights debate is that the fight to protect a woman's right to choose has diverted attention from the other, equally important issues surrounding reproductive rights. I think that one of the most successful elements of the anti-choice campaign has been its ability to divide women on the issues of reproductive health by creating a threat-based need to constantly defend a woman's right to abortion. The relentless attack on abortion has created a focus and a consciousness among mainstream women's rights organizations so that they spend their energy on abortion, often prioritizing abortion over the range of issues that makes up "reproductive freedom." There is a legitimate threat to the legal right to abortion, but there are also other reproductive issues that have long been neglected. One such issue is the critical fight to protect women from unnecessary medical treatments without their consent; sterilization, hysterectomies, and episiotomies are just a few of the common procedures that have been performed on women without informed consent—and which have become so common that consent is often assumed.

In fact, reproductive health incorporates a wide variety of health-care issues for women. From menstruation to menopause, from sexuality to birth control, from pregnancy to infertility, from abortion to adoption, from breast health to osteoporosis, women face these issues daily. The feminist movement is dedicated to educating women, incorporating them into research, and empowering them to make informed decisions for themselves. But the focus on abortion has diverted many resources and energies from these other important health issues. This diversion has served as a major source of division among women activists. Notably, women of color have voiced their frustration over the lack of attention given to the critical issue of forced sterilization that exists in epidemic proportions.

Dorothy Roberts, author of *Killing the Black Body: Race, Reproduction and the Meaning of Liberty,* details numerous accounts of such abuses—including "the practice of sterilizing Southern Black women through trickery or deceit," surgeries performed for "training purposes," lack of adequate education and explanation prior to medical procedures, sterilization emphasized over information about other birth control methods, the performance of hysterectomy in place of abortion, and the lack of accurate documentation of such procedures in medical records.[48] Women of color have long fought to bring these and other issues to the forefront of society and to the agenda of the feminist movement. However, these issues have far too often taken a back seat to issues championed by white women, furthering the divide among activists. Roberts describes the divide between women of color and white women in the feminist movement, writing that "the disparate experiences of women of color and white women led to a clash of agendas concerning sterilization."[49] The fight of white women to gain access to voluntary sterilization and other birth control methods undervalued the fight of women of color to end forced sterilization. Roberts writes, "there is nothing contradictory about advocating women's freedom to use birth control while opposing coercive birth control practices. The focus on the interests of white privileged women led to a myopic vision of reproductive rights."[50]

Unfortunately, this limited vision continues to impact the debate and fight for reproductive health rights—including all issues related to women's reproductive health care.

Similarly, the issues of lesbian and queer women are neglected in healthcare discussions that are heterosexually based. Much emphasis is placed on pregnancy prevention and female-male relationships. As a result, lesbians are often marginalized in the health community. According to the Lesbian Health Research Center, lesbians face a number of critical barriers to access—including structural, financial, personal, and cultural barriers. Homophobia and a heterosexual norm, combined with the lack of sensitivity and education among healthcare providers, further limit the lesbian community's access to health care. Additionally, lesbians are less likely to be insured than their heterosexual counterparts—largely because of the lack of spousal benefits.[51] Political battles regarding sexuality education, sexual orientation, gender identity, marriage equality, rights to adoption, and parental rights further marginalize the GLBTQQI community, seriously undermining access to services and education.

Reproductive rights needs to include the rights of queers to reproduce and to have legal guardianship of their kids.
Noemi, 28, white and Jewish, queer, California

Lesbian and gay adoption is complex. State laws vary from state to state. In many cases, courts determine the rights of same-sex couples to adopt. The Human Rights Campaign (www.hrc.org) has comprehensive information about laws and regulations impacting the lesbian, gay, bisexual and transgender community, including state-by-state regulations on adoption.

For supportive, nondiscriminatory, feminist adoption services, contact Adoption Choices at http://www.womenshealthspecialists.org/adoption/adoption-Choices.shtml or call (530) 891–0302. Birthparents can call (800) 607–9200 toll-free for more information.

TAKING BACK THE DEBATE

In order for this movement to continue and to be successful, we must take back the debate. We need to confront the stereotypes about women's health, combat the negative imagery in our media, broaden our discussion and policy work regarding women's health, and empower women to have respect for and pride in their bodies. Far too often, our society sends the message that women are unable to consider their options, evaluate their lives, and make decisions for themselves. Whether we are looking at abortion care or prenatal care, whether a woman is considering adoption or infertility treatments, hospital or home births, medical doctors or midwives, we must ensure that women have access to needed services. Politically and economically, we have not made women's health a priority. Approximately twelve million women of reproductive age are uninsured; the proportion of women covered by Medicaid dropped 21% between 1994 and 1998.[52] Women pay 68 percent more than men in out-of-pocket medical costs, primarily due to lack of coverage for contraception and other reproductive health costs,[53] and the Bush administration has further limited contraceptive coverage by cutting funding in the federal budget and by supporting religious exemptions for reproductive health services, thus allowing religious hospitals and/or health centers to deny services and contraceptives to women.

We must take back the women's health agenda. No longer should the radical right control the discussion of women's bodies, nor should extremists control women's access to services. The feminist health movement began because women were not receiving the information and services they deserved. A feminist health agenda says that *all* women have the right to health care and health information that is supportive, respectful, and nonjudgmental. We have to say "no more" to limitations on treatment that are based on race, economics, class, sexual orientation, or age. No more to forced sterilization. No more to the denial of reproductive health information and services for young women. It is not enough to fight for women's rights to abortion or other reproductive healthcare options. We must also fight for women's freedom to make these choices—from abortion, to birthing, to adoption, to the decision not to have children—without shame or blame. Women must have access to all their health information, from education about their bodies, to funding and support, to participation in decisions about what to research and fund. We can stand collectively and send the message that women will fight back, that we will not stand for limitations on our healthcare options and services, that our sexuality is ours, and that decisions about our bodies belong to us.

SPOTLIGHT ON ACTIVISM

Emergency contraception, or the "morning-after pill," is a key focus of activism for young women today. Often confused with RU-486, the abortion pill, emergency contraception is not an abortion but rather an effective and important form of birth control. Used up to five days after unprotected intercourse, emergency contraception contains the same hormone as that used in birth control pills and works to prevent a pregnancy by stopping the release of the egg, preventing fertilization or preventing the egg from implanting in the uterus. Emergency contraception is up to 95 percent effective if used within the first twenty-four hours after unprotected intercourse. Emergency contraception is a safety-net method in case a birth control method fails, the couple has not used birth control, or in cases of rape. It is estimated that emergency contraception has the potential to reduce the number of unintended pregnancies in half. EC is incredibly safe, in fact statistically safer than aspirin. It should be noted that emergency contraception does not protect against sexually transmitted infections, including HIV/AIDS.

Young women throughout the country have been working to make emergency contraception available over-the-counter and without a prescription. But, despite a twenty-four-to-three vote by two FDA advisory panels in favor of making emergency contraception (plan B) available over the counter, in May 2004, the FDA (and Commissioner Mark McClellan) rejected the request for over-the-counter status. As of 2006, we continue this fight for over-the-counter access. To support efforts to make emergency contraception widely available, the Feminist Majority has launched grassroots and campus activism throughout the country. For more information and to get involved, visit www.feminist.org.

TAKE ACTION

Getting Started

Know the facts! There is a successful slam campaign against abortion. It is our responsibility to *set the record straight* and to dispel the myths about abortion.

Discuss contraceptive choices and sexual histories with your sexual partners *before* you have sex. What you don't know could hurt you.

Carry condoms for you and your friends when you go out for the evening. There's no shame in being smart and protected.

Visit http://www.guttmacher.org/pubs/state_data/index.html to see how your state meets women's need for birth control services.

The Next Step

Take part in a Walk for Breast Cancer; most major cities host walks throughout the spring and summer. See www.avonwalk.org.

Write your local school board in support of open and honest sex education in our public schools.

Refuse to support companies (local and national) that don't support women's reproductive health options—for example, only after intense activist pressure did Wal Mart agree to provide emergency contraception pills in its pharmacies, and Curves' founder and CEO, Gary Heavin, financially supports anti-choice organizations with the profits from Curves fitness centers.

Write to your health care insurer questioning its practice of not fully covering contraceptive products for women.

Call or e-mail your local, state, and federal representatives when a hearing, a bill, or a nomination, comes up regarding reproductive rights.

Getting Out There

Hold a V-Day event such as a benefit production of *The Vagina Monologues;* see www.vday.org.

Become a clinic escort. Contact local feminist organizations for more information or work with local clinics to start your own escort program. NOW and the Feminist Majority are great resources for this.

Join the efforts of organizations like NOW, Feminist Women's Health Centers, Feminist Majority, Choice USA, ACCESS, Medical Students for Choice, Planned Parenthood, NARAL, and local organizations in your area.

ON MY BOOKSHELF

Natalie Angier, *Woman: An Intimate Geography* (New York: Anchor Books, 1999).

G. J. Barker-Benfield, *The Horrors of the Half-Known Life* (New York: Routledge, 2000).

Ruth Bell, *Changing Bodies, Changing Lives: The Book Every Teenager Should Have* (New York: Random House/Times Books, 1998).

Judy Blume, *Are You There, God? It's Me, Margaret* (New York: Dell, 1970).

Angela Bonavoglia, ed., *The Choices We Made: 25 Women and Men Speak Out About Abortion* (New York: Random House, 1991).

Boston Women's Health Collective, *Our Bodies, Ourselves* (New York: Touchstone, 2005).

Suzie Bright, *Sexual State of the Union* (New York: Simon and Schuster, 1997).

Suzie Bright, *Full Exposure: Opening Up to Your Sexual Creativity and Erotic Expression* (San Francisco: Harper San Francisco, 1999).

Rebecca Chalker, *The Clitoral Truth: The Secret World at Your Fingertips* (New York: Seven Stories Press, 2000).

Rebecca Chalker and Carol Downer, *A Woman's Book of Choices: Abortion, Menstrual Extraction and RU-486* (New York: Four Walls Eight Windows, 1992).

Betty Dodson, *Sex for One: The Joy of Self-Loving* (California: Three Rivers Press, 1996).

Barbara Ehrenreich and Deirdre English, *Witches, Midwives and Nurses: A History of Women Healers* (New York: Feminist Press, 1972).

Barbara Ehrenreich and Deirdre English, *For Her Own Good: 150 Years of Experts' Advice to Women* (New York: Anchor Books, 1978).

Federation of Feminist Women's Health Centers, *A New View of a Woman's Body* (Los Angeles: Feminist Health Press, 1995).

Gloria Feldt, *The War on Choice: The Right-Wing Attack on Women's Rights and How to Fight Back* (Bantam Books, 2004).

Judy Grahn, *Blood, Bread and Roses: How Menstruation Created the World* (Boston: Beacon Press, 1993).

Laura Kaplan, *The Story of Jane: The Legendary Underground Feminist Abortion Service* (New York: Pantheon Books 1995).

Merri Lisa Johnson, ed., *Jane Sexes It Up* (New York: Four Walls Eight Windows, 2002).

Kristen Luker, *Abortion and the Politics of Motherhood* (Berkeley: University of California Press, 1984).

Emily Martin, *The Woman in the Body: A Cultural Analysis of Reproduction* (Boston: Beacon Press, 1987).

Patricia Miller, *The Worst of Times: Illegal Abortion—Survivors, Practitioners, Coroners, Cops, and Children of Women Who Died Talk About Its Horrors* (New York: Harper Perennial, 1993).

Sandra Morgen, *Into Our Own Hands: The Women's Health Movement in the United States, 1969–1990* (New Brunswick: Rutgers University Press, 2002).

Inga Muscio, *Cunt: A Declaration of Independence* (Seattle: Seal Press, 1998).

Christiane Northrup, M.D., *Mother-Daughter Wisdom: Creating a Legacy of Physical and Emotional Health, The Wisdom of Menopause,* and *Women's Bodies, Women's Wisdom* (New York: Bantam Dell, 2005).

Laura Owen, *Her Blood Is Gold* (San Francisco: Harper San Francisco, 1993).

Laura Owen, *Honoring Menstruation* (Freedom: Crossing Press, 1998).

Janice Raymond, *Women as Wombs: Reproductive Technologies and the Battle Over Women's Freedom* (San Francisco: Harper San Francisco, 1993).

Dorothy Roberts, *Killing the Black Body: Race, Reproduction and the Meaning of Liberty* (New York: Vintage Books, 1997).

Barbara Seaman, *The Doctors' Case Against the Pill* (Alameda, CA: Hunter House, 1969, updated   1995).

Rickie Solinger, *Beggars and Choosers: How the Politics of Choice Shapes Adoption, Abortion and Welfare in the United States* (New York: Hill and Wang, 2001).

Rickie Solinger, *Pregnancy and Power: A Short History of Reproductive Politics in America* (New York: New York University Press, 2005).

Sarah Weddington, *A Question of Choice: By the Lawyer Who Won* Roe v. Wade (New York: Penguin Books, 1992).

Susan Weed, *Wise Woman Herbal for the Childbearing Year* (New York:' Ash Tree Publishing, 1986).

Rose Weitz, ed., *The Politics of Women's Bodies: Sexuality, Appearance, and Behavior* (New York: Oxford University Press, 1998).

Cathy Winks and Anne Semans, *The Good Vibrations Guide to Sex* (San Francisco: Cleis Press, 1994).

Gail Elizabeth Wyatt, *Stolen Women: Reclaiming Our Sexuality, Taking Back Our Lives* (New York: Wiley, 1997).

FABULOUS FEMINIST WEB RESOURCES

Alan Guttmacher Institute   www.agi-usa.org
Great source for statistics and fact sheets about reproductive health care issues.

Asian Community for Reproductive Justice   www.apirh.org
"To achieve Reproductive Justice, we are building the social, political, and economic power of Asian women and their communities. Our model of social change utilizes two core strategies: Community Organizing and Movement Building."

Babes in Toyland   www.babeland.com
Operated by women, this site is plush with sex education and plenty of fun toys.

Betty Dodson   www.bettydodson.com
The mother of sex education and empowerment in sexuality. Her site is full of great information.

Black Women's Health Imperative   www.blackwomenshealth.org
Founded in 1983 by Byllye Avery, the Black Women's Health Imperative, previously the National Black Women's Health Project, serves as an important resource for education, leadership training, advocacy, and research on African American women's health issues.

Boston Women's Health Collective   www.ourbodiesourselves.org
The authors of the feminist health classic Our Bodies Ourselves *and a number of other important books with a woman-centered approach to health information. Web site includes a wealth of women's health information and resources.*

Catholics for Free Choice   www.cath4choice.org
Information and resources for Catholics who support a woman's right to choose.

Choice USA   www.choiceusa.org
  Started by Gloria Steinem, Choice USA "mobilizes and provides ongoing support to the diverse, upcoming generation of leaders who promote and protect reproductive choice both now and in the future."

Feminist Women's Health Centers   www.fwhc.org
  Women-centered health care information and services nationwide.

Good Vibrations   www.goodvibes.com
  A great store in Berkeley and San Francisco—and online! Toys, books, education for sex and sexuality. Will make you comfortable the moment you walk in the door. Staff is readily available and helpful.

Latino Issues Forum   www.lif.org
  Focused on California, LIF provides research, advocacy, and information about Latino health issues.

Lesbian Health Research Center   www.lesbianhealthinfo.org
  Affiliated with the University of California, San Francisco, the Lesbian Health Research Center provides comprehensive health information and research geared toward lesbians, bisexual women, and transgender individuals.

Medical Students for Choice   www.ms4c.org
  An international organization for medical students interested in learning and providing abortion services. Great source of information and support for student leaders.

National Abortion Federation   www.pro-choice.org
  An organization made up of abortion providers. Site provides statistical information and internship and job opportunities.

National Abortion Rights Action League   www.naral.org
  NARAL Pro-Choice America is an advocacy organization working to protect abortion rights. Site contains updated legislative information, along with NARAL action campaigns.

National Asian Women's Health Organization   www.nawho.org
  "The mission of NAWHO is to improve the health status of Asian American women and families through research, education, leadership, and public policy programs, and to address broader social justice issues for underserved communities in the United States."

National Latina Institute for   www.latinainstitute.org
Reproductive Health
  "The mission of NLIRH is to ensure the fundamental human right to reproductive health for Latinas, their families and their communities through public education, policy advocacy, and community mobilization."

National Organization for Women   www.now.org
A national nonprofit organization fighting for women's equality. Site includes information on a host of women's rights issues, including abortion and reproductive rights. Can also locate local chapters action and find contact information to get involved.

Physicians for Reproductive Choice and Health   www.prch.org
An organization for physicians who want to participate in providing universal reproductive health care.

Planned Parenthood   www.plannedparenthood.org
Provides a variety of reproductive healthcare services for women and men. Site includes health information, as well as political action updates.

Pro-Choice Public Education Project   www.protectchoice.org
"The Pro-Choice Public Education Project (PEP) is a collaborative project of the country's leading national pro-choice organizations dedicated to empowering this new generation of pro-choice activists and supporters. With the input of young pro-choice leaders, PEP puts choice on the radar screens of today's young women, educates them about threats to reproductive rights, and provides them with tools for action."

Scarleteen   www.scarleteen.com
A fun, contemporary site with sex education geared toward teens.

Sistersong—Women of Color   www.SisterSong.net
Reproductive Health Collective
Site includes information, resources, and events geared toward the reproductive healthcare needs and activism of women of color.

Women's Health Specialists   www.womenshealthspecialists.org
A member of the Federation of Feminist Women's Health Centers, Women's Health Specialists provides reproductive healthcare information and services to women and men in northern California (Chico, Redding, Sacramento, and Santa Rosa). Also provides resources for cervical self-exam. Adoption Choices is a program of Women's Health Specialists.

Young Survival Project   www.youngsurvival.org
The only international, nonprofit organization dedicated to the concerns of women with breast cancer under the age of forty. Web site has advocacy, action, and educational information about breast-self exam and breast cancer.

7

Fighting Back

It's dark as she enters the parking garage. No one is around. She is walking in high heels to her car. The camera scans the garage, and the viewer sees the dreaded but expected shadow lurking in the background. She notices, too. Distinctly male in his shadowed size, he begins to slowly follow her. She picks up her step, her high heels quickly clicking against the cement. His speed increases, too. Suddenly, he is gaining on her. She begins to run, toward what we are not sure. He is running. She is running. We're on the edges of our seats watching this unfold. Suddenly, she falls. We scream, "Get up! Get up! Run!" knowing it is only a matter of moments before this stranger is upon her—to do the unspeakable violence that we hear about everyday.

Why is this story played out over and over? Why is this scene so common in the media and in our minds? Why don't we hear more stories about women who fight back? Instead of this ever-so typical garage scene where the woman runs and falls and becomes a victim, why don't we see her turn around and yell, "Get the fuck away from me!" Why aren't there more movies about girls who kick ass? Why aren't we our own superheroes? Why don't we hear more real-life stories of women who defend themselves—like the South Philadelphia high school girls who ran down the twenty-five-year-old man who had been exposing himself in front of their high school campus and beat the crap out of him until the police arrived?[1] Why don't we hear more stories of the countless women who fight back in the streets, on our campuses, and in our homes? Why isn't the lead news story about the woman who apprehended her attacker and not about the woman who was brutally raped and murdered? More important, why are news accounts of women who are brutally violated so commonplace? Why isn't the storyline about the shock of the nation—shock at the fact that violence against a woman occurred in the first place? And why don't we live in a culture where we wouldn't think to show images of women victimized in movies for entertainment and that those who dared to do so would be shunned by audiences and the Academy Awards alike (as opposed to being recognized with the highest Hollywood honors)? Why don't we learn the history of women warriors? Perhaps, if they knew these stories, more girls and women would know their strength, believe in their worth, and not internalize fear-based assumptions about their ability and safety. And maybe more men would learn to appreciate and respect women's strength. A reach? Perhaps. But this vision requires us to imagine a society that does not yet exist.

Women Are Warriors

Women have always been warriors—from Greek and Roman times to the modern day, across the globe and in every culture. We have fought in wars, we have been spies, we have volunteered, we have served as nurses, we have been prisoners of war, we have died in battle, and occasionally we have been recognized as heroes alongside men. Women fought in the American Revolution—like Margaret Corbin, who took over her husband's cannon in the Battle of Fort Washington. She was the first woman in U.S. history to be awarded a disability pension for being wounded during military service. Disguised as men, women served on both sides of the conflict during the War of 1812 and during the Civil War. Dr. Mary Walker received the Congressional Medal of Honor for her service with the Union Army. Harriet Tubman served as a nurse, spy, and scout for the Union Army during the Civil War. Women served as nurses in the army in World War I, and those who were not nurses enlisted in the marines and the navy. Edith Cavell and Mata Hari were both prisoners of war, and both were executed as spies during World War I. Virginia Hall was awarded America's Distinguished Service Cross after eluding the Nazis for years while working for the French and the United States as a spy. Women served in World War II, in Vietnam, in the Persian Gulf, and, most recently, in Iraq. Many women have served, and many have given their lives in the line of duty. But, as with most areas of history, women's contributions and sacrifices in the armed forces have largely been ignored.

What would it be like for little girls if they grew up knowing their history as fighters? I wonder how this knowledge would have impacted our self-esteem when it came time to defend ourselves—physically but also emotionally. We need to reclaim our history as warriors, respect the fight within us, at the same time we seek peaceful resolution. We need to recognize and respect that women fight everyday for safety, self-determination, and freedom.

I know that we currently live in a culture where many women are afraid to fight back, where most women are taught that we can't fight back, and where some are even disempowered and believe that we are not worth fighting for. We live in a culture where, on a conscious, semiconscious, or unconscious level, men are encouraged to see women as property and believe that we exist for their amusement and convenience. Think Hooters, *Playboy*, Miss America. We live in a culture where rape and gender-based violence is condoned—either actively or by inaction. But we must realize that we create this reality. Our movies, news media, and television shows create a culture of fear for women and desensitize men (and women) to the realities of violence against women. And so we watch the actor-police officer step over the rape victim to get to the "real" story; we watch women slapped and shoved and pushed and punched in music videos; we see images of brutalized women on the pages of our magazines to sell products; we see images of male dominance and control in advertising; image after image inundates us, the viewer, until we believe that violence against women is insignificant or, worse, that such violence is entertainment—*just part of the story line.*

Violence against women is real. It is not entertainment. One in three women in her lifetime will experience some form of sexual violence. One in four will experience domestic violence.[2] Fifty to 70 percent of women will experience sexual harassment on the job, and 83 percent of girls will experience sexual harassment at school.[3] Women experience sexual harassment, sexual assault, rape, dating violence, domestic abuse, sexual trafficking, and many other heinous acts of violence. Many of us survive. But, tragically, many of us do not.

Vi·o·lence *n.* **an unjust or unwarranted exertion of force or power.**

INTIMATE-PARTNER VIOLENCE

We are taught the magic of love. We believe that love will be enough. We believe that *we* will be enough. Intimate-partner violence—whether in a dating, live-in, marriage, or partner relationship—is devastating. The person who hurts us is the person who is supposed to love us. The fairy tale of falling in love and living happily ever after can go desperately wrong. And for one out of every four women, it does.[4]

Intimate-partner violence—also referred to as domestic violence, spousal abuse, battering, courtship, or dating violence—is the intimidation, assault, battery, verbal, or sexual abuse perpetrated by one intimate partner against another. Intimate-partner violence occurs in both heterosexual and gay/lesbian relationships, among married and nonmarried couples, and across all economic and racial lines. Gender, however, does seem to make a difference in the statistics about intimate-partner violence. While men are victims and survivors of intimate-partner violence, women represent the vast majority of those being violated. A National Crime Victimization survey "found that women were six times more likely than men to experience violence at the hands of an intimate partner."[5] Intimate-partner violence consists of a number of abusive behaviors, including these:[6]

> I have often heard jokes and comments regarding women and "their place" in school, my workplace and in social circles. Some people may say it is only a joke or tell me to lighten up, and I constantly find myself fighting these comments. I feel that even though someone may be joking, it is creating an acceptance of these issues, without challenging them, which I see as contributing to the problem. Christine, white, heterosexual, Massachusetts

Physical abuse: Hitting, shoving, slapping, punching, and so on—any physical violence or force inflicted upon a partner.

Sexual abuse: Any unwanted sexual behavior. Though legal at one time, marital rape is now illegal in all fifty states. Rape is a key form of violation in dating relationships.

Mental/emotional abuse: Also referred to as psychological or verbal abuse, the breaking down of a person's self-esteem, often through derogatory and demeaning comments that often serve to keep the abused individual in the relationship. Individuals are broken down and come to believe that they are worth nothing and that no one will ever love them.

Financial abuse: Tight control over financial resources by controlling bank accounts, allotting a strict allowance, and making the abused individual account for every penny spent. When these "regulations" are violated, the victim is likely to be physically or emotionally attacked.

Legal abuse: Withholding alimony or child support payments, hiding financial assets, dragging out custody hearings or legal proceedings, fighting for custody just to avoid making child support payments to control victim's whereabouts.

Communal abuse: Also referred to as "spiritual abuse." This category encompasses activities such as prohibiting one's partner from attending social activities, such as churchgoing; visiting friends or family; or participating in a social club. This tactic isolates the abused individual from potential sources of help and support.

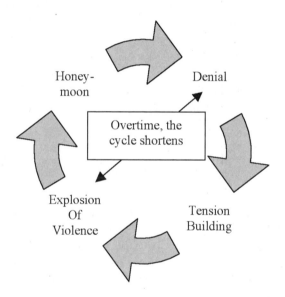

Intimate-partner violence often occurs in a cycle that is perpetuated until the woman either leaves the relationship or dies.[7] As with any cycle, it is difficult to determine which stage begins first, and certainly individuals begin this cycle in different places, but for explanatory purposes let's begin with the "walking on eggshells," or *tension-building*, stage. In this stage, the woman is unsure when the physical abuse will occur but is certain that physical abuse is imminent. She feels as if she is "walking on eggshells," waiting for the abuse to occur. One strategy for dealing with this stage is to attempt to make everything "perfect" to prevent the explosion from the abusive partner. Unfortunately, this is only a temporary band-aid, because perfection is impossible, and eventually the abusive partner will abuse. Another way to handle this stage is to provoke abuse in order to get the attack out of the way. Many who have never lived in an abusive relationship have a hard time understanding this response, but provoking violence can be the only form of control an abused individual may have. This strategy can be as simple as controlling when the abuse occurs to avoid an explosion in front of children or to allow bruises to heal sufficiently that they can be covered with make-up before a family member is scheduled to visit. It is important to note that the best solution is to leave the relationship, but it is equally important to understand that everything is a process, and gaining control in any aspect of your life is an important step to taking back your life.

> It is inexcusable that this war on women continues on a daily basis in our country and around the world . . . until we can protect half our citizens, give them the right to protect and feel safe in their bodies—I find all other issues to be secondary. Julia, 24, Hispanic/Caucasian, bisexual, California

The next stage is the *explosion-of-violence* stage. Fairly self-explanatory, it is the stage of physical abuse—slapping, hitting, punching, beating, or sexual abuse. Physical abuse can take many different forms and can inflict bodily damage ranging from bruising to death. Approximately 1.5 million women are raped and/or physically assaulted every year by an intimate partner.[8] Though the actual numbers are difficult to account for, the National Violence Against Women Survey estimates that 500,000 women are injured every year and require medical treatment.[9] Sadly, this figure doesn't include the thousands of others who are prohibited from seeking or too embarrassed or fearful to seek medical treatment. Physical violence is known to rise during a woman's pregnancy, with an estimated 324,000 women annually experiencing intimate-partner violence while pregnant.[10] Violence during pregnancy among teens is particularly alarming, with more than 70 percent of pregnant teens and teen parents experiencing violence inflicted by their intimate partners.[11] Women are far more likely than men to be murdered as a result of intimate-partner violence, with women between the ages of twenty and twenty-nine reportedly at highest risk.[12]

Following the explosion of violence is the *honeymoon* stage, perhaps the most dangerous stage because it creates a false picture of the relationship, often leading the abused individual into believing that all is well. The honeymoon stage is the make-up stage—the flowers and candy, the "I'm sorry and will never do it again" stage. Bruises and breaks are healing, our abusers are sweet and kind and vulnerable, we're told they can't live without us, we believe our love will make them better . . . excuses are believed, and we head right into the next stage.

The *denial* stage is the key to perpetuating the cycle of abuse. During the denial stage, the abused individual is convinced that the violence is isolated and not part of a cycle. It is during this stage that excuses replace questions and we make the ultimate decision to stay. A common question arises: why do we stay? Women stay in abusive relationships for a wide array of reasons: love, fear, religious and cultural beliefs, low self-esteem, isolation, self-blame, for the children, as a response to pressure from family or friends, embarrassment, shame, a belief that no one will help, economic dependency, a belief that the abuser will change, and opposition to divorce, among other reasons. And, as with many life events, it takes a catalyst to propel us to leave the situation—a near-death experience, a threat to a child. In absence of this experience, we continue through the cycle. Over time, the cycle shortens until we are ricochet between denial and the explosion-of-violence stage. This continues until someone leaves or someone gets killed.

TEENS AND INTIMATE-PARTNER VIOLENCE

Intimate-partner violence is increasingly prevalent among teenagers. According to the National Center for State Courts' Family Violence Forum, more than one-fourth of high school girls have been victims of physical or sexual abuse.[13] As with intimate-partner violence among adults, teen women are more likely to be abused than their male counterparts; studies have found that teen women are twice as likely as teen men to experience dating violence and that teen women suffer significantly more physical injuries than teen men.[14] Young women between the ages of sixteen and twenty-four experience the highest rates of violence perpetrated by intimate partners.[15] Many explanations can be offered to better understand these occurrences—the imagery of violence against women in our media, violence in the home modeled to young adults, lack of education and empowerment training, and attitudes about violence against women perpetrated throughout our society. Some studies point to the use of heavy alcohol or drug use, the presence of sexually aggressive peers, male acceptance of dating violence, traditional sex roles, negative attitudes about relationships, and the prevalence of rape myths.[16] Whatever the reason, young women are at risk.

Rape *n.* any act of sexual intercourse that is forced upon a person.

RAPE

Rape. Just the word itself invokes a kind a fear that is truly gender specific. While it is true that men are raped, women live with the constant reminder that they are at risk. The U.S. Department of Justice estimates that 91 percent of rape victims are female.[17] Approximately 1.3 women are raped every minute in the United States.[18] Rape is a kind of abuse that is so specific, so violating, that it thrives off our fear and insecurity and strips us of our dignity and our freedom. The myths and misconceptions surrounding rape are further violating in that they create a culture of blame and responsibility targeted at women. Some of the most prevalent myths about rape include these:

> Rape is part of men's biological nature (they need to "spread their seed").
> Men cannot control their sexual desires/arousal.
> Rape is sex.
> Women provoke rape by the clothes they wear, their make-up, the way they act—all "victim-blaming" myths.
> Rapists are always strangers.
> Rape occurs only when a woman is alone.
> Rape occurs only at night.
> Rape doesn't occur in the safety of your own home.
> Rape cannot occur in intimate relationships (or with someone that you have previously had sex with).

The truth, of course, is that rape has nothing to do with sex and everything to do with power, control, and violence. Women don't cause rape;

rapists do. Marriage and intimate relationships do not guarantee intimacy, security, or protection and far too often are the source of violence. And, despite the myths, 75 to 80 percent of the time, a woman knows her rapist.[19]

In fact, a number of different categories for understanding rape exist:

Stranger rape—The most recognized type of rape and the one that most believe to present the majority of risk. In reality, stranger rape accounts for only about 20 percent of all rapes that occur. Yet, this is the type of rape that is most represented in our media—the dark stranger in the bushes awaiting his victim and ready to pounce. The threat of stranger rape is often at the heart of self-defense programs and cautionary advisories for women as they traverse their worlds.

Acquaintance rape—Rape committed by anyone that the victim knows—a boyfriend, a work colleague, a schoolmate. Acquaintance rape accounts for 75 to 80 percent of all rapes. Date rape, particularly common on college campuses, has become the subject of a great deal of criticism, misconception, and debate. Survivors of acquaintance rape are often not believed by others because they knew, or were involved with, the perpetrator. As a result, acquaintance rape is seriously underreported.[20]

Spousal rape—Rape that occurs within the confines of marriage or domestic partnerships.

Substance-related rape—Rape that occurs while the victim is under the influence of alcohol or drugs. While this type of rape can occur when drinking or drug use is consensual, most states have now determined that sex under the influence is not consensual. Additionally, the prevalence of so-called date-rape drugs like Rohypnol and GHB (gamma hydroxybutyrate) has led to an increase in substance-related rape, particularly on college campuses. Marketed outside the United States as a short-term treatment for insomnia, Rohypnol (commonly referred to as "rophies") has become one of the most common drugs used in the United States as a date-rape drug. Not manufactured or legal in the

United States, this inexpensive drug is easily available over the Internet, from street dealers, in clubs, and at raves.[21] Rophies dissolve quickly in a drink and take effect within thirty minutes. Combined with alcohol, rophies can cause "blackouts," with memory loss and decrease in defenses. Because the drug has no taste, odor, or visual residue, attackers can slip it into a drink and violate someone with little or no resistance. Gamma-hydroxybutyrate, or GHB, is another common form of the "date-rape drug." GHB has a sedative and euphoric effect and has been referred to as "liquid ecstasy." Like Rohypnol, GHB has been used in a growing number of sexual assaults.

Multiple-assailant rape—Also referred to as "gang rape." This type of rape occurs when there is more than one attacker. Professor Peggy Reeves Sanday's *Fraternity Gang Rape* details her extensive research on multiple-assailant rape on college campuses. She focuses upon sexual aggression as part of the definition of masculinity, stating that "sexual aggression is the means by which some men display masculinity and induct younger men into masculine power roles."[22] This type of male aggression is supported through peer acceptance and the practice of blaming the victim. Sanday writes, "by blaming the victim for provoking their own sexual aggression, men control and define acceptable and unacceptable female sexual behavior through the agency of fear."[23] While her work emphasizes behavior among members of college fraternities, Sanday notes that "gang rape" is also prevalent among "many other exclusively male contexts at colleges and universities in the United States, such as organized sports."[24]

Clearly, women have more to fear from the men they know than from strangers. Unfortunately, many believe the opposite and can be duped into keeping their defenses high in public while lowering them in private situations. Additionally, these misconceptions can cause others to distrust women's accounts of date and acquaintance rape. Rape myths have far too often been used against women—leading to the assumption that rape between acquaintances is somehow *just the result of a miscommunication,* a misunderstanding.

Because of these misconceptions about rape, the response women receive after the rape can feel like a second violation, adding to the trauma of the initial attack. From family and friends to police and the courts, women confront an intense blame-the-victim mentality that asks them to account for the behavior that left them "vulnerable" to rape. More energy is spent on dissecting women's behavior and clothing than on locating and prosecuting the attackers. While coping with her rape, the woman's sense that she is somehow at fault is confirmed by questions like, Why were you at that bar? Why were you drinking? Were you being "flirtatious"? Were you wearing a short skirt?

WHY WOMEN GET BLAMED

Why do we blame women for being raped? I think that there are many reasons, but the strongest have to do with the culture surrounding women's sexuality and male entitlement and the need to create a sense of security, false though it may be. The first reason, I believe, is deeply rooted in history. As Estelle Freedman recounts in her excellent history of feminism, *No Turning Back*, rape didn't exist as a category in patriarchal societies prior to the 1800s but was seen as a "theft of virginity," a category that applied only to those women who had not yet married and/or women who were virgins. The crime was actually considered to be one against her father or her promised husband and not against the woman herself.[25] In addition, rape has also been viewed historically as a crime against family property. This not only meant that a woman had no personal recourse for sexual violation but also laid the foundation for the concept of male entitlement to women's bodies—especially as property. Men were not legally accountability for acts against their own personal property. Marital rape was not recognized as a crime in the United States until 1976 and was not considered a crime in all 50 U.S. states until 1993— how do you rape something that you own?[26] Indeed, for generations, to some extent, women have been viewed as men's property, creating a very unbalanced power dynamic.

In recent years, while we have instituted laws to protect women, we have also perpetuated a victim-blaming culture as means to check women's sexuality. Perhaps one of the most effective ways in which we restrict women's sexuality is through categorizing and labeling. In *Slut!*

Growing Up Female with a Bad Reputation, Leora Tanenbaum discusses the power of the "slut" label. She writes that

> girls who are singled out for being "sluts" are by no means a mono-
> lithic group. And contrary to what most people think of when they vi-
> sualize a "slut," many have no more sexual experience than their peers
> do, and some have no sexual experience at all. Whether or not a girl is
> targeted because of her sexual behavior, the effect is nonetheless to po-
> lice her sexuality.[27]

This "policing" is a powerful influence over female adolescent sexuality, one that deeply impacts young women's exploration and self-
definition. As a result, young women spend a tremendous amount of
energy trying to adhere to teenage sexual norms and avoid the "slut"
label. But the unfortunate reality is that young women have little control over whether they are labeled sluts.

Tanenbaum identifies multiple reasons that girls are labeled sluts,
including being outsiders, developing breasts earlier than other girls,
suffering from revenge, or being the victim of abuse or rape. The slut
label is particularly powerful in response to rape; as Tanenbaum writes,
"the 'slut' reputation protects rapists because it makes the victims believe that they are partly to blame."[28] In other words, the slut label carries with it the assumption of consent. As a slut, it is presumed, the girl
in question wants sex with anyone, anytime, and that consequently she
did something to "ask for it" or "led him on" and therefore is to blame.

Another reason women get blamed is that this creates a false sense
of security. I find this particularly to be the case when it comes to acquaintance or date rape. Society at large does not want to believe
women who are raped by a date or acquaintance. Instead, assertions
that the attack resulted from a miscommunication, derogatory assumptions about women's sexuality, the slut myth, or accusations of morning-after regret are used to justify this type of rape. I believe that these
justifications reflect fear. Often, it is believed that if a specific behavior
or behaviors can be identified, then we can ensure our own safety. In
other words, if the woman who was raped drank too much, then we can
avoid rape by not drinking. If she wore "provocative" clothing, then we
can prevent rape by rejecting similar clothing. But there is no
justification for the perpetration of violence. Recognizing that rape is
out of our control is scary, for what do we do then? We want to date, we

want to have sex, but how do we prevent violence? Are men the enemy? But what happens to our quest for a man if men become the enemy? And what becomes of us if we pursue dating relationships? Are we at risk, as well? Not if the rape was her fault; then we are safe. This line of reasoning doesn't have to be so all-or-nothing; not all men are rapists or enemies, and aligning ourselves with other women for the protection of all women doesn't have to mean deciding to have girlfriends but no boyfriends. Instead, we could create a world where women are valued. If we collectively stood together, we could change the consciousness of what it means to be female. We could define ourselves independent of our male counterparts, where our sexuality is ours regardless of whether or not we choose to have sex with men. We could take back control over our own sexuality so that we no longer are forced to feel shame or be seen in terms of male desire. While this may not eradicate violence against women, it can expand existing supportive and safe communities for women, where we address the realities of rape, work to end violence, and feel free from shame and blame.

According to the National Crime Victimization Survey, conducted by the Department of Justice Bureau of Justice Statistics, only about half of rape and sexual-assault victims report their attacks.[29] While trust is increasing in law enforcement's ability to effectively and sensitively handle rape cases (thanks in large part to the activism and training of the sexual-assault awareness and prevention movement), experts in the field with whom I have spoken say that the number of women who go directly to the police following their rape is still very low. While the rate at which rape is reported may have gone up in the past few years, factors such as poverty, racism, marriage, or military service can drastically impact the rate of reporting. Women understandably fear that no one will believe them, that their personal sexual history will be used against them, that they will lose friends, and that their family will blame them. In date or acquaintance rape, women question whether their behavior led to or caused the rape. They question whether what happened could even be called rape. Was it their fault? Unfortunately, instead of standing together with women speaking out against violence, some women have taken center stage on this issue—loudly sending the message that women are to blame. Katie Roiphe's book, *The Morning After*, made headlines (thanks to a great deal of support from the conservative right) when she claimed that date rape couldn't exist because, to her knowledge, none of her friends had been raped. In a 1993 *New York*

Times magazine article based upon her book, Roiphe states, "if I was really standing in the middle of an 'epidemic,' a 'crisis'—if 25 percent of my women friends were really being raped—wouldn't I know it?"[30] Throughout her book, Roiphe misrepresents statistics and research on date rape and dismisses the realities and secrecy surrounding rape— what makes her think that her friends would tell her they had been raped? While we have heard little from Roiphe in recent years, I reference her work because it presents an important debate that we continue to engage in today. Similarly, the author Camille Paglia has created a tone that blames women and demonizes our sexuality with comments like "if you're advertising, you better put out," implying that we are obligated to provide sex and that men are justified in taking it.[31] It's the classic message to women that our appearance and behavior are designed to illicit responses from men and not to serve ourselves. In other words, our actions are viewed in the context of men and not independent of them. While the views of Roiphe and Paglia may have received a lot of press at the time, suggesting the increasing influence of the right on the media, the research on rape does not support their views. Are the millions of women who claim to have been date raped all wrong?

Rape Kits

Rape kits consist of DNA evidence that is gathered from a survivor of rape. Kits cost about $500 each to test. But often in cases without a suspect, rape kits go untested due to inadequate funding. The Department of Justice estimates that there are 350,000 kits nationwide that have not been tested (Ryan, 2003). Other estimates have shown that as many as a million untested rape kits exist throughout the country (Valdivieso, 2002).

Fortunately, the feminist community has led the way in trying to end rape and to help those who have been raped. Education, crisis lines and centers, the enactment of new laws and regulations have all been part of the effort. This work has made inroads in changing the consciousness around violence against women and led the way to establishing important and needed programs and services. Today, more than 1,260 organizations provide rape crisis services, more than 820 programs provide sexual-assault and domestic-violence services and campuses around the country are involved in awareness campaigns.[32] In fact, any institution of higher education that receives federal funds is required to provide some form of sexual-assault awareness program (the extent to which this occurs is dependent on the campus; usually, student activists rather than administrators head these efforts). While this is a success story of activism creating change and addressing needs, the ideal success story would be the end of the need for any of these programs because sexual violence no longer exists. But, until that day comes, college campuses; community centers; churches, temples, synagogues, and mosques; apartment complexes; coffee houses; and bookstores can all serve as great vehicles for spreading information about rape resources.

> I'm a man against rape and I'm a man who sees that my fellow males have a responsibility to do something. Rishi, 20, Indian, Chicago, hetero-flexible/queer

Supporting and providing resources to rape survivors is a critical piece of feminist activism, but if we want rape to end, we have to target rapists. While I absolutely believe that we should continue to support education, shelters, and self-defense, I also think that we need to expose rapists. Why not shame them instead of shaming women? We need to stop blaming women for rape and using women's sexuality against them. We must stop the message that what we wear, say, or do invites sexual abuse. Let's place blame on the perpetrators and not on those who are abused.

MEN, VIOLENCE, AND FEMINISM

This fight is not just ours. Men must step up and change the consciousness of other men. It is no surprise that the vast majority of rapes are perpetrated by men—nearly 99 percent, according to the U.S. Department of Justice. As a result, we fear men and the rape that they could enact. In my classes, I ask my male students to be aware of women's responses to them on the street. I ask them to observe the body language of women and their behaviors. They usually come back shocked to learn that women avert their eyes, switch their purses to their opposite arm, change the side of the street they are walking on, or hurry their step. This is an eye-opening exercise for my male students because while men fear violence from other men, they rarely fear it from women. And if they don't see themselves as perpetrators, they rarely believe that others would. To see the reaction of women who don't know them can serve as a wakeup call regarding their role in violence against women.

Fortunately, some men are heeding this call. There are great men and male-led organizations working to realize true political, social, and economic equality between women and men. One such man is Jackson Katz.[33] His film *Tough Guise: Violence, Media and the Crisis in Masculinity* suggests that while we learn violence and ideas of masculinity from many sources, one powerful source is the media. From video games to wrestling to the movie screens, we see a masculinity defined for boys and men that reinforces and supports violence as integral to this definition and to the real-life behavior of men. And, in fact, as cited by Jackson Katz in his work:[34]

> Males are the victims and the perpetrators in 90 percent of homicides.[35]
>
> Ninety percent of people who commit violent physical assault are men.[36]
>
> Men perpetrate 95 percent of all serious domestic violence.[37]
>
> Of the people in prison who have been convicted of rape, 99.8 percent are men.[38]
>
> Out of ten thousand cases of road rage, more than 95 percent were committed by men.[39]
>
> An estimated one in four men will use violence against his partner in his lifetime.[40]

I fear that violence, specifically male-perpetrated violence, has become so commonplace that it is largely accepted. As a culture, we make excuses for male temper, we flock to violent movies for entertainment, we watch rape scenes on prime-time television without a flinch, we buy *Grand Theft Auto III*[41] and other video games for boys' birthdays—and what this all contributes to is an overall desensitization to violence—particularly violence against women. Jackson Katz addresses this concern well in stating:

> The reality is that messages that link being a man with being violent, controlling and intimidating are everywhere in the culture—from gun magazines, sports and wrestling, to romantic comedies and talk radio—as well as in the more obvious places like video games and tel-

evision. If we want to deal seriously with reducing violence, we have to turn away from thinking about violence as "kids imitating violence," and focus instead on the incredible diversity of ways that we as a society are actively constructing violent masculinity as a cultural norm; not as something unusual or unexpected, but as one of the ways that boys become men.[42]

Katz eloquently outlines the challenges of masculinity in today's American society. From the violent actions of boys to the trivializing of the importance of violence by adults, violent masculinity undermines the quest for true equality and creates a greater barrier to raising boys into nonviolent men.

Violence prevention is a key area of activism for feminist men. In Canada, the White Ribbon Campaign: Men Working to End Men's Violence Against Women has grown into the largest worldwide effort of men working to end violence. Founded in 1991, this volunteer organization pledges "never to commit, condone nor remain silent about violence against women."[43] The White Ribbon Campaign encourages men and boys to wear ribbons for one to two weeks starting November 25—the International Day for the Eradication of Violence Against Women. The campaign brings awareness to the prevalence of violence against women and the role that men can play in eradicating such violence. Additionally, in the United States, Men Stopping Rape programs are starting up at college campuses, working with already existing women's centers and women's organizations to address the epidemic of date rape.

The work of Jackson Katz and of organizations like the White Ribbon Campaign and Men Stopping Rape has made significant inroads in deconstructing the attitudes of masculinity, confronting the realities of male violence, and fostering respectful and egalitarian relationships between women and men. Men must stand up against the harmful attitudes of their peers toward women. Men can speak out and actively work to change the cult of masculinity that embraces and promotes violence against women. Malcolm X used to be asked by white people, What can I do to end racism? He would tell them to go back and talk to other white people to try to change their ideas about racism. Similarly, men need to talk to other men about their behavior and attitudes toward women. Rape will not end when women stop wearing short skirts; it will end when men stop overpowering and violating women.

This is not to say that women have no role in changing ideas about rape or that they are only powerless victims, but it is to recognize that without men' involvement and change, the violations will only continue. Real change requires both men and women to make it happen.

SEXUAL HARASSMENT IN THE WORKPLACE

Sexual harassment in our schools, on our jobs, and in our communities is intended to intimidate and threaten women and girls. Sexual harassment is a power trip, allowing the harasser to exert control over another. An estimated 40 to 90 percent of women in the United States have been victims of some form of sexual harassment on the job.[44] This estimate covers such a broad range because more than half of those who experience sexual harassment on the job say and do nothing about the harassment.[45] Women who do not report this abuse cite reasons ranging from fears of retaliation to fear that they will not be believed, that they will receive no support, or that they will lose their jobs.

Typically, sexual harassment in the workplace occurs between an employee and her supervisor. A study of Fortune 500 companies found that two-thirds of sexual harassment complaints involved an immediate supervisor.[46] Because of the power dynamic, supervisors are more likely to initiate acts of harassment and are also more likely to get away with it. Equal Rights Advocates, based in San Francisco, is a women's law center that litigates, educates, and organizes for women's rights. It explains this power dynamic:

> [P]ower is central to a supervisor's harassment of a subordinate. As a result, a victim of sexual harassment is more likely to submit to and less likely to complain when the harasser is a supervisor. Not only do supervisors have, by definition, greater authority and power than do their subordinates, but they also control the norms of the workplace. In addition to determining assignments, evaluating performance and recommending promotions, they influence the "climate" of work: what behaviors are acceptable, what standards exist and how communication occurs. Individuals in higher status positions believe and are believed to have the right to make demands of those in lower status roles. Some managers view harassing behavior as an extension of that right. They expect lower status individuals to comply.[47]

There are two main types of sexual harassment, *quid pro quo* and *hostile environment*. Quid pro quo is a Latin term that means "this for that" and, when used in reference to sexual harassment, refers to scenarios in which a boss offers job benefits or threatens job status in exchange for sexual favors. Individuals can often find themselves in a no-win situation, forced to choose between keeping a job and dealing with unwanted sexual advances. A

> They tell me I should expect sexual harassment and get used to it because I am working a man's job. Allegra, 30, equipment operator, California

hostile environment occurs "when physical, verbal or visual sexual harassment is severe or pervasive enough to create a hostile or abusive work environment."[48] Making comments, sending inappropriate e-mails, displaying pornographic pictures, touching, and grabbing are all examples of actions that make a workplace a hostile environment. I know of one case where a male superior sent e-mails of women's breasts to a female worker. When she opened the e-mail (which came titled as work-related), the breasts grew until they exploded. Cases of sexual harassment can also take on more extreme elements in which women's lives are put in danger. For example, a friend of mine is a scientist and frequently works in remote locations. She had a supervisor who pulled a gun on her out in the field after she rejected his advances. She survived and did go through the process of reporting him, but her fear was not diminished. Unfortunately, despite the severity of sexual harassment, many women are fearful to come forward about this abuse. As with the other types of violence against women, they fear not being believed, they fear that the abuse will escalate, and, in the case of workplace harassment, they fear losing their jobs.

SEXUAL HARASSMENT AT SCHOOL

Sexual harassment is not limited to just the workplace. The American Association of University Women estimates that 83 percent of girls experience sexual harassment at school.[49] From experience, I can tell you that harassment in the classroom is humiliating, frightening, and disempowering. Peer-to-peer sexual harassment is the most common and consists of physical and/or nonphysical abuse. Seventy-six percent of students have experienced nonphysical harassment, which includes teasing, jokes, rumors, and gestures, while fifty-eight percent have experienced physical abuse.[50] Of those students who have reported sexual harassment in school, seven percent report being harassed by a teacher.[51] Harassment in any situation is difficult and damaging, but, when it comes from a teacher, a whole new element of abuse is introduced. The abuse of power and trust can make a student feel even more unsafe and isolated. Adults—and certainly teachers—are touted as being there to protect and educate students. When you move out of the peer situation and sexual harassment is perpetrated by teachers, it becomes that much more difficult to speak up and have others believe you.

> Sexual harassment straight out of college has left me reelin' in the truth that objectification of women is the fearful reaction of threatened men.
> Amanda, 27, botanist, California

We must increase our awareness about sexual harassment in our schools. We need to support trainings, speak-outs, resources, educational materials, and a safe place to talk about harassment. We need comprehensive and uniform nationwide training for teachers and administrators about the signs and symptoms of sexual harassment and about the services available to its victims. And, while sexual harassment in education is prohibited under Title IX of the Education Amendments of 1972, we must dedicate the resources necessary and institutionalize a commitment to enforcing this provision.

Ho·mo·pho·bi·a: *n.* unreasoning fear of or antipathy toward homosexuals and homosexuality.

POWER, GENDER, AND HOMOPHOBIA

Violence within the gay, lesbian, bisexual, trans, queer, questioning, and intersex (GLBTQQI) communities is much the same as violence among heterosexuals. There are similar rates of occurrence, and the types of violence perpetrated are similar, as well. An added power dynamic, however, is the threat to "out" the abused individual to family, friends, or workplace colleagues. This threat serves to keep an individual in an abusive relationship for fear that the abuser will retaliate by revealing the victim's sexuality. Homophobia is present throughout our society, within our workplaces and our families. "Coming out" as lesbian, gay, queer, or trans is often a significant event, bringing with it fear of being ostracized by family, friends, and co-workers. Institutional homophobia works to control an abused individual by creating a fear (and, far too often, a reality) that the person will not be believed, that resources for help are limited, that the person will not be accepted in shelters or group programs, and that service environments will be hostile toward the person's sexuality. Additionally, there is often an added pressure to protect the GLBTQQI community by not exposing intimate-partner violence. The queer community is under such scrutiny that its members fear that exposure of violence within same-sex relationships will reinforce the accusation that homosexuality is immoral.

Social attitudes have influenced legal and structural realities for same-sex couples. For example, the battle over the legal definition of marriage has left many same-sex couples without basic protections in cases of domestic violence. Most states have gender-neutral language within their domestic-violence laws, which leaves discretion to the courts. As a result, in many cases, judges deny protective orders to individuals seeking help in cases of same-sex domestic violence. In fact, only three states—Ohio, Illinois, and Kentucky—consistently interpret their laws to include same-sex relationships, and only Hawaii has a domestic-violence law that explicitly gives members of same-sex couples the right to obtain restraining orders against abusive partners.[52] In contrast, Arizona, Delaware, Louisiana, Montana, New York, South Carolina, and Virginia all have state laws that specifically exclude same-sex partners from domestic-violence laws.[53] The lack of legal protection, combined with the social stigma, leaves many same-sex partners without resources and protection to fight violence in their lives.

All people, regardless of sexual or gender identity, should be guaranteed the right to safety. The fact that domestic- or intimate-partner violence exists in same-sex relationships is not evidence that same-sex relationships are wrong. The same standard applied to heterosexual relationships would certainly create controversy. The sad tragedy is that abuse happens in all relationships. To create a healthy world, we need to recognize the prevalence of abuse, confront its stereotypes, identify signs and symptoms, and provide resources, services, and education to all. Additionally, we need to guarantee partners in same-sex relationships the same protections under the law that are available to heterosexuals and to eradicate homophobia so that sexual identity does not serve to further victimize individuals who are fighting for their security.

GLOBAL VIOLENCE

Millions of women around the globe live with violence in their lives—across socioeconomic and educational classes, across cultural and religious lines, and in every region of the world. From intimate-partner violence, to rape, to sexual trafficking, to child abuse, to female genital mutilation, violence is a reality known to women worldwide. And violence against women, anywhere in the world, is about control, power, and the devaluing of women. Violence during wartime, violence against refugee women, abuses of women in prison occur in manners perpetuated, condoned, and ignored by local governments. And the international community is only recently recognizing and taking action to end these abuses.

VIOLENCE AGAINST WOMEN AROUND THE GLOBE

An estimated 100 to 140 million women and girls have undergone female genital mutilation—a procedure that removes a varying degree of female genitalia, usually including the clitoris and some portion of the vulva—with an additional estimated two million girls at risk annually.[54]

At least sixty million girls who would otherwise be expected to be alive are "missing" from various populations, mostly in Asia, as a result of sex-selective abortions, infanticide, or neglect.[55] In a study conducted in a large Bombay hospital, 95.5 percent of fetuses identified as female through amniocentesis were aborted.[56]

In India, despite the 1961 Anti-Dowry Act, an estimated seven thousand women died at the hands of their husband and in-laws in dowry-related deaths in 2001.[57]

In Peru, 70 percent of all crimes reported to the police involve a woman beaten by her husband.[58] In 2000, in Cusco, Peru, 46.7 percent of women experienced an attempted or completed rape by an intimate partner.[59]

In Zimbabwe, more than 60 percent of murder cases that go through the high court are domestic-violence cases.[60]

In 2003, an estimated 631 women in Pakistan were victims of "honor
    killings." Honor killings are enacted to restore honor to male
    members of a family by killing a woman who has been accused of
    wrongdoing.[61]
Laws exist in Ethiopia, Lebanon, and Uruguay to protect a rapist from pros-
    ecution if he chooses to marry his victim.
Two million girls between the ages of five and fifteen are coerced, abducted,
    sold, or trafficked into the illegal sex market annually.[62]
Rape is systematically used as a weapon of war all over the world. In
    Chiapas, Rwanda, Kuwait, Haiti, and Colombia, soldiers from both sides
    of a conflict gang-rape women and girls.[63] An estimated ten thousand
    to sixty thousand women were raped in Bosnia and Herzegovina
    alone.[64]
In Jordan, Morocco, and Syria, women who commit adultery can legally be
    killed by their husbands.
In Bangladesh, 47 percent of adult women report physical assault by a male
    partner.[65]
Every ten minutes, a woman or child is trafficked into the United States for
    forced labor.[66]

Awareness is rising about global violence against women—
thanks to the many grass-roots efforts of women around the globe.
From community marketplaces to prostitution outreach, from local
organizing to nationwide commissions, women work to challenge
traditional gender roles and practices, to create and maintain services,
and to educate the world's political system to work to eradicate all
discrimination against women. When a 1999 court overturned a 1998
rape conviction in Italy, ruling that rape could not occur because the
woman was wearing jeans and would need to participate in their re-
moval, thus giving consent, women throughout Italy and the world
responded. Female lawmakers wore jeans to Parliament in Rome in
protest—and Jeans for Justice was born. Jeans for Justice is an international campaign in which women wear jeans to work, protesting
not just the Italian ruling but general attitudes about rape and violence against women. Women in Thailand, Nepal, and the Philippines
are working to increase education and access to jobs to end the sexual trafficking of women and girls. Women throughout the developing world are attempting to unionize their labor in an attempt to
have more control over their own wages and working conditions.
The Asante market women in Ghana, West Africa, have taken control

of the central market place, controlling trade and commerce, thereby giving women greater financial independence. In the United States, the Coalition to Abolish Slavery and Trafficking (CAST) has established the first and only shelter for survivors of trafficking in the United States. Incorporating crisis and transition services, the CAST shelter embraces a holistic approach to wellness, providing garden and art therapy and teaching computer and job training skills. On a global scale, women from around the world came together in Beijing in 1995 to reconfirm CEDAW (Convention on the Elimination of All Forms of Discrimination Against Women) and set forth an agenda for the self-determination of women worldwide. Since then, many nations have taken action to end violence against women. A number of countries, including Austria, Belarus, Mexico, and Hungary, for the first time have criminalized sexual violence against women by their husbands. The Philippines has initiated a program to combat trafficking in women and children. And Tanzania has enacted laws criminalizing female genital mutilation.[67] While abuses continue and the amount of violence against women is staggering, we can find hope in the fact that we join our sisters throughout the world to fight back.

> I came across an issue of Time magazine in 1995 about how rape was used as a war tool in the civil war in Yugoslavia. I started doing more research on female genital mutilation, forced sterilizations in China, and the illegal trafficking of young girls in Thailand for prostitution and I started to realize that in the world over, the attitude towards women is destructive, oppressive and unacceptable. This point has been particularly brought home over the years as women I know have been victims of domestic violence, rape and molestation, and I started to realize how much violence is directed at women both in my own life and at women around the world. Lisa, 25, Indo-American, straight, Connecticut

FIGHTING BACK

Fighting back is about more than physically fighting our attacker. It is about fighting back against violence on every level—fighting for recognition, fighting so that violence against women will be taken seriously, fighting for legislative provisions that will protect women and punish perpetrators (and not the other way around), fighting that our law enforcement and our courts do not re-victimize women in their pursuit for justice, fighting to hold men accountable—both as those who perpetrate violence and as those who stand by in a culture that allows this violence—fighting to change the consciousness of our global culture, fighting to ensure that rape continue to be recognized and treated as a violation of human rights whether or not it occurs during wartime, and fighting to create a social and political no-tolerance policy about violence.

The sexual assaults and the coercive, abusive marriage I survived led me to the decision to reclaim my life and the lives of other women. Sharon, 33, Asian/White, California, bisexual

The epidemic of violence against women is so vast and so pervasive that it is nearly unspeakable. But, fortunately, women are speaking. We are speaking out and saying NO MORE. Events like Take Back the Night exist for just that purpose—to create a safe venue for women to tell their stories, band together and, for at least one day, take back the night. Take Back the Night originated in England, in 1877; the first Take Back the Night march and rally in the United States took place in San Francisco in 1978 to bring awareness to and to protest violence against women. This San Francisco march followed the first feminist conference on pornography and brought together more than ten thousand people who gathered to march in the streets, protesting the harms of pornography.[68] Today, Take Back the Night events focus on sexual violence in all forms and occur throughout the world in hundreds of communities. Often associated with Take Back the Night, the Clothesline Project further raises awareness about violence against women through the artistic display of multicolored t-shirts on a clothesline. Started in 1990 by a small group of women in Massachusetts, the Clothesline Project serves to educate about intimate violence while honoring both victims and survivors. Today it is estimated that more than five hundred projects exist nationally and internationally, with between fifty thousand and sixty thousand shirts created.[69]

Grass-roots activism is the cornerstone that serves as the foundation for political change. Not only do events like Take Back the Night create a safe place to heal; they also raise awareness about societal and governmental responsibility. It was from grass-roots activism that we achieved the Violence Against Women Act (VAWA) in 1994 and helped win its reauthorization in 1998, 2000, and 2005. While VAWA is not the cure-all for violence against women, it is a strong start to prioritizing funding, resources, and education to end violence against women. Administered by the Department of Health and Human Services and the Department of

Justice, VAWA includes grants for battered women's shelters; a National Domestic Violence 24-hour hotline (1.800.799.SAFE / 1.800.787.3224); outreach to runaway, homeless youth; for programs to reduce sexual assault; and coordinated community programs. Expanded in 2000 and again in 2005, VAWA now also addresses issues related to trafficking, battered immigrant women, dating violence, services for disabled women, services for elderly women, and transitional housing. But we're not done yet. It is important that we elect representatives who will continue to support and expand VAWA until the violence stops.

A world free of violence against women benefits EVERYONE. Nicole, 25, biracial, heterosexual, Connecticut

Indeed, efforts throughout the world are under way to end violence against women—from the international campaign for CEDAW to local outreach, education, and crisis programs. College campuses have widely taken up the issue of rape and dating violence, hosting Clothesline Projects, Take Back the Night rallies, dorm outreach programs, Men Stopping Rape projects, and V-Day activities. We continue to raise awareness in our communities, to support our local shelters and hotlines, and to raise money through walk-a-thons and charity events. We continue to fight for the support of the Violence Against Women Act in Congress and for federal funding for and prioritizing of programs to end violence against women. We can all be part of this fight; whether we are on the floor of our legislatures making policy or talking to a friend or family member who is in an abusive relationship, we can make a difference. We must change the consciousness of this culture to end violence. Remember, no act is too small. We never know whose life we are helping with our activism.

SPOTLIGHT ON ACTIVISM

Eve Ensler and the V-Day Campaign

Eve Ensler is one of the coolest feminist chicks out there. She's also an amazing visionary. Who knew that she would take the world by storm with her one-woman show and subsequent 1998 book, *The Vagina Monologues?* Refusing to be ashamed of the v-word, Ensler encouraged women to tell their stories about menstruation, sex, masturbation, violence, and all things vagina. These stories became a catalyst for raising awareness, consciousness, and important funding to end violence against women around the world. Ensler soon transformed *The Vagina Monologues* and created the V-Day

Campaign—"a worldwide movement to stop violence against women." As
of 2006, *The Vagina Monologues* has been performed in more than one
thousand venues throughout the world—including in Africa, Asia, Europe,
and Great Britain. But the V-Day Campaign now extends far beyond
performances to include the 1 Percent Campaign, which demands that the
United States donate 1 percent of its defense budget to end violence
against women and girls; "Africa, Middle East and Asia," an initiative that
works to eradicate violence in these areas of the world; V-Day Spotlight
Campaigns, which highlight a particular group of women that is experiencing violence, with the goal of raising awareness and funds to support the
group's efforts to end the violence; and public service announcements,
heard throughout the world, that encourage an end to violence against
women. For more information and to get involved with the V-Day
Campaign, visit www.vday.org.

TAKE ACTION

Getting Started

Take a woman-centered self-defense class.

Institute the buddy system among your friends—decide ahead of time that
you are coming and leaving together, watch each others' drinks, watch
each others' "back."

Contact the Rape, Abuse, and Incest National Network (www.rainn.org) and
request materials about violence against women to hand out to your
friends or in your community.

Take educational materials about date-rape drugs to your local clubs and
bars, and ask the management if you can put them up in bathrooms (best
if you go during the day, before they are busy with the club scene). Pass
out materials at the clubs during club hours.

Support rape-kit funding—contact your legislators to support increased
funding.

Counter the myths about violence against women. Speak up.

Educate yourself about global acts of violence against women (see Fabulous
Feminist Web Resources for on-line resources).

The Next Step

Donate clothes, books, and household goods to a local domestic-abuse shelter. Many cell-phone vendors now take donations of old phones to sup-

port domestic violence centers. See the appendix "Where to donate stuff" for more information.

Participate in your local Take Back the Night event. Bring a friend.

Talk to your friends about violence. Reach out to those whom you suspect are dealing with abuse in their lives. Let them know that they are not alone, that they are not to blame, and that resources are available.

Get involved with campaigns to end violence against women worldwide. See Fabulous Feminist Web Resources for on-line resources.

Getting Out There

Host an informational forum at your school, at a local bookstore, at a coffee house. Invite a speaker from your local shelter to facilitate.

Start a Clothesline Project on your campus or in your community. Visit www.clotheslineproject.org for more information.

Support the V-Day campaign. Bring a performance of *The Vagina Monologues* to your campus or community. Participate in a local performance.

Volunteer at a local domestic-abuse shelter.

Volunteer for a rape crisis line. Volunteer to be an on-call language interpreter.

Take Action for Men

Join the fight to end violence against women.

Talk to your friends.

Speak out.

Pay attention.

Deconstruct the myth of masculinity.

Commit to living a nonviolent life.

Recognize and support November 25, the International Day for the Eradication of Violence Against Women, and support the White Ribbon Campaign. See www.whiteribbon.ca for more information.

Give money to domestic-violence and sexual-assault-prevention organizations.

ON MY BOOKSHELF

Anne Brodsky, *With All Our Strength: The Revolutionary Association of the Women of Afghanistan* (New York: Routledge, 2003).

Susan Brownmiller, *Against Our Will: Men, Women and Rape* (New York: Fawcett, 1975).

Denise Caignon and Gail Groves Harper, *Her Wits About Her: Self-Defense Success Stories by Women.* (New York: Perennial Library, 1987).

Gavin De Becker, *The Gift of Fear* (New York: Dell, 1998).

Eve Ensler, *The Vagina Monologues* (New York: Villard, 1998).

Estelle Freedman, *No Turning Back: The History of Feminism and the Future of Women* (New York: Ballantine, 2002).

Rus Ervin Funk, *Stopping Rape: A Challenge for Men* (Philadelphia: New Society, 1993).

Margaret Gordon and Stephanie Riger, *The Female Fear: The Social Cost of Rape* (Champaign: University of Illinois Press, 1991).

Kerry Lobel, *Naming the Violence: Speaking Out About Lesbian Battering* (Seattle: Seal Press, 1986).

Nancy Matthews, *Confronting Rape: The Feminist Anti-Rape Movement and the State* (New York: Routledge, 1994).

Charlotte Pierce-Baker, *Surviving the Silence: Black Women's Stories of Rape* (New York: Norton, 1998).

Michael Penn and Rahel Nardos, *Overcoming Violence Against Women and Girls: The International Campaign to Eradicate a Worldwide Problem* (New York: Rowman and Littlefield, 2003).

Jessica Amanda Salmonson, *The Encyclopedia of Amazons: Women Warriors from Antiquity to the Modern Era* (New York: Paragon House, 1991).

Peggy Reeves Sanday, *Fraternity Gang Rape* (New York: New York University Press, 1990).

Leora Tanenbaum, *Slut! Growing Up Female with a Bad Reputation* (New York: Perennial Harper Collins, 2000).

Alice Walker and Pratibha Parmar, *Warrior Marks* (New York: Harcourt Brace, 1993).

Alice Walker, *The Temple of My Familiar* (San Diego: Harcourt Brace Jovanovich, 1989).

Alice Walker, *Possessing the Secret of Joy* (New York: Washington Square Press, 1997).

Robin Warshaw, *I Never Called It Rape: The Ms. Report on Recognizing, Fighting and Surviving Date and Acquaintance Rape* (New York: Harper and Row, 1988).

Emily White, *Fast Girls: Teenage Tribes and the Myth of the Slut* (New York: Scribner, 2002).

FIGHTING BACK FILM RESOURCES

The Accused (1988)

Bastard Out of Carolina (1996)

Beloved (1998)

Boys Don't Cry (1999)

The Burning Bed (1984)

The Color Purple (1985)

Crimes of the Heart (1986)

The Crying Game (1992)

Date Rape Backlash: Media and the Denial of Rape (1994)

Defending Our Lives (1993)

Double Jeopardy (1999)

Dreamworld and *Dreamworlds II* (1991 and 1995)

Enough (2002)

Fear (1996)

Freeway (1996)

Fried Green Tomatoes (1991)

Girlfight (2000)

Girls Town (1996)

The Joy Luck Club (1993)

Kiss the Girls (1997)

Long Kiss Goodnight (1996)

Monster (2004)

North Country (2005)

Once We Were Warriors (1994)

Senorita Extraviada Missing Young Women (2001)

Sleeping with the Enemy (1991)

Thelma and Louise (1991)

Tough Guise (1999)

The Vagina Monologues with Eve Ensler (2002)

What's Love Got to Do with It? (1993)

Where the Heart Is (2000)

FABULOUS FEMINIST WEB RESOURCES

American Women's Self Defense Association   www.awsda.org
Dedicated to ending violence against women, AWSDA provides a central place for information, referrals, training and resources for self-defense.

Amnesty International   www.amnesty.org
An international campaign working for human rights and peace. Web site includes a wealth of information, including information on campaigns to end violence against women, protect refugee rights, end torture, and control arms.

Anti-Asian Violence Network janet.org/~ebihara/aavn/aav_org.html
A network of organizations working to end violence against Asian Americans.

BRAVE People   www.bravepeople.com
A division of Defending Ourselves, BRAVE People is dedicated to Building Resources for Anti-Violence Education.

California Coalition Against Sexual Assault   www.calcasa.org
A coalition of sexual rape crisis and prevention centers throughout California.

Center for Young Women's Development   www.cywd.org
Dedicated to improving the lives of young women, the Center for Young Women's Development provides training, resources, referrals, and education—including programs like the Street Survival Project and Girls' Detention Advocacy Project.

The Clothesline Project   www.clotheslineproject.org
Information about the Clothesline Project, including history and starting a project locally.

Coalition to Abolish Slavery and Trafficking   www.castla.org
Resources, services, and information about forced labor and slavery. Provides case management, advocacy, public education, and training.

Defending Ourselves   www.selfdefenseschool.com
Woman-centered self-defense and empowerment education. Site includes information for training and education about self-defense. Classes offered in northern California.

Equal Rights Advocates   www.equalrights.org
A great resource for sexual harassment, includes legal case history, advice for dealing with harassment, information on resources, litigation and advocacy

Equality Now   www.equalitynow.org
International campaigns to end violence against women, including female genital mutilation, trafficking, rape, and domestic violence.

Feminist Majority   www.feminist.org
National and international information, resources, and activism. The Feminist Majority Web site is a great source of information on how to get involved and make a difference in the lives of women worldwide.

Jackson Katz   www.jacksonkatz.com
Official site for Jackson Katz and his work. Includes antiviolence education and resources specifically for men.

Maiti Nepal   www.maitinepal.org
Information on working to protect Nepalese girls from prostitution, sex trafficking, domestic violence, child labor, and torture.

National Coalition Against Domestic Violence   www.ncadv.org
Education and resources about domestic violence; includes information about starting a domestic violence shelter in your area.

National Coalition of Anti-Violence Programs   www.ncav.org
National advocacy for local GLBT communities. Web site includes information and resources for programs around the nation. Also includes reports on hate crimes and domestic violence.

National Organization for Men Against Sexism   www.nomas.org
Pro-feminist, gay-affirmative, antiracist organization dedicated to enhancing men's lives.

National Sexual Violence Resource Center   www.nsvrc.org
A collection of resources and referral regarding sexual violence; includes statistics, information, and resources for state, community, and tribal programs.

The Network   www.thenetworklared.org
English- and Spanish-language Web site providing information and resources about domestic violence against the GLBT community.

NYC Alliance Against Sexual Assault   www.nycagainstrape.org
Based in New York City, site provides resources and referrals for area services. Also includes extensive library, research, fact sheets, and information about training program.

Rape, Abuse and Incest National Network   www.rainn.org
Comprehensive resources, statistics, research, and program information.

Revolutionary Association   www.rawa.org
of the Women of Afghanistan
The oldest sociopolitical organization of Afghan women fighting for justice.

Street Harassment Project (NYC)   www.streetharassmentproject.org
In response to the harassment of fifty-six women in New York's Central Park, the Street Harassment Project meets weekly to work to end harassment of women in public places. It hosts workshops and street theater to raise awareness about and to stop street harassment.

The Survivor Project   www.survivorproject.org
Information and resources for intersex and trans survivors of domestic and sexual violence. Web site also provides great resources regarding language, definitions, and building allies for the trans community.

Toolkit to End Violence Against Women   www.toolkit.ncjrs.com
Extensive research and resources dedicated to ending violence against women.

VAW Net   www.vawnet.org
A network of referrals and resources for violence-against-women programs, research, and projects on the Internet.

V-Day—Stop Violence Against Women   www.vday.org
 The Vagina Monologues' V-Day Campaign, working to eradicate violence against women around the globe.

WEAVE   www.weave.org
(Women Escaping a Violent Environment)
 Sacramento-based WEAVE provides services, information, training, and referrals for violence prevention and violence-against-women services.

White Ribbon Campaign   www.whiteribbon.ca
 Canadian-based organization of men working to end men's violence against women.

Women for Women International   www.womenforwomen.org
 International program working to aid women in war-torn regions in the world. Program provides financial and emotional support, vocational training, and micro-credit loans and financial assistance and works to promote women's rights.

8
. . . Like A Girl

The Center for Young Women's Development, in San Francisco, California, works from the belief that young women are themselves experts on their lives and are therefore the best ones to lead. They did exactly that in 1997 when they took over full leadership of the center, making it the nation's first youth-led social service agency. The center is dedicated to empowering the lives of low-income young women who have lived and/or worked on the streets and have been involved with the juvenile justice system.

Sisters in Action, in Portland, Oregon, works with low-income young women of color. Through empowerment programs, Sisters in Action addresses issues of racism, harassment, and violence to raise awareness and confidence. It has trained more than six hundred girls in political activism through Oregon's only girl-based leadership program. With more than half of its board made up of women under the age of eighteen, Sisters in Action is another great example of young women leaders making a difference.

The Young Survival Coalition, based in New York City, was founded by three breast cancer survivors who were all under the age of thirty-five when diagnosed. Founded in 1998, The Young Survival Coalition works to bring awareness, advocacy, and education to issues of breast cancer in women under the age of forty. Encouraging breast self-exams, the Young Survival Project also hosts on-line discussion boards and chat rooms, shares research, and advocates and fundraises for research and services for breast cancer in young women. It is the only international nonprofit organization dedicated to young women with breast cancer.

Students Take Action for New Directions (STAND) was founded in 1982 by twelve high school students and is a program of Women's Action for Nuclear Disarmament (WAND). With national offices in Massachusetts, Washington, D.C., and Georgia, and with chapters throughout the country, STAND works to empower young women to take political action, including voting and working with legislators. Their mission in-

218

cludes a commitment to peace and justice, and the group brings together young leaders through conferences and on-line communities.

Beyond Media Education is a Chicago organization working to make media tools available to young women so that they can speak for themselves. Projects include Think Beyondmedia, which provides media- and technology-infused curricula to underserved communities in Chicago's public schools. The group offers a Girls! Action! Media! workshop where young women can discuss issues and promote leadership. Through these workshops, young girls learn media, arts, and technology skills. The Women and Prison group offers a program for former and current prisoners and their families and provides these young women with media access and training to tell their stories of life behind bars.

Feminism is not a static thing. It should be changing with every day. Listen and learn to the people who came before but do not be afraid to move forward with what you've learned. Jay, 22, genderqueer/trans, Doukhobor, Canada

Based in Philadelphia, the Student Environmental Action Coalition is a "network of progressive organizations and individuals whose aim is to uproot environmental injustices through action and education."[1] SEAC is a national grass-roots organization run by students and youth. Its work emphasizes the physical, economic, political, and cultural conditions that impact our lives. Campaigns include Youth Power Shift, a national, youth-led project to engage students, schools, and the government in an effort to reduce their negative impact on the environment; Global Finance Campaign, a program to bring awareness to corporate globalization; Militarism and the Environment, a project to take a stand regarding the global environmental impact of war and the "military-industrial-entertainment complex"; and Tampaction, a national youth-led program to encourage positive attitudes toward women's bodies and menstruation, to address the concerns of unhealthy menstrual products, and to introduce the use of sustainable alternatives.

The Third Wave Foundation has been essential to third-wave feminist activism. Organized and led by young women in New York City, the Third Wave Foundation serves as a national resource for organizations and efforts headed by young women ages fifteen through thirty. The Third Wave Foundation provides funding, resources, public education, and networking opportunities. Its Reaching Out Across Movements (ROAMS) program, which brings together young feminist activists and social justice organizations across the nation, is fabulous.

From these organizations to the many young women who are working in community centers, in campus task forces, or as individuals, young women are making change everywhere. Whether we are working on body image, violence prevention, reproductive rights, clean air, economic justice, or free trade, young women are fighting for a better world. Some of us call ourselves feminists, while others do not. Some of us belong to long-established organizations, while others are forging a new path. Some of us work within the system, some of us work outside it—and sometimes we do both. While not all of my generation is active, there is a strong presence of young women—young people—who are plugged in. As Vivien Labaton and Dawn Lundy Martin write in their anthology, *The Fire This Time: Young Activists and the New Feminism,* "young feminists are not only creating new organizations, new models of organizing, and new forms of cultural work but reenvisioning the world in which we live, and placing a renewed feminism at its center."[2]

WOMEN WHO HAVE MADE A DIFFERENCE

Abigail Adams wrote her now-famous letter to her husband, John Adams, asking him to "remember the ladies" while writing the Declaration of Independence, 1774.

Judith Sargent Stevens Murray advocated for equal education for women and men in *On the Equality of the Sexes,* published in 1790.

Emma Hart Willard founded Troy Female Seminary, the first endowed school for girls, 1821.

The first women's rights convention in the United States took place in Seneca Falls, New York, where the Declaration of Sentiments was written, calling for equal rights for women, 1848.

The first four-year college for women, Mount Holyoke College, in Massachusetts, was founded by **Mary Lyon,** 1837.

Harriet Tubman, in the 1850s, ran the Underground Railroad to help slaves escape.

Sojourner Truth delivered her famous "Ain't I a Woman" speech in Akron, Ohio, 1851.

The American Equal Rights Association, advocating for universal suffrage, was formed by **Elizabeth Cady Stanton** and **Susan B. Anthony,** 1866.

Victoria Woodhull is the first woman to campaign for the U.S. presidency, 1872.

Ida B. Wells created a national antilynching campaign, 1892.

Charlotte Perkins Gilman first published *The Yellow Wallpaper,* 1892.

Hannah Greenbaum Soloman founded the National Council for Jewish Women (NCJW), 1893. The National Association of Colored Women (NACW) was formed by **Mary Church Terrell, Ida B. Wells-Barnett, Margaret Murray Washington, Fanny Jackson Coppin, Frances Ellen Watkins Harper, Charlotte Forten Grimké, and Harriet Tubman,** 1896.

Marie Curie was the first woman to win the Nobel Prize for physics, 1903.

Maggie Lena Walker, the first woman bank founder and president, founded St. Luke Penny Savings Bank in 1903 and served as its president until 1930.

Mary McLeod Bethune started a school for African American girls in Florida with $1.50, 1904.

Lois Weber, the first female movie director, began directing in 1913.

Jeannette Rankin, of Montana, was the first woman to serve in the U.S. House of Representatives, 1916.

Alice Paul and other members of the National Women's Party first proposed, and drafted, the Equal Rights Amendment, 1923.

Amelia Earhart was first woman to fly solo across the Atlantic Ocean, 1932.

Frances Perkins became the first woman to hold a Cabinet position in U.S. politics when she was appointed secretary of labor by Franklin D. Roosevelt, 1932.

The National Council of Negro Women was founded by **Mary McLeod Bethune,** who also became the organization's president, 1935.

Eleanor Roosevelt was the first U.S. delegate to the United Nations, 1945–1951.

Alice Coachman was the first black woman to win an Olympic gold medal for the high jump, 1948.

Rosa Parks touched off the Montgomery, Alabama, bus boycotts when she refused to sit in the back of the bus, 1955–1956.

Daughters of Bilitis, the first lesbian rights organization in the United States, was founded by **Del Martin** and **Phyllis Lyon,** 1955.

Jerrie Cobb was the first female astronaut candidate for NASA, 1959.

Wilma Rudolph was the first woman to win three gold medals in a single Olympiad, 1960 (Rudolph had had polio as a child and was told that she would never walk).

Delores Huerta co-founded the United Farm Workers to advocate for farm workers' rights, 1962.

Patsy Takemoto Mink, Democrat of Hawaii, was the first Asian/Pacific Islander woman elected to the House; she served from 1965 through 1977 and was re-elected in 1990 and 1992.

Shirley Chisholm, Democrat of New York, became the first black woman U.S. representative in 1968. She ran for U.S. president in 1972, becoming the first woman and the first African American to seek the nomination of the Democratic Party.

Feminist Women's Health Center was founded in Los Angeles by **Carol Downer** and **Lorraine Rothman** in effort to create women-centered health care, 1971.

In 1969, a young lawyer in Texas took on a pro bono case to fight for one woman's right to abortion. The case went to the Supreme Court in 1971. It was *Roe v. Wade,* and **Sarah Weddington** was the attorney. On January 22, 1973, women won the right to an abortion in the first trimester.

Aileen Hernandez, a labor organizer and a black feminist activist, became NOW's second national president, 1971.

Ms. magazine was founded by **Gloria Steinem** and **Pat Carbine,** 1972.

The first woman producer to win an Oscar was **Julia Phillips,** who won for *The Sting,* 1974.

Julia B. Robinson was the first mathematician to be elected to the National Academy of Science, 1976.

Sarah Caldwell was the first woman to conduct the orchestra at the Metropolitan Opera; Beverly Sills refused to sing until Caldwell was allowed to conduct, 1976.

Bette Nesmith Graham, a single mother who had not finished high school and who was working as a secretary, invented Liquid Paper ("white-out"). In 1979, she sold her invention to Gillette for $47.5 million, plus royalties.

The National Women's History Project is founded, 1980.

Maya Lin, a twenty-one-year-old Chinese-American architectural design student, won the competition for the design of the Vietnam Veterans Memorial in Washington, DC, 1981.

Sally Ride was the first female American astronaut to go into space, 1983.

Alice Walker was awarded a Pulitzer Prize for her novel *The Color Purple,* 1983.

Geraldine Ferraro is the first woman to run on a national political party ticket for vice president, 1984.

The **Guerrilla Girls** was founded by a group of anonymous women with the goal of bringing recognition to women artists, 1984.

Emily's List was founded by **Ellen Malcolm**. Emily's List gives money to Democratic, pro-choice, women political candidates, 1985.

Wilma Mankiller was the first female chief of the Cherokee Nation, 1987.

Toni Morrison received the Pulitzer Prize for *Beloved* and the rest of her work, 1988.

Ileana Ros-Lehtinen, Republican of Florida, became the first Cuban American (male or female) and the first Hispanic woman to be elected to the U.S. Congress, 1989.

The first woman to wear pants on the U.S. House floor was **Susan Molinari,** a Republican from New York, 1990.

Sylvia Rhone, CEO of EastWest Records, became the first woman and the first African American woman to head her own record label, 1990.

Anita Hill testified before the Senate Judiciary Committee, bringing sexual harassment to national awareness as she confronted her harasser, Supreme Court nominee (now Justice) Clarence Thomas, 1991.

Nydia Velazquez, Democrat of New York, was the first Puerto Rican congresswoman, 1992.

Dr. Mae Jemison was the first black female astronaut to successfully complete a space shuttle mission, 1992.

Rebecca Walker founded the Third Wave Direct Action Corporation in 1992, which later became the Third Wave Foundation.

Carol Moseley-Braun, Democrat of Illinois, was the first woman of color to serve in the U.S. Senate, elected 1992. She later ran for president of the United States, 2004.

Lucille Roybal-Allard, Democrat of California, was the first Mexican American congresswoman, elected 1993.

Dr. Joycelyn Elders, former U.S. surgeon general, dared to speak about masturbation at the United Nations World AIDS Day in 1994 conference. She was fired the following week.

Andi Zeisler and **Lisa Jervis** found *Bitch* magazine, in 1996.

Lilith Fair, an international women's music festival that critics said would never happen, was created by **Sarah McLachlan,** 1997.

At just fifteen years of age, **Shelby Knox** took a stand against the abstinence-only curriculum at her school in Lubbock, Texas, prompting the creation of a PBS documentary film, "The Education of Shelby Knox," by the filmmakers **Marion Lipschultz** and **Rose Rosenblatt**.

Katie Couric became the first solo network anchorwoman when she joined CBS in 2006.

CHALLENGES WE FACE

Throughout this book, I have highlighted the many issues we face as women, both in society and within the movement itself. If our voices are to impact the decisions of a society, we must achieve equal representation. No longer can we stand for government without equal representation; nor can we allow business, media, military, religion, or education to exist without fair representation for women. Our safety and health cannot be negotiable. Accessible and comprehensive health care, health research, funding, and services that meet all women's needs—at every stage of

What you say matters. Stand up, shout it out. Rachel, 26, Caucasian/American, heterosexual, Nebraska

her life—are what we need. Women must have economic justice. Our relationships need to be by choice and not dictated by government. Our sexuality must belong solely to ourselves—in definition and in practice. And we need to be taught from the earliest stages that we are valuable, powerful, beautiful beings. Some would say this is too much to ask for, but I argue that it is the bare minimum for a safe, healthy, equal society. I also argue that it is worth the fight. But, as we have learned from our past, this fight is neither a quick nor an easy one. Those who have taken up the challenge in the past risked, and lost, a great deal. Far too many never lived to see their work realized. But they fought, not just for themselves, but for the vision of a better world for all. Now it is our turn. Phyllis Chesler tells us in her book *Letters to a Young Feminist*, "know that you too may be punished for fighting back, whether you do so alone or with others. But know that if you persevere, you *may* improve the fate of future generations."[3] Many of us have stepped up to the challenge; we work every day to make sure women and girls have a fair chance at a life of quality and equality. Still others must join us, for freedom and justice are not yet fully realized.

Feminism is the vision and practice of a truly just society. It is about believing in our worth as women and girls. It is about the opportunity to dream and to see those dreams realized. It is a movement to have our stories told, our experiences recognized, our bodies protected, our lives valued, and our voices counted in all levels of decision making and leadership.

BEING THE CHANGE WE WANT TO SEE

Alix Olson, a fabulous feminist slam poet whom I met years ago at a conference in Los Angeles, California, has a great collection of poetry about social justice and activism. In one of my favorite poems, *Warriors*, she says,

. . . cause if this is a movement we're making, we have got to get moving.
In this crazy maze we've been handed, we've got to quit losing ourselves.
We gotta use our big fat mouths to talk,
We gotta use our big thick thighs to walk.
We got to follow those who choose a different way to knock.[4]

And she is right, because we are not just the future. The fight is today, and we have a stake in it. Every day, decisions are made that impact every level of our lives. We need to be part of the decision-making process. We need to believe in our individual and collective strength, to respect the connections we share—that what one does impacts another. We need to take on this fight together, addressing all issues of discrimination. Men need to join the feminist movement, be partners in this fight for equality—a fight whose success will also benefit them. We need to broaden our understanding and definition of gender and allow people to define themselves. We need to ensure that we all are at the table, sharing our analysis and strategizing for our futures. We need to break the barriers of race, age, gender, sexuality and sexual orientation, physical ability, and all other identities that keep us separate. We must fight sexism, racism, ageism, homophobia—all the isms to recognize that, collectively, we are stronger and that, while we experience discrimination uniquely and individually, there is a commonality to oppression. It is with this commonality that we can come together and fight so that we all experience a life of quality and equality. We must believe that we are worth fighting for—because we are. It's our fight. It's our rights. The torch of feminism is in our hands. So, say it with me . . .

Play like a girl. Act like a girl. Eat like a girl. Think like a girl. Organize like a girl. Write like a girl. Vote like a girl. Throw like a girl. Laugh like a girl. Move like a girl. Dream like a girl. Invent like a girl. Dance like a girl. Heal like a girl. Study like a girl. Run like a girl. Resist like a girl. Raise money like a girl. Celebrate like a girl. Dress like a girl. Invest like a girl. Argue like a girl. Raise Hell like a girl. Speak like a girl. Stand up like a girl. Strategize like a girl. Speak out like a girl. Love like a girl. Yell like a girl. Do it like a girl. Act up like a girl. Lead like a girl. *Fight like a girl!*

Appendix A
Timeline and Checklist for Action

Note to the Reader: I hope that the ideas in this and the following appendices will assist you in fighting like a girl.

6 Weeks Prior to Event

Choose a site, date, and time.
Apply for any needed permits and make room reservations.
Contact potential speakers and performers.

5 Weeks Prior to Event

Create a flyer listing the date, site, time, and purpose of the event and contact information.
Mail flyer to supportive groups.
Begin posting flyers in public locations (e.g., coffee houses, laundromats, bookstores, college campuses).

4 Weeks Prior to Event

Contact local newspaper calendar listings departments and send event notices.
Continue spreading information on the event.

3 Weeks Prior to Event

Confirm speakers and guests.
Make arrangements for necessary equipment.
Send mailing on event to local supporters and members.

2 Weeks Prior to Event

Send press advisories and public service announcements to local media.

Plan visuals for the event, such as signs, banners, and stage backdrops.

Plan volunteer roster for event.

I Week Prior to Event

Phone-bank group membership to inform about the event. Get commitments to attend.

Send press releases to local media.

Poster-blitz community.

Make any visuals for event as previously planned.

3–5 Days Prior to Event

Make final adjustments to program.

Get biographical data on speakers for introductions.

Hold volunteer trainings (especially for peacekeepers and facilitators).

I–2 Days Prior to Event

Make follow-up calls to media.

Confirm equipment arrangements, including delivery and set-up time and costs.

Make reminder calls to volunteers, speakers, and performers.

Day of Event

Assemble volunteers on-site at least 1 1/2 hours in advance.

Hang banners and signs.

Check equipment.

Greet performers and speakers, and confirm time limits and program with them.

Start on time, and stick to the program.

After Event

Clean up event area.
Return rented or borrowed equipment.
Meet with organizers and de-brief.
Videotape news coverage and clip newspaper stories.
Write thank-you notes to speakers and helpers.

(Timeline and Checklist reprinted with permission from CA NOW's *Action for Justice Training Manual*, 2003).

Appendix B
Building an Activist Kit

An activist kit is something to take with you to events or to leave in your car or bag for last-minute outreach opportunities. A few things to consider putting in your kit:

1. Flyers for upcoming events and meetings (make sure to always include your contact information)

2. Sign-up list for volunteers and/or people who wish to be contacted about upcoming meetings or events

3. Clipboard

4. Pens

5. Information cards and flyers about your organization or effort, with contact and meeting information

6. Rubber bands (use rubber bands to keep flyers from flying away in outdoor settings)

7. Wrapped candy to give to visitors to your table (it's amazing how a bit of sweets can draw people in)

Appendix C
How to Write a Press Release

1. Use letterhead and type the release (do not handwrite . . . *ever!*).

2. Label the top NEWS RELEASE, PSA (public service announcement), CALENDAR LISTING, PRESS ADVISORY, or PRESS CONFERENCE, as appropriate. When you use all caps, you are signifying to the reporters that this is for their information, and not part of the text to be printed.

3. Provide one or two contact names and phone numbers (ALL CAPS).

4. Date it in this way—For Immediate Release MONTH, DATE, YEAR. Use today's date or the date the organization will receive the release. If you're sending in a calendar listing, you may wish to add an END DATE or EFFECTIVE UNTIL.

5. Write a headline for your press release. Make it catchy, and use a present-tense verb for action or interest. Note: reporters rarely use your headline, but it is still important to provide one.

6. Double-space the body of your story, and leave wide margins on both sides. The editor uses this space for rewriting or marking special printing instructions. If you must go beyond one page, number each page and end each page with MORE until the end, where you should write END at the bottom of the page.

7. Get your press release off to a good start—be interesting and intriguing. Include all pertinent information—who, what, when, where—in the first paragraph, often in the

first sentence, or the lead, and the only sentence allowed to be so long.

8. Provide information in order of importance, or top down, which is why you have the pertinent information in the lead sentence. This way you catch all the readers who will not read the entire press release. Editors often cut from the bottom up without rereading or rewriting.

9. Use short sentences (except for the lead sentence) and multiple paragraphs. Ignore what you learned in English class! News paragraphs are kept short so that they can be cut to fit the space available.

10. Quote the statements of others. Such quotations add human interest and can assert your position.

11. Keep the verb in simple tenses; present, simple past, or simple future. This makes for a quicker, more lively read. Use active, not passive, verbs.

12. Contractions may be used in quotations, but never in copy writing. You may quote "it's" and "can't" and "she's," but, otherwise, write, "it is" and "cannot" and "she is."

13. Use only one side of the page.

14. If you do not have a contact name, address the envelope to "News Desk" or "Assignment Desk" or "Calendar Editor," as appropriate.

15. Proofread!

(Guidelines adapted with permission from CA NOW's *Public Relations/Media Guidelines for NOW Chapters,* April 1999).

Appendix D
Guidelines to a Good Media Interview

1. *First and foremost, interviews are not conversations.* You are speaking to the public, not the reporter. The reporter represents the public and is there to get information to relay to the public, and he or she will probably ask difficult or leading questions. Don't feel that you have to give detailed answers to every question or that you have to answer every question. Remember, you can say "no comment" to questions that you do not know how to answer or that are unrelated to the issue at hand.

2. *Don't be hostile or evasive.* Maintain your professionalism even when confronted with hostile interviewers. Don't fall into the trap of saying anything that will hurt your cause; stay focused, and remember why you are doing the interview.

3. *Prepare, prepare, prepare.* Have friends or fellow activists create practice questions to help prepare you for the interview. Think of at least one question you are least prepared for, or least want to address, and be ready to handle it in case it comes up.

4. *Set your own agenda.* Create talking points on the topic, outlining what you will say. Repeat them several times during the interview.

5. *Give good quotations.* Create sound bites, or concise quotations, for your issue(s). A sound bite does not need to be more than a sentence or two. Make it catchy; make it memorable. Be clever and original, but not melodramatic. If you can express yourself well and catch the attention of

the reporter, you will most likely not only end up in print but also earn a relationship with the reporter for future stories.

6. *Remember, there is no such thing as "off the record."* Be aware that, as soon as you grant an interview, anything that you say may end up in print. Many reporters will respect a request to go "off the record," but be careful. Remember that you are not having a conversation with a friend; you are both doing a job.

7. *As an interviewee, you have rights.*

a. *You have the right to be comfortable.* You can set the time, location, and length of an interview, particularly if the reporter has requested the interview. Depending on how important the interview is to you, you may need to be flexible. Negotiate.

b. *You have the right to request the topics to be discussed.* You have the right to know the purpose of the interview and to request an overview of the questions to be asked. Asking for specific questions is not usually appropriate; most reporters will not give this information, nor will editors allow interview subjects that kind of control over the story.

c. *You have the right to ask questions of the reporter.* Reporters are supposed to be objective, but this is not usually the case. Ask a question to get the sense of the reporter's position on the issue or agenda under discussion. If you sense that the reporter is in opposition to you on the issue, stick to your main message and stay professional.

d. *You have the right to make a follow-up call to the reporter to clarify any statements that you feel may have been misunderstood.* However, you do not get final approval of the story. The reporter is not your publicist. While you may ask for quotations to be read back to you, a reporter may not appreciate a request to have them confirmed and is not obligated to change them if you disagree with how you are quoted. It is best not to ask unless the story is particularly controversial or you have a reason to believe that the reporter misunderstood you during the interview.

e. *You have the right to confirm spelling of names and titles.* This is always a good thing to do, as you want the public to have accurate information about you and/or your organization.

f. *You have the right to share contact information to be relayed to the public.* Reporters usually want this information, anyhow, but it is always a good idea to confirm this information with the reporter, especially Web site references. You want the those who hear or read the story to know how to get involved with your work.

(Guidelines adapted with permission from CA NOW's *Public Relations/Media Guidelines for NOW Chapters,* April 1999).

Appendix E
Guidelines to Creating and Earning Effective Media

1. Remember, there are many kinds of media—print, TV, radio, and Internet—and each can be effective for getting your message across.

2. Know your local press, and create a media list; compile a comprehensive listing of your local print, radio, and television news contacts. Be sure to include a contact name, title, address, phone number, fax number, and e-mail address.

3. Identify your allies—who are the feminist reporters? Which reporters write stories on the issues that concern you? Identifying your allies can help get your event covered or your stories told.

4. Take time to make personal contacts with people in the media—send an introductory letter when first setting up your contacts, and include information about the issues you focus on, as well as your contact information.

5. Remember that reporters sometimes have a hidden agenda, or something that they want you to say. Approach every media interview with caution, and be wary of responding to stories or issues that trivialize your cause. If you don't have sufficient information to answer a question, decline to comment ("no comment"), rather than being pressured into answering something you do not know enough about or trying to meet the interviewer's deadline or agenda. Remember, there is no "off the record" when you are talking to reporters; they are not your friends. They have a job to do, and so do you—so stick to your message.

6. When working in a group, designate a media spokesperson(s). Make it clear to the group that these are the only people authorized to speak to the press and refer the press to these folks. Spokespeople need to be articulate and charismatic speakers. They need to be well informed on the issue and able to answer reporters' questions concisely, with "sound bites" that have been predetermined. Have a brainstorming session with your group prior to the event or in connection with the issue about which you will be interviewed to come up with ideas, points, and effective responses. Practice with one another.

7. Keep your message simple. Identify three key points or themes that are concise and to the point. Repeat these themes in your press release and during your interview. Saying less is more; keep to your points even when you feel you're being repetitive.

8. Write a news press release or media advisory. A release informs the media about your event or position on an issue. An advisory informs the media about an action or event and informs them about the date, time, location, and purpose. Mail, fax, or e-mail the advisory or release a few days before the event, and follow up with phone calls. The morning of the event, make reminder phone calls.

9. Come up with sound bites, which are thirty-second statements about your event or the issue you are working on. Practice your sound bites on your colleagues or fellow activists. Make them catchy, make them interesting, make them powerful—you want to catch the interest of the interviewer and your audience, not bore them.

10. Target your audience. Identify whom you are trying to reach, taking into consideration your choice of medium and the time of coverage.

11. Target the media. Explore the media "angles" to your story. Who is most likely to cover your event or issue? If you are working on pay equity, try the business reporters or one from the lifestyle section. If you are working on a reproductive rights, try the health reporters, legal writers, or national reporters. Shop around for reporters who have a

good understanding of the issue, and make your press release relevant to their work (this increases your chances of getting coverage).

12. When doing a press conference or inviting the press to cover an event, remember to make your media visual. Create a backdrop for your speakers. Location is important for this. If talking about a legislative issue, hold your event or press conference in front of the Capitol; if dealing with a legal issue, stand before a courthouse. Make signs or banners with clear messages (not too many words). Chose the right time—check press schedules and conflicting events, avoid Fridays and the 10 A.M. news rush, and don't schedule past 2 P.M. Create press packets with information about the event or issue and the participating organizations, with contact information.

13. Be timely and relevant, be accessible, be prepared, be reliable, and be consistent.

   a. Timeliness = Relevance. This makes a difference in whether you get your message printed or broadcast.

   b. Accessibility. If a story breaks, be available to comment. This is a great opportunity to get into the press and also helps to establish your relationship with the press.

   c. Preparedness. Never succumb to pressure to respond. Be prepared before you respond. Tell the reporter that you will call right back so that you can gather your thoughts and decide on your comment.

   d. Reliability. Be accurate in your facts and statistics.

   e. Literacy (related to reliability). Correct grammar, sentence structure, and punctuation in writing and body language while speaking create your credibility.

   f. Consistency. Sending out news releases or PSAs regularly is impressive and earns you respect and credibility.

14. Don't be afraid to ask for corrections when you are misquoted or your statements are taken out of context.

15. Follow up with the reporter. Send a thank-you note for good coverage, and take the opportunity to confirm your contact information for future stories. This is about maintaining and supporting your working relationship. A little effort can keep the relationship strong for years to come.

(Guidelines adapted with permission from CA NOW's *Public Relations/Media Guidelines for NOW Chapters*, April 1999).

Appendix F
Feminist Shopping Guide

Note: There are many criteria for what makes a socially responsible or feminist business. The list of companies given here is not a complete one, nor can I guarantee that the companies on this list will be in synch with your personal politics. For more information on socially responsible shopping, go to www.responsibleshopper.org and www.sweatshopwatch.org.

Aveda

Plant-based hair, face, and body products. No animal testing, uses organic materials when possible.

Ben & Jerry's

Socially and environmentally conscious ice cream. Indulge!

The Body Shop

Pro-choice, pro-woman, environmentally conscious body, hair, and makeup products.

Buffalo Exchange

Used clothing, clothing exchange with a company purpose that includes intent of "acting with integrity" and "functioning in a socially responsible manner." See www.buffaloexchange.com for stores near you.

Burt's Bees

A variety of environmentally safe beauty products. Available at herbal and natural food stores and some bookstores.

Costco/Price Club

The CEO of Costco voluntarily accepted a cap on his salary to create a more equitable distribution of profits. According to the Center for Responsive Politics, 98 percent of the company's political campaign contributions went to Democrats in the 2004 election.

Esprit de Corp

Clothing, shoes, and apparel. Esprit has great girls' programs, grants, and fellowships.

Femail Creations

One of my favorite catalogs! Great gift ideas. Products are by, for, and/or about women. The Web site is www.femailcreations.com.

Glad Rags and The Keeper

Cotton washable menstrual pads. Available in natural food stores and at www.gladrags.com. Keeper is a reusable menstrual cup, available at www. thekeeperinc.com.

Good Vibrations

Feminist, sex-positive sex shop—great resources, information, toys, and very helpful, nonjudgmental staff. Stores in Berkeley and San Francisco and also on line at www.goodvibes.com.

Hansen's Natural Soda

A great alternative to other sodas. And Hansen's has an annual program to donate to breast cancer research.

Kiss My Face

Natural body-care products. Available at natural food stores and co-ops.

L'Occitane

Body products that have natural ingredients and use recycled products. L'Occitane makes a commitment not to test on animals and not to use child labor. Additionally, its recycled packaging has Braille labeling, and its shopping bags are made from recycled algae from the Venetian canals in a partnership to reduce pollution. The Web site is www.loccitane.com.

Luna Bars

Nutritional bars geared toward women.

Seat Belt Bags

Really cool U.S.-made bags, with proceeds donated to MADD. For store locations or to order on-line, visit www.seatbeltbags.com.

Tom's of Maine

Natural and cruelty-free personal hygiene products (e.g., deodorant, toothpaste, mouth wash).

Working Assets

Socially responsible wireless, long-distance, and credit card company. A portion of every customer's charges goes to support progressive organizations; more than $50 million generated since 1985. The Web site is www.working assets.com.

For feminist bookstores, visit
http://www.litwomen.org/WIP/stores.html.

For listings of women-owned businesses, visit feminist.com's
Women-Owned Businesses site at
www.feminist.com/market/wombus.

It is difficult to keep up with those companies that do and do not use
sweatshop labor. I suggest checking with www.sweatshopwatch.org
for up-to-date information. Also, as SweatShopWatch recommends,
look for products made by fair-trade organizations and co-ops and
those with a union label.

For information about political contributions by companies to candidates and campaigns, visit the Center for Responsive Politics at
www.opensecrets.org.

Working Mother magazine publishes an annual list of the best companies for working mothers, as well as the best companies for women
of color.

Business Ethics: The Magazine of Corporate Responsibility publishes a
"Business Ethics' Corporate Social Responsibility Report," naming
companies that conduct business ethically. Its Web site also maintains a "Business Ethics Directory." For more information, see the
magazine or the Web site at www.business-ethics.com.

Appendix G
Where to Donate Stuff

First and foremost, check with your local resources—domestic-violence shelters, reproductive-health centers, food banks, transitional living programs, and various outreach programs. Many domestic-violence shelters have thrift stores and shelter relief programs where you can donate clothes, books, and toys. Also, check with local reproductive-healthcare providers, which may need donated supplies and cell phones to support their work.

DONATING CLOTHES

Women's Alliance

Organization can direct you to programs in your area that accept business clothing for women in transition. The Web site is www.thewomensalliance.org.

Dress for Success

An international nonprofit program that takes business clothing donations and trains women in transition for successful job interviews. The Web site is www.dressforsuccess.org.

The Glass Slipper Project

Accepts donations of prom-ready formal wear and accessories for women that are given to help high school women in financial need get ready for the prom. The group is Chicago based, but the Web site has links to similar programs around the country (e.g., the Cinderella Project in California and Georgia, the Fairy Godmother Project in Maine and Texas, and Princess Project in California, New Hampshire and New York). The Web site is www.glassslipperproject.org.

DONATING OLD CELL PHONES

The Body Shop

Bring your old cell phones to Body Shop stores, and they will be recycled and given to domestic-violence shelters.

Susan G. Komen Breast Cancer Foundation

The Susan G. Komen Foundation works to fund research and provide community-based outreach and education programs. It hosts an annual Race for the Cure throughout the United States. The group recycles phones so that they don't end up in landfills. It will send you a prepaid shipping label for you to use when you send in your old cell phones. It also takes toner cartridges and PDAs. The Web site is www.recycleforbreast cancer.org; the mailing address is PO Box 2929 San Ramon, CA 94583.

Today's Chicago Woman Foundation

TCWF, "a not-for-profit organization, is dedicated to developing awareness and providing funds to Chicago-area organizations and projects that help women and children in crisis situations, particularly those responding to situations resulting from domestic violence and abuse." For guidelines to donating cell phones, visit www.tcwfoundation.com.

Verizon Wireless Hopeline

From the company's Web site: "Verizon Wireless embraces a philosophy of commitment to the community. Its exclusive HopeLine program puts wireless products and services to work to the benefit of the community. HopeLine is a multi-faceted program, primarily focusing on the prevention of domestic violence and increasing community awareness of this national epidemic. Verizon Wireless' HopeLine program also makes financial grants to regional and national domestic violence organizations." The Web site is www.verizonwireless.com/hopeline.

Sprint Project Connect

"In April 2002, Sprint launched Sprint Project Connect^{SM}, a wireless phone donation and recycling program, to raise money and support for people with disabilities while providing an environmentally friendly way to dispose of used wireless phones. Through Sprint Project Connect, donated wireless phones are either recycled or resold with 100% of net proceeds going to charity; the Wireless Foundation shares the net proceeds with Easter Seals and the National Organization on Disability (N.O.D.)" Donate phones at a local Sprint Store or through participating Easter Seals. For more information, visit www.sprintpcs.com/projectconnect.

DONATING HAIR

Locks of Love

Takes donations of hair ten inches or longer to make hairpieces for children under the age of eighteen who are fighting long-term medical hair loss. For details and to donate, contact Locks of Love at www.locksoflove.org or call the group tollfree at 1.888.896.1588.

Wigs for Kids

Takes donations of hair ten to twelve inches long for kids "affected by hair loss due to chemotherapy, alopecia, burns and other medical conditions." Contact Wigs for Kids on the Internet at www.wigsforkids.org.

DONATING BLOOD

Check your local area for the location of the American Red Cross. Visit www.givelife.org for more information and to schedule an appointment.

DONATING RESOURCES

A great organization for donating livestock for sustainable living is Heifer International. Visit its Web site at www.heifer.org.

Notes

NOTES TO THE PREFACE

1. There were three key grape boycotts in the history of the UFW, the first beginning in 1967. The boycott that I joined in 1987 was a part of the third boycott, which began in 1984 and continued until 2000, seven years after Chavez's death. Chavez's intention through this boycott was to call attention to the use of dangerous pesticides—a concern that continues today.

2. According to the National Center for Farmworkers' Health, farmworkers seldom have access to disability compensation, occupational rehabilitation, or workers' compensation and are seldom able to prove claims for Social Security despite a lifetime of work. Additionally, the Environmental Protection Agency estimates that 300,000 farmworkers are poisoned by pesticides every year (www.ncfh.org).

NOTES TO THE INTRODUCTION

1. Title IX is the 1972 federal law that prohibits gender discrimination in education. Title IX states: "no person in the United States shall, on the basis of sex, be excluded from participation in, be denied the benefits of, or be subjected to discrimination under any educational program or activity receiving federal financial assistance."

2. Discrimination and oppression based upon physical ability.

3. Discrimination and oppression based upon body size.

4. Rosen, 2000, p. 160.

5. Ibid.

6. Rape, Abuse, Incest National Network, 2002, citing the U.S. Department of Justice, 1998.

7. U.S. Department of Justice, November 1998.

8. Oppenheimer, 1995–1996.

9. American Association of University Women, 2001; 1993.

10. Center for American Women and Politics, 2006.

11. Catalyst, "2005 Catalyst Census of Women Board Directors of the Fortune 500," 2005.

12. Costello and Stone, 2001.

13. National Women's Law Center, "The Paycheck Fairness Act: Helping to Close the Wage Gap for Women," April 2006.

14. Ibid.

15. National Women's Law Center, 2003.

16. National Women's Law Center, 2003; Gold, 1999.

17. Alan Guttmacher Institute, 2006; Gold, 1990.

18. NARAL, "Talking Points About Freedom of Choice: 10 Important Facts About Abortion," March 26, 2002 (citing Warren M. Hern, *Abortion Practices* [Philadelphia: Lippincott, 1984], pp. 23–24.)

NOTES TO CHAPTER 1

1. Count taken by march organizers.

2. The Steps to Taking Action are in large part taken from California NOW's *Action for Justice: Making a Difference for Women and Girls Activist Training Manual*, 2003.

3. People for Better TV, Fact Sheet, 2002.

4. From the Web site www.MoveOn.org.

NOTES TO CHAPTER 2

1. Freedman, 2002.

2. Rosen, 2000; Schlafly, 1972.

3. Hernández and Leong, April 21, 2004.

4. Chesler, 1997, p. 43.

5. Just to share a few of these realities: globally, at least one in three women and girls has been beaten or sexually abused in her lifetime (U.N. Commission on the Status of Women, February 28, 2000); 4 million women and girls are trafficked annually (UNFPA, 2000); at least 130 million women and girls are victims of female circumcision or other forms of genital mutilation (UNFPA, 2000); honor killings take the lives of thousands of young women every year, mainly in North Africa, western Asia, and parts of South Asia (in 1999, at least one thousand women in Pakistan were victims of honor crimes) (UNFPA, 2000); in Papua, New Guinea, 67 percent of adult women report physical assault by a male partner (UNFPA, 2000); in Peru, 33 percent of women are abused by their partners (G. E. Rein, D. M. Le Roux, J. Jaschinski, P. Haines, and D. R. Barnes, *The Prevalence and Related Factors of Domestic Violence Against Women in the Mamre Community [Epidemiology Project, September 1996]*); in Zimbabwe, domestic violence accounts for more than 60 percent of murder

cases that go through the high court in Harare (Zimbabwe Women's Resource Centre and Network, 1995).

6. Fraser, 2001, p. 57.

7. Ibid.

8. Dauer, 2001, pp. 65–66.

9. U.N. Division for the Advancement of Women (2006). A list of countries that have ratified CEDAW is available at www.un.org/womenwatch.

NOTES TO CHAPTER 3

1. Findlen, 2001, p. 71.

2. hooks, 2000, p. 55.

3. McIntosh, 1988.

4. Pamphlet *Uprooting Racism* from New Society Press.

5. Kivel, 2002, pp. 97–98.

6. Rousso, 2002.

7. Jan and Stoddard, 1999.

8. Ibid.

9. Vaid, 1999.

10. Severson, 1998.

11. For more information about the fight for gay marriage in Massachusetts, visit the Freedom to Marry Coalition of Massachusetts Web site at www.equalmarriage.org.

12. The U.S. Senate voted in June 2004 to expand hate-crime legislation to include crimes based on sexual orientation, gender, and disability. The legislation needs to be signed into law and enforced. To keep track of this and other hate-crime-related legislation, visit the Gender PAC Web site at www.gpac.org.

13. Bornstein, 1998, p. 31.

14. More information on NOMAS is available at www.nomas.org.

NOTES TO CHAPTER 4

1. I have heard Nancy Pelosi in person recount this experience, which gave me chills. This quotation is from "Nancy Pelosi's Aha! Moment," an article she wrote for *O, The Oprah Magazine* in April 2004.

2. Center for American Women and Politics, "Women in elective office 2006 fact sheet," 2006; Center for American Women and Politics, "Women of color in elective office 2006 fact sheet," 2006.

3. Ibid.

4. Ibid.

5. U.S. Census Bureau, 2000.

6. International Women's Democracy Center, 2002.

7. Portions of this section are part of CA NOW's *21st Century Women in the Workplace Taskforce Report* (2003), written by Rachel Allen, Helen Grieco, and myself.

8. Girls Incorporated, 1992.

9. The National Association of Child Care Resource and Referral Agencies Report, "Childcare in America," 2006.

10. Bureau of Labor Statistics, Women's Bureau, "20 Leading Occupations of Employed Women Full-Time Wage & Salary Workers, 2004 Annual Averages."

11. Bureau of Labor Statistics, "November 2004 National Occupational Employment and Wage Estimates," 2004.

12. Bureau of Labor Statistics, *Occupational Outlook Handbook, 2006–2007.*

13. U.S. Glass Ceiling Commission, November 1995.

14. Meyerson and Fletcher, 2000.

15. Ibid.

16. Ibid.

17. Annenberg Public Policy Center, 2003.

18. Lauzen, 2001.

19. Media Awareness Network, "Media and Girls," 2005.

20. Lauzen, 2001.

21. Ibid.

22. Baumgardner and Richards, 2000.

23. Statistics available at www.religioustolerance.org.

24. Additional information on this organization is available at www.we-are-church.org.

25. American Association of University Women (AAUW), 2001.

26. Title IX does not usually extend to military or religious schools, fraternities or sororities.

27. For more information on these cases or on Title IX, visit www.aauw.org.

28. AAUW, 2001.

29. AAUW Public Policy and Government Relations Department, January 2001; California Women's Law Center, 2000; Women's Sports Foundation, 1998; Zimmerman and Reavill, 1998; Page, 1998; Sabo and Oglesby, 1995.

30. Lopiano, 2001.

31. National Coalition for Women and Girls in Education, June 2002.

32. National Women's Law Center, March 8, 2001.

33. Ibid.

34. Murray, 2002.

35. Ibid.

36. Curphey, 2003.

37. Suggs, 2000.

38. Murray, 2002.

39. As reported from The Official Web Site of Wimbledon, 2005, "Guide: Prize Money," http://scoreboard.wimbledon.org/en_GB/about/guide/prize.html.

40. AAUW, 2001.

41. U.S. Department of Education, 2000.

42. AAUW, 2006.

43. Curtis, 2003–04.

44. Wal-Mart Class Media Advisory, "Federal Judge Orders Wal-Mart Stores, Inc., the Nation's Largest Private Employer, To Stand Trial for Company-Wide Sex Discrimination," June 22, 2004.

45. Wal-Mart Class Press Release, "Women Present Evidence of Widespread Discrimination at Wal-Mart; Ask Judge to Expand Case to Be Largest Ever Sex Discrimination Case," April 28, 2003.

46. Drogin, 2003.

NOTES TO CHAPTER 5

1. Chernik, 2001.

2. Clance, 1985.

3. Anorexia Nervosa and Related Disorders, 2002; Thompson, 1998.

4. Adams, 2000.

5. Steele, 2001, p. 152.

6. Ibid., p. 143.

7. Bordo, 1993, p. 164.

8. Honey, 1984, p. 113.

9. Ibid., p. 119.

10. Strodder, 2000, p. 55.

11. Bordo, 1993, p. 102.

12. Haubegger, 1994.

13. U.S. Census Bureau, 2001.

14. Croteau and Hoynes, 2000.

15. U.S. Census Bureau, 2001.

16. Jean Kilbourne, 2000.

17. Ibid.

18. Klein, 2002.

19. Ibid.

20. National Eating Disorders Association, 2002; Smolak, 1996.

21. Fraser, 1997, p. 8. In her notes, she writes, "The often quoted $34 billion figure for the diet industry comes from John LaRasa, diet industry analyst at Marketdata Research. It includes, in order to size, diet soft drinks, artificial

sweeteners, fitness clubs, commercial weight-loss programs, medically super-vised weight-loss programs, diet foods, meal replacements and appetite sup-pressants, and diet books, videos and audio cassettes. That number, however, doesn't account for the amount we spend on weight-loss surgeries and liposuc-tion, pharmaceutical diet drugs, the estimated $5 billion to $6 billion we spend on fraudulent diet products (according to Frances Berg, editor of *Healthy Weight Journal*), or the $1.4 billion we spend on diet books, lectures, seminars and workshops, which is why I think the total is closer to $50 billion."

22. Reuters, 2005.

23. Research conducted by Ann Kearney-Cooke, physician-scholar with the Partnership for Women's Health at Columbia University and funded by *Seventeen* magazine and Procter & Gamble; Paula Gray Hunker, 2000, "Pres-sure to Be Perfect (Teenagers and Plastic Surgery)" (electronic version), Insight on the News, March 13, 2000.

24. Hunker, 2000, "Pressure to Be Perfect (Teenagers and Plastic Surgery)."

25. Ibid.

26. American Society of Plastic Surgeons (ASPS), 2003.

27. Ibid., 2003.

28. American Society of Plastic Surgeons, 2004.

29. CNN, "Gastric Bypass Coverage Dropped by Insurer," March 3, 2004 http://www.cnn.com/2004/HEALTH/03/03/gastric.bypass.ap.

30. Taren et al., 2001.

31. Schmidt, 2003.

32. National Association for Sport and Physical Education (NASPE), 2001.

33. Feminist Majority, "Frequently Asked Questions About Sweatshops," 2001.

34. Greenhouse, 1999; Carlsen, 1999; Miller, 1999.

35. Sweatshop Watch, Summer 2001.

36. Sweatshop Watch, "Frequently Asked Questions" accessed June 12, 2006, www.sweatshopwatch.org/index.php?s=18.

37. Ehrenreich, 2001.

38. Sweatshop Watch, "Frequently Asked Questions" accessed June 12, 2006, www.sweatshopwatch.org/index.php?s=18.

39. National Labor Committee (reports), "Disney's Children's Books Made with Blood, Sweat and Tears of Young Workers in China," August 18, 2005; "Chi Fung Factory, Apopa, El Salvador: Nike, NBA, Jordan, Adidas, Wal-Mart, VF Corporation," 2005; "Update: Maternity Leave in Bangladesh," January 13, 2005.

40. Sweatshop Watch, 2002.

41. *The Seattle Syndrome,* directed by Steve Bradshaw. Bull Frog Films, 2000.

42. Ibid.

43. Ibid.

44. Fraser, 1997, p. 283.

NOTES TO CHAPTER 6

1. Most women with a tipped uterus don't experience any problems. Some women, however, experience pain during sexual intercourse or menstruation.

2. Black, 2005; Cloutier-Steele, 2003; West and Dranov, 2002.

3. Schiebinger, 2003; Carnes, 1999.

4. For more information about the Feminist Women's Health Centers, visit www.fwhc.org and www.womenshealthspecialists.org, or read *A New View of a Woman's Body* (Feminist Health Press, 1991) and *A Woman's Book of Choices* (Chalker and Downer, 1992).

5. Martin, 1992, p. 93.

6. Ibid., p. 84.

7. Alan Guttmacher Institute, *Sex Education: Needs, Programs and Policies*, 2003, pp. 16–17; Landry, Kaeser, and Richards, 1999.

8. Alan Guttmacher Institute, *Sex Education: Needs, Programs and Policies*, 2003.

9. Ibid.; Darroch, Landry, and Singh, 2000.

10. Alan Guttmacher Institute, *Sex Education: Needs, Programs and Policies*, 2003.

11. Alan Guttmacher Institute, *Sex Education: Needs, Programs, and Policies*, 2003; Kaiser Family Foundation, 2000; Kirby, 1999.

12. Waxman, 2004.

13. Ibid.

14. Ibid.

15. Alan Guttmacher Institute, *Sex Education: Needs, Programs and Policies*, 2003.

16. Ibid., p. 13; Darroch et al., 2001.

17. Alan Guttmacher Institute, *Sex Education: Needs, Programs and Policies*, 2003, p. 14; Darroch et al., 2001; Boonstra, 2002, pp. 7–10.

18. Alan Guttmacher Institute, *State Facts About Abortion*, 2003.

19. Women's Health Specialists: A Feminist Women's Health Center, at www.womenshealthspecialists.org, and the Federation of Feminist Women's Health Centers, at www.fwhc.org.

20. Alan Guttmacher Institute, 2002.

21. Ibid.; National Abortion Federation, "Women Who Have Abortions" fact sheet, 1997.

22. National Abortion Federation, "Women Who Have Abortions" fact sheet, 1997; Alan Guttmacher Institute, 2002.

24. NARAL, "Talking Points About Freedom of Choice: 10 Important Facts About Abortion," March 26, 2002, citing Warren M. Hern, *Abortion Practice* (Philadelphia: Lippincott, 1984), pp. 23–24.

25. Alan Guttmacher Institute, 2002.

26. Ibid.

27. Alan Guttmacher Institute, *State Facts about Abortion*, 2003.

28. Ibid.

29. National Abortion Federation, 1996.

30. Luker, 1984, pp. 12–13.

31. Barker-Benfield, 2000.

32. Ehrenreich and English, 1970.

33. Ibid., p. 21.

34. Barker-Benfield, 2000, p. 61.

35. Luker, 1984, p. 15.

36. Ibid., pp. 14–15.

37. Ibid., p. 15.

38. Ibid.

39. Ibid., pp. 15–16.

40. Miller, 1993, p. 63.

41. Ibid., pp. 12–13.

42. To learn more about this case, visit www.now.org.

43. National Organization for Women, *NOW v. Scheidler Timeline: The Complete Story,* 2002 available at www.now.org.

44. Ibid.

45. Ibid.

46. National Abortion Federation, *NAF Violence and Disruption Statistics,* 2003.

47. Ibid.

48. Roberts, pages 90–91.

49. Ibid., p. 95.

50. Ibid., p. 96.

51. Diamant et al., 2000.

52. Gold, 1999.

53. National Women's Law Center, 2003.

NOTES TO CHAPTER 7

1. "High School Girls Pummel Man Who Exposed Himself," Reuters, October 31, 2003.

2. Centers for Disease Control (CDC), *Intimate Partner Violence: Factsheet,* 2004; and Tjaden, 2000a.

3. American Association of University Women (AAUW), 2001.

4. Centers for Disease Control, *Intimate Partner Violence: Factsheet*, 2004; and Tjaden and Thoennes, 2000a.

5. National Center for Inquiry Prevention and Council (NCIPC), 2003; R. Bachman and L. E. Saltzman, August 1995.

6. The types of intimate-partner violence are widely published and are available from a number of domestic violence centers that provide resource information and from state-based alliances.

7. I was first introduced to this chart through a presentation from a domestic-violence-prevention educator at Women Escaping a Violent Environment (WEAVE) in Sacramento, California.

8. Tjaden and Thoennes, 2000a.

9. Ibid.

10. Gazmararian et al., 2000.

11. Dancy, 2003.

12. Paulozzi et al., 2001.

13. Dancy, 2003.

14. Gray and Foshee, 1997; Makepeace, 1986.

15. Dancy, 2003.

16. NCIPC, 2003.

17. Women ages eighteen and over. California Coalition Against Sexual Assault (Cal CASA), 2000–2002; Lawrence A. Greenfield, "Sex Offenses and Offenders: An Analysis of Data on Rape and Sexual Assault," Bureau of Justice Statistics, Office of Justice Programs, U.S. Department of Justice (Washington, DC, 1997).

18. Cal CASA, 2000–2002; D.G. Kilpatrick, C. N. Edmunds, and A. Seymour, "Rape in America: A Report to the Nation," National Victim Center, Arlington, VA, 1992.

19. Tjaden and Thoennes, 2000b.

20. National Advisory Council on Violence Against Women, 2001.

21. Loder, 2004, and Woodworth, 1999.

22. Sanday, 1990, p. 9.

23. Ibid., p. 13.

24. Ibid., p. 4.

25. Freedman, 2002, pp. 279–280.

26. Racquel Kennedy Bergen, "Marital Rape," Applied Research Forum National Electronic Network on Violence Against Women (March 1999), and Ann-Marie Imbornoni, "Timeline of Key Events in the American Women's Rights Movement," available at www.infoplease.com/spot /womenstimeline1.html#1961.

27. Tanenbaum, 2000, p. 7.

28. Ibid., p. 9.

29. Loder, 2003.

30. *New York Times* magazine, "Rape Hype," June 13, 1993.

31. Sut Jhally, 1994 (videocassette).

32. The number of programs and services is taken from the National Sexual Violence Resource Center, which maintains an annual list of State Sexual Assault Coalition members. The Center notes that these numbers do not always include community-based, campus-based, or tribal programs.

33. For more information about Jackson Katz and his work, visit his Web site at www.jacksonkatz.com.

34. J. Katz and J.Earp, *Tough Guise Study Guide*, 1999, available at http://www.mediaed.org/videos/MediaGenderAndDiversity/ToughGuise/studyguide/ToughGuise.pdf.

35. U.S. Department of Justice, Bureau of Justice Statistics, Homicide Trends in the U.S.: Gender, available at http://www.ojp.usdoj.gov/bjs/homocide/gender.htm.

36. U.S. Department of Justice, Bureau of Justice Statistics, Sourcebook of Criminal Justice Statistics Online, available at http://www.albany.edu/sourcebook.

37. Ibid.

38. National crime statistics, as reported by Katz and Earp, 1999.

39. AAA Foundation for Traffic Safety, "Aggressive Driving," available at www.aaafts.org/Text/agdr3study.pdf.

40. M. Paymar, *Violent No More: Helping Men End Domestic Abuse* (Alameda, CA: Hunter House, 2000).

41. One of the most offensive video games designed for a male audience; a player (depicted as a male) can have sex with a prostitute (shown by a bouncing car) to restore his health. While paying the prostitute decreases the player's funds, he can beat her to death and get his money back. Supposedly restricted to players seventeen years and older, the game is frequently available to younger players who are often well aware of its premise. To take action, contact Rockstar Games and its owner, Take-Two Interactive Software, Inc., as well as the maker of PlayStation 2, Sony Computer Entertainment, Inc.

42. Katz and Earp, 1999.

43. For more information, visit www.whiteribbon.ca/about_us.

44. "Exacerbating the Exasperated: Title VII Liability of Employers for Sexual Harassment Committed by their Supervisors," 81 *Cornell Law Review*, as cited at www.equalrights.org/sexhar/work/workfact.htm.

45. H.R.1, 102nd Congress, 1st Session, "Estimating the Cost of Sexual Harassment to the Fortune 500 Service and Manufacturing Firms," as cited at www.equalrights.org/sexhar/work/workfact.htm.

46. Equal Rights Advocates, "Sexual Harassment in the Workplace," 2004. Visit www.equalrights.org for great resources on how to deal with sexual harassment.

47. Ibid.

48. Ibid.

49. American Association of University Women, 2001.

50. Ibid.

51. Ibid.

52. Kingsbury, 2004.

53. Ibid.

54. World Health Organization, June 2001.

55. United Nations Population Fund (UNFPA), 2000.

56. United Nations, 1996.

57. Ash, 2003.

58. United Nations, 1996.

59. World Health Organization, 2002.

60. Zimbabwe Women's Resource Centre and Network, "Sexual Violence Factsheet," 1995.

61. United Nations Foundation, "'Honor Killings' in Pakistan Reach 631 This Year, Group Says," U.N. Wire, September 15, 2003.

62. UNFPA, 2000.

63. United Nations, 1996.

64. World Health Organization, 2002.

65. UNFPA, 2000.

66. King, 2004.

67. United Nations, 2000.

68. Lederer, in *The Reader's Companion to U.S. Women's History*, 1998.

69. For additional information, visit www.clotheslineproject.org.

NOTES TO CHAPTER 8

1. For more information on the Student Environmental Action Coalition, visit www.seac.org.

2. Labaton and Martin, 2004, p.289.

3. Chesler, 1997, p. 45.

4. Olson, 2001. For more of Alix's poetry, visit www.alixolson.com.

Bibliography

Adams, Jane Meredith. "Mommy, Am I Fat?" WebMD Feature, June 12, 2000. www.wemd.com/content/article/1111739_50367#.

Agosín, Marjorie, ed. *Women, Gender and Human Rights: A Global Perspective.* New Brunswick, NJ: Rutgers University Press, 2001.

Alan Guttmacher Institute. *Facts in Brief: Facts on Induced Abortion in the United States.* AGI: New York and Washington, DC, May 4, 2006.

Alan Guttmacher Institute. *Facts in Brief: Sexuality Education.* AGI: New York and Washington, DC, 2002.

Alan Guttmacher Institute. *State Facts About Abortion.* AGI: New York and Washington, DC, 2003.

Alan Guttmacher Institute. *Sex Education: Needs, Programs and Policies.* AGI: New York and Washington, DC, September 2003.

American Association of University Women. *Affirmative Action.* AAUW, 2006.

American Association of University Women. *Hostile Hallways: Bullying, Teasing and Sexual Harassment in School.* AAUW, 2001.

American Society of Plastic Surgeons. *People choosing cosmetic plastic surgery triples since 1992* (electronic version). PR Newswire, April 19, 2002. http://findarticles.com/cf_0/m4PRN/2002_April_19/85897203/.

American Society of Plastic Surgeons. "2003 gender distribution cosmetic procedures." American Society of Plastic Surgeons, Department of Public Relations, media@plasticsurgery.org or www.plasticsurgery.org.

American Society of Plastic Surgeons. "Gastric bypass surgery popularity leads to jump in plastic surgery procedures, according to ASPS statistics." ASPS Press Release, March 10, 2004.

Annenberg Public Policy Center. "The glass ceiling persists: 3rd annual APPC report on women leaders in communications companies." Annenberg Public Policy Center, Washington, DC, December 19, 2003.

Anorexia Nervosa and Related Eating Disorders (ANRED). "Statistics: How many people have eating disorders?" *ANRED,* January 2004.

Ash, Lucy. "India's dowry death." *BBC News UK Edition,* July 16, 2003.

Associated Press. "Gastric bypass coverage dropped by insurer." CNN, March, 3, 2004. http://www.cnn.com/2004/HEALTH/03/03/gastric.bypass.ap.

Associated Press. "CDC overstated risks of being overweight." MSNBC, April 19, 2005. http://www.msnbc.msn.com/id/7561422/.

Bachman, R., and L. E. Saltzman. "Violence against women: Estimates for the redesigned survey." *Bureau of Justice Statistics, Special Report, U.S. Department of Justice*, August 1995.

Barker-Benfield, G. J. *The Horrors of the Half-Known Life: Male Attitudes Toward Women and Sexuality in Nineteenth-Century America*. New York: Routledge, 2000.

Baumgardner, Jennifer, and Amy Richards. *Manifesta: Young Women, Feminism, and the Future*. New York: Farrar, Straus and Giroux, 2000.

Bergen, Racquel Kennedy. "Marital rape." *Applied Research Forum National Electronic Network on Violence Against Women*, March 1999.

Black, Alexis. "Unnecessary surgery exposed! Why 60% of all surgeries are medically unjustified and how surgeons exploit patients to generate profits." *Newstarget*, October 7, 2005.

Boonstra, H. "Teen pregnancy: Trends and lessons learned." *The Guttmacher Report on Public Policy*, Vol. 5, No. 1 (2002).

Bordo, Susan. *Unbearable Weight: Feminism, Western Culture, and the Body*. Berkeley: University of California Press, 1993.

Bornstein, Kate. *My Gender Workbook*. New York: Routledge, 1998.

Bradshaw, Steve (dir.). *The Seattle Syndrome*. Bull Frog Films, 2000.

Brumberg, Joan Jacobs. *The Body Project: An Intimate History of American Girls*. New York: Random House, 1997.

Business Wire. "Diet Drug—Fen-Phen Litigation Settlement." May 13, 1999. http://www.findarticles.com/p/articles/mi_mOEIN/is_1999_may_13/ai_54625436.

California Women's Law Center Policy Brief. "Sex discrimination and athletics." *Policy Brief*, 2000.

Carlsen, William. "Sweatshop conditions alleged on U.S. island retailers sued for selling 'Made in USA' garments." *San Francisco Chronicle*, January 14, 1999.

Carnes, Molly, M.D. "Health care in the U.S.: Is there evidence for systematic gender bias?" *Wisconsin Medical Journal*, December 1999: 15–19, 25.

CBS SportsLine. "U.S. intercollegiate study: Men make up majority of women's sports coaches." June 12, 1998. http://www.caaws.ca/whas_New/June/coaches_study_Jn13.htm.

Center for American Women and Politics. "Women in elective office 2006 fact sheet." Eagleton Institute of Politics, Rutgers University, New Brunswick, NJ, 2006.

Center for American Women and Politics. "Women of color in elective office 2006 fact sheet." Eagleton Institute of Politics, Rutgers University, New Brunswick, NJ, 2006.

Chalker, Rebecca, and Carol Downer. *A Woman's Book of Choices: Abortion, Menstrual Extraction, RU-486.* New York: Four Walls, Eight Windows, 1992.

Chernik, Abra Fortune. "The body politic." In Barbara Findlen (ed.), *Listen Up: Voices from the Next Feminist Generation* (pp. 103–111). Seattle: Seal Press, 2001.

Chesler, Phyllis. *Letters to a Young Feminist.* New York: Four Walls, Eight Windows, 1997.

Clance, Pauline Rose. *The Impostor Phenomenon: Overcoming the Fear That Haunts Your Success.* Atlanta, GA: Peachtree, 1985.

Cloutier-Steele, Lise. *Misinformed Consent: Women's Stories About Unnecessary Hysterectomy.* Chester, NJ: Next Decade, 2003.

Costello, Cynthia, and Anne Stone, eds. *The American Woman 2001–2002.* New York: Norton, 2001.

Croteau, David, and William Hoynes. *Media Society: Industries, Images and Audiences.* Thousand Oaks: Pine Forge Press, 2000.

Curphey, Shauna. "Number of stay-at-home dads rising." *Women's eNews,* July 4, 2003.

Curphey, Shauna. "Women losing ground in coaching college athletes." *Women's eNews,* December 15, 2003.

Curtis, John W. *Faculty Salary and Faculty Distribution Fact Sheet 2003–04,* Washington, DC: American Association of University Professors, 2003–04.

Dancy, Denise. "Dating violence in adolescence." *National Center for State Courts' Family Violence Forum,* Vol. 2, No. 4 (Winter 2003).

Dao, James. "Legislators push for state action on gay marriage." *New York Times,* February 27, 2004, available at www.nytimes.com.

Darroch, J. E., D. J. Landry, and S. Singh. "Changing emphasis in sexuality education in U.S. public secondary schools, 1988–1999." *Family Planning Perspectives,* Vol. 32, No. 5 (2000): 204–211, 265.

Darroch, Jacqueline E., Jennifer J. Frost, and Susheela Singh. *Teenage Sexual and Reproductive Behavior in Developed Countries: Can More Progress Be Made?* Occasional Report, New York, Alan Guttmacher Institute, No. 3, 2001.

Dauer, S. "Indivisible or invisible: Women's human rights in the public and private sphere." In M. Agosín (ed.), *Women, Gender and Human Rights: A Global Perspective* (pp. 65–82). New Brunswick, NJ: Rutgers University Press.

Diamant, A. L., C. Wold, K. Spritzer, and L. Gelberg. "Health behaviors, health status and access to and use of health acre: A population-based study of lesbian, bisexual and heterosexual women." *Archives of Family Medicine,* Vol. 9, N0.10 (2000): 1043–1051.

Drogin, Richard. "Statistical analysis of gender patterns in Wal-Mart workforce." Prepared for expert testimony on behalf of Drogin, Kakigi and Associates, Berkeley, CA. (February 2003).

Ehrenreich, Barbara. *Nickel and Dimed: On (Not) Getting By in America.* New York: Metropolitan Books, 2001.

Ehrenreich, Barbara, and Deirdre English. *Witches, Midwives and Nurses: A History of Women Healers.* New York: Feminist Press, 1970.

Findlen, Barbara, ed. *Listen Up: Voices from the Next Feminist Generation.* Seattle: Seal Press, 2001.

Foshee, V.A., G. F. Linder, K. E. Bauman, S. A. Langwick, X. B. Arriaga, J. L. Heath, P. M. McMahon, and S. Bangdiwala. "The safe dates project: Theoretical basis, evaluation design, and selected baseline findings." Youth Violence Prevention: Description and baseline data from 13 evaluation projects (K. Powell, D. Hawkins, eds.), *American Journal of Preventive Medicine, Supplement,* Vol. 12, No. 5 (1996): 39–47. Cited at www.cdc.gov/ncipc/factsheets/datviol.htm.

Fraser, Arvonne S. "Becoming human: The origins and development of women's human rights." In Marjorie Agosín (ed.), *Women, Gender, and Human Rights: A Global Perspective* (pp. 16–64). New Brunswick, NJ: Rutgers University Press, 2001.

Fraser, Laura. *Losing It: American's Obsession with Weight and the Industry That Feeds on It.* New York: Dutton, 1997.

Freedman, Estelle. *No Turning Back: The History of Feminism and the Future of Women.* New York: Ballantine, 2002.

Garland-Thomson, Rosemarie. "Re-shaping, re-thinking, re-defining: Feminist disability studies." Barbara Waxman Fiduccia Papers on Women and Girls with Disabilities. Washington, DC: Center for Women Policy Studies, 2001.

Gazmararian, J. A., R. Petersen, A. M. Spitz, M. M. Goodwin, L. E. Saltzman, and J. S. Marks. "Violence and reproductive health; current knowledge and future research directions." *Maternal and Child Health Journal,* Vol. 4, No. 2 (2000): 79–84. Cited at www.cdc.gov/ncipc/factsheets/ipvfacts.htm. .

Girls Incorporated, *Past the Pink and Blue Predicament: Freeing the Next Generation from Sex Stereotypes.* Indianapolis: Girls Incorporated National Resources Center, 1992.

Gold, Rachel Benson. "Implications for Family Planning of Post-Welfare Reform Insurance Trends." *The Guttmacher Report on Public Policy.* New York and Washington, DC: The Alan Guttmacher Institute, December 1999.

Gold, R. B., S. K. Henshaw, and L. D. Lindberg. *Abortion and Women's Health: A Turning Point for America?* New York: Alan Guttmacher Institute, 1990.

Gray, H. M., and V. Foshee. "Adolescent dating violence: Differences between one-sided and mutually violent profiles." *Journal of Interpersonal Violence,* Vol. 12, No. 1 (1997): 126–141. Cited at www.cdc.gov/ncipc/factsheets/datviol.htm.

Greenfield, Lawrence A. "Sex offenses and offenders: An analysis of data on rape and sexual assault." Bureau of Justice Statistics, Office of Justice Programs, U.S. Department of Justice, Washington, DC, 1997.

Greenhouse, Steven. "18 major retailers and apparel makers are accused of using sweatshops." *New York Times,* January 14, 1999.

Haubegger, Christy. "I'm not fat, I'm Latina." *Essence,* Vol. 25, No. 8 (December 1994).

Heery, William J. "Corporate mentoring: Shattering the glass ceiling." *Harrington Group Newsletter,* Vol. 3, Issue 7 (August, 9, 2002).

Herman, Edward, and Noam Chomsky. *Manufacturing Consent: The Political Economy of the Mass Media.* New York: Pantheon Books, 2002.

Hernández, Daisy, and Pandora L. Leong. "Feminism's future young feminists of color take the mic." *In These Times,* April 21, 2004.

Hesse-Biber, Sharlene. *Am I Thin Enough Yet?: The Cult of Thinness and the Commercialization of Identity.* New York: Oxford University Press, 1996.

Hewlitt, Sylvia Ann. *Creating a Life: Professional Women and the Quest for Children.* New York: Talk Miramax Books, 2002.

Honey, Maureen. *Creating Rosie the Riveter: Class, Gender, and Propaganda during World War II.* Amherst: University of Massachusetts Press, 1984.

hooks, bell. *Feminism Is for Everybody: Passionate Politics.* Cambridge, MA: South End Press, 2000.

Hunker, Paula Gray. *Pressure to Be Perfect (Teenagers and Plastic Surgery).* Insight on the News, March 13, 2000.

Imbornoni, Ann-Marie. *Timeline of Key Events in the American Women's Rights Movement.* Available at www.infoplease.com/spot/womenstimeline1.html#1961.

International Women's Democracy Center. *Fact Sheet: Women's Political Participation,* 2002.

International Women's Democracy Center. *Women in Politics: A Timeline,* 2002.

Isidore, Chris. "Less pay for more popular play." *CNN Money,* June 23, 2003.

Jan, S., and S. Stoddard. *Chart Book on Women and Disability in the United States.* An InfoUse Report. Washington, DC: U.S. National Institute on Disability and Rehabilitation Research, 1999.

Jhally, Sut. *Date Rape Backlash.* Media Education Foundation, 1994 (videocassette).

Kaiser Family Foundation. *Sex Education in America: A View from Inside the Nation's Classrooms.* Menlo Park: Kaiser Family Foundation, 2000.

Katz, Jackson and Jeremy Earp. *Tough Guise.* Media Education Foundation, 1999 (videocassette).

Kilbourne, Jean. *Killing Us Softly 3: Advertising's Image of Women.* Northampton, MA: Media Education Foundation, 2000.

Kilpatrick, D. G., C. N. Edmunds, and A. Seymour. "Rape in America: A report to the nation." National Victim Center, Arlington, VA, 1992.

King, Gilbert. *Women, Child—For Sale: The New Slave Trade in the 21st Century.* New York: Penguin, 2004.

Kingsbury, Kathleen. "Few laws help gays in cases of domestic violence." *Columbia News Service,* July 21, 2004.

Kirby, Douglas. "Sexuality and sex education at home and school." *Adolescent Medicine: State of the Art Reviews,* Vol. 10, No. 2 (1999): 195–209.

Kivel, Paul. *Uprooting Racism: How White People Can Work for Racial Justice.* Gabriola Island, BC, Canada: New Society Publishers, 2002.

Klein, Naomi. *No Logo.* New York: Picador USA, 2002.

Labaton, Vivien, and Dawn Lundy Martin (eds.). *The Fire This Time: Young Activists and the New Feminism.* New York: Anchor Books, 2004.

Landry, D. J., L. Kaeser, and C. L. Richards. "Abstinence promotion and the provision of information about contraception in public school district sexuality education policies." *Family Planning Perspectives,* Vol. 31, No. 6 (1999): 280–286.

Lauer, Nancy Cook. "Studies show women's role in media shrinking." *Women's eNews,* May 21, 2002.

Lauzen, Martha M. "The Celluloid ceiling: Behind-the-scenes employment of women in the top 250 films of 2000." School of Communication, San Diego State University, 2001.

Loder, Asjylyn. "Statistics suggest more rape victims speak up." *Women's eNews,* September 4, 2003.

Loder, Asjylyn. "Date rape drugs still available, despite crackdown." *Women's eNews,* January 16, 2004.

Lopiano, Donna. "Dropping men's sports—the Division I football/basketball arms race is the culprit in the cutting of men's Olympic sports: The Foundation's position." *Women's Sports Foundation,* May 9, 2001.

Luker, Kristen. *Abortion and the Politics of Motherhood.* Berkeley: University of California Press, 1984.

Makespeace, J. M. "Gender differences in courtship violence victimization." *Family Relations,* Vol. 35 (1986): 383–388. Cited at www.cdc.gov/ncipc/factsheets/datviol.htm.

Mankiller, Wilma, Gwendolyn Mink, Marysa Navarro, Barbara Smith, and Gloria Steinem (eds.). *The Reader's Companion to U.S. Women's History.* New York: Houghton Mifflin, 1998.

Marshall, Carolyn. "More than 50 gay couples are married in San Francisco." *New York Times,* February 13, 2004. Available at www.nytimes.com.

Martin, Emily. *The Woman in the Body: A Cultural Analysis of Reproduction.* Boston: Beacon Press, 1992.

Mathis, Nancy. "Health and environment: Global statistics on women's health are chilling." *Women's eNews,* June 7, 2001.

McIntosh, Peggy. *White Privilege and Male Privilege: A Personal Account of Coming to See Correspondences Through Work in Women's Studies.* Working Paper, Wellesley College, 1988.

Meyerson, Debra E., and Joyce K. Fletcher. "A modest manifesto for shattering the glass ceiling." *Harvard Business Review,* January–February 2000.

Miller, Michael. "Major U.S. retailers sued in sweatshop law case." *Los Angeles Times,* January 14, 1999.

Miller, Patricia. *The Worst of Times: Illegal Abortion—Survivors, Practitioners, Coroners, Cops, and Children of Women Who Died Talk About Its Horrors.* New York: Harper Perennial, 1993.

Moore, Michael. *Stupid White Men . . . and Other Sorry Excuses for the State of the Nation.* New York: Regan Books, 2001.

Moskowitz, Daniel B. "The skinny on diet drug settlement." *Business and Health,* October 2000: 23.

Murray, Sarah. "Posting up in the pink ghetto." *Women's Sports Foundation,* April 10, 2002.

National Abortion Federation. *Teenage Women, Abortion and the Law Fact Sheet,* 1996.

National Abortion Federation. *Women Who Have Abortions Fact Sheet,* 2003.

National Abortion Federation. *NAF Violence and Disruption Statistics,* 2003.

National Advisory Council on Violence Against Women. *Toolkit to End Violence Against Women,* November 2001.

National Association for Sport and Physical Education (NASPE). "Shape of the Nation Executive Summary," October 2001.

National Center for Injury Prevention and Council (NCIPC), "Dating Violence Fact Scheet," Center for Disease Control, accessed on-line 12/11/2003 at http://www.cdc.gov/ncipc/factsheets/datviol.htm.

National Coalition for Women and Girls in Education. "Title IX at 30: Report Card on Gender Equity," National Coalition for Women and Girls in Education, June 2002.

National Eating Disorders Association. (2002). "Statistics: Eating disorders and the precursors." Seattle: National Eating Disorders Association.

National Women's Law Center. "Women and Health Insurance," Washington, DC: April 2003.

National Women's Law Center. "GAO report shows schools added athletic opportunities for women by raising revenue, not cutting men's teams," March 8, 2001 (press release).

Olson, Alix. "Warriors." *Built Like That* (CD), 2002.

Oppenheimer, David Benjamin. "Exacerbating the exasperated: Title IV liability of employers for sexual harassment." *Cornell Law Review,* Vol. 81 (1995–1996).

Orenstein, Peggy. *Flux: Women on Sex, Work, Love, Kids and Life in a Half-changed World.* New York: Doubleday, 2000.

Page, R. M., J. Hammermeister, A. Scanlan, L. Gilbert. "Is school sports partici- pation a protective factor against adolescent health risk behavior?" *Jour- nal of Health Education,* Vol. 29 (3) (1998): 186–192.

Paulozzi, L. J., L. A. Saltzman, M. J. Thompson, and P. Holmgren. "Surveil- lance for homicide among intimate partners—United States, 1981–1998." *CDC Surveillance Summaries* Vol. 50 (SS-3) (2001): 1–16. Cited at www.cdc.gov/ncipc/factsheets/ipvfacts.htm.

PBS *Frontline. Merchants of Cool,* 2001 (videocassette).

Penn, Michael, and Rahel Nardos. *Overcoming Violence Against Women and Girls: The International Campaign to Eradicate a Worldwide Problem.* New York: Rowman and Littlefield, 2003.

Pipher, Mary. *Reviving Ophelia: Saving the Selves of Adolescent Girls.* New York: Grosset/Putnam Books, 1994.

Pipher, Mary. *Hunger Pains: The Modern Woman's Tragic Quest for Thinness.* New York: Ballantine Books, 1995.

Reuters. "Obesity in U.S. carries hefty price tag." MSNBC, June 27, 2005. http://www.msnbc.msn.com/id/8376790/.

River, F., and J. Erlich. *Community Organizing in a Diverse Society.* Boston: Allyn and Bacon, 1998.

Roberts, Dorothy. *Killing the Black Body: Race, Reproduction and the Meaning of Liberty.* New York: Vintage Books, 1997.

Rosen, Ruth. *The World Split Open: How the Modern Women's Movement Changed America.* New York: Penguin Putnam, 2000.

Rousso, Harilyn. "Strong proud sisters: Girls and young women with disabili- ties." Center for Women Policy Studies, Barbara Waxman Fiduccia Papers on Women and Girls with Disabilities, 2001.

Rousso, Harilyn. "Briefing on girls and young women with disabilities." Cen- ter for Women Policy Studies, September 19, 2002.

Ryan, Harriet. "Ending rape kits wait puts price on justice." CNN, April 25, 2003. http://www.cnn.com/2003/LAW/04/25/ctv.rape.kit.

Sabo, D., and C. Oglesby. "Ending sexual harassment in sport: A commitment whose time has come." *Women in Sport and Physical Activity Journal.* Vol. 4 (2) (1995): 84–104.

Sanday, Peggy Reeves. *Fraternity Gang Rape.* New York: New York University Press, 1990.

Schiebinger, Londa. "Women's health and clinical trials." *Journal of Clinical In- vestigation,* Vol. 112 (2003): 973–977.

Schlafly, Phyllis. "The right to be a woman." *The Phyllis Schlafly Report* 6 (No- vember 1972).

Schmidt, Charles. "Obesity a weighty issue for children." *Environmental Health Perspectives,* October 2003.

Schmitt, Eric. "Female GIs report rapes, assaults by fellow troops." *San Francisco Chronicle*, February 26, 2004.

Severson, Kristen. "Identity politics and progress: Don't fence me in (or Out)." *Off Our Backs*, April 1998.

Smolak, L. *National Eating Disorders Association/Next Door Neighbors Puppet Guide Book*, 1996.

Steele, Valerie. *The Corset: A Cultural History*. New Haven: Yale University Press, 2001.

Strodder, Chris. *Swingin' Chicks of the 60s*. San Rafael, CA: Cedco, 2000.

Suggs, Welch. "New study finds a decline in the number of female coaches." *Chronicle of Higher Education Bulletin*, May 2, 2000.

Sweatshop Watch, California Garment Industry: Pyramid of Power and Profit, 2002.

Sweatshop Watch. Sweatshop Watch newsletter. Vol. 7 (2) (Summer 2001).

Tanenbaum, Leora. *Slut! Growing up Female with a Bad Reputation*. New York: Perennial, 2000.

Taren, Douglas, Cynthia A. Thomson, Nancy Alexander Koff, Paul R. Gordon, Mary J. Marian, Tamsen L. Bassford, John V. Fulginiti, and Cheryl K. Ritenbaugh. "Effect of an integrated nutrition curriculum on medical education, student clinical performance, and student perception or medical-nutrition training." *American Journal of Clinical Nutrition*, Vol. 73, No. 6 (June 2001): 1107–1112.

Thompson, Becky W. "Eating disorders." *The Reader's Companion to U.S. Women's History*. New York: Houghton Mifflin, 1998.

Tjaden, P., and N. Thoennes. "Full report of the prevalence, incidence, and consequences of intimate partner violence against women: Findings from the National Violence Against Women Survey." National Institute of Justice and the Centers for Diseases Control and Prevention, Washington, DC, 2000a.

Tjaden P., and N. Thoennes. "Full report of the prevalence, incidence, and consequences of violence against women: findings from the national violence against women survey." Report NCJ 183781, National Institute of Justice, Washington, DC, 2000b.

United Nations, Division for the Advancement of Women, "Online Updates for the Convention on the Elimination of All Forms of Discrimination Against Women (CEDAW)," www.un.org/womenwatch, June 2006.

United Nations. "Human rights: Women and violence fact sheet." United Nations Department of Public Information (DPI/1772/HR), February 1996.

United Nations. "Review and appraisal of the implementation of the Beijing Platform for Action: Report of the Secretary-General" (E/CN.6/2000/PC/2). United Nations Department of Public Information, May 2000.

United Nations Population Fund (UNFPA). "Ending violence against women and girls." *State of the World Population 2000,* 2000.

U.S. Census Bureau. *Profile of General Demographic Characteristics: 2000.* Washington, DC: U.S. Census Bureau, 2000.

U.S. Census Bureau. *Statistical Abstract of the United States: 2001. The National Data Book.* Washington, DC: U.S. Census Bureau, 2001.

U.S. Department of Education. *Trends in Educational Equity of Girls and Women,* June 2000.

U.S. Department of Justice, National Institute of Justice, Centers for Disease Control and Prevention. "Prevalence, incidence, and consequences of violence against women: Findings from a National Violence Against Women survey." Washington, DC, November, 1998.

U.S. Department of Labor, Bureau of Labor Statistics. November 2004 National Occupational Employment and Wage Estimates, Building and Grounds Cleaning and Maintenance Occupations. Available at www.bls.gov/oes /current/oes_37bu.htm (visited May 19, 2006).

U.S. Department of Labor, Bureau of Labor Statistics. Occupational Outlook Handbook, 2006–07 Edition, Automotive Service Technicians and Mechanics. Available at http://www.bls.gov/oco/ocos181.htm (visited May 19, 2006).

U.S. Department of Labor, Bureau of Labor Statistics. Occupational Outlook Handbook, 2006–07 Edition, Child Care Workers. Available at http://www.bls.gov/oco/ocos170.htm (visited May 19, 2006).

U.S. Department of Labor, Bureau of Labor Statistics, Women's Bureau. "20 leading occupations of employed women full-time wage and salary workers, 2004 annual averages." Washington, DC, 2004.

U.S. Glass Ceiling Commission. *A Solid Investment: Making Full Use of the Nation's Human Capital,* November 1995.

Vaid, Urvashi. "Linking arms and movements: Lesbian rights summit of the National Organization for Women, April 23–25 in Washington, DC, 1999." *The Advocate,* June 8, 1999.

Valdivieso, Veronica. "DNA warrants: A panacea for old, cold rape cases?" *Georgetown Law Journal,* Vol. 90 (2002): 1009–1053.

Waxman, Henry. *The Content of Federally Funded Abstinence-Only Education Programs.* U.S. House of Representatives Committee on Government Reform; Minority Staff, Special Investigations Division, December 2004.

West, Stanley, and Paula Dranov. *The Hysterectomy Hoax: The Truth About Why Many Hysterectomies Are Unnecessary and How to Avoid Them.* Chester, NJ: Next Decade, 2002.

White, Emily. *Fast Girls: Teenage Tribes and the Myth of the Slut.* New York: Scribner, 2002.

Women's Sports Foundation Report. *Sport and Teen Pregnancy.* East Meadow, NY: Women's Sports Foundation, 1998.

Women's Sports Foundation. "Title IX and race in intercollegiate sport." East Meadow, NY: Women's Sports Foundation, 2003.

Woodworth, Terrance. DEA Congressional Testimony before the House Commerce Committee Subcommittee on Oversight and Investigation, March 11, 1999.

World Health Organization. *Female Genital Mutilation: Integrating the Prevention and the Management of the Health Complications into the Curricula of Nursing and Midwifery. Policy Guidelines for Nurses and Midwives.* New York: World Health Organization, 2001.

World Health Organization. "Sexual violence fact sheet." New York: World Health Organization, 2002.

Zimmerman, Jean, and Gil Reavill. *Raising Our Athletic Daughters: How Sports Can Build Self-Esteem and Save Girls' Lives.* New York: Main Street Books, 1998.

Index

Abelism, 251n2

Abortion, 43, 158-174; access, 159; anti-choice activity, 9, 158-160, 164-165, 168-169, 170-171; courts, 159, 171-173; demographics, 163-164; global gag rule (Mexico City Policy), 160; history, 166-169; language, 173-174, 177-178; legality, 9, 149, 168-169; *NOW v. Scheidler*, 172-173; politics of, 161-162, 164-165, 170-171; *Roe v. Wade*, 34, 43, 46, 149, 160, 165, 169, 170; safety, 9, 164-165; violence, 159, 165; why women have abortions, 162-163; womanhood vs. "fetushood," 170-171; young women and abortion, 165-166. *See also* Reproductive health

Activism, xi-xii, 15-19, 218-220, 223-225; building an activist kit, 231; in daily life, 24; definition of, 16; steps to taking action, 19-22; 2004 March for Women's Lives, 38, 40; timeline, 227-229; violence, 208-212; where to donate, 247-250; Women's Equality Day, 40

Adams, Abigail, 23, 93

Anorexia. *See* Eating disorders

Anthony, Susan B., 29, 41, 95, 220

Aptheker, Bettina, xii

Baumgardner, Jennifer, 37, 47, 103

Body image: advertising and media influence, 4, 129-130, 133; body dysmorphic disorder (BDD), 132; changing the image, 127-129, 140-141; corsets, 125; dieting, 130-132; history of, 124-129; Hollywood, 127-128; myths of feminism, 5-6; plastic surgery, 132-134; power, 127; race/racism, 125-126; sports and Title IX, 127; young women, 131-132. *See also* Women globally

Bulimia. *See* Eating disorders

CEDAW, 52-53, 55, 57, 98, 115, 210, 253n9

Chavez, Cesar, xi

Chesler, Phyllis, 50

Clothesline Projects, 209, 210, 215

Consciousness raising, 62

Declaration of Sentiments, 40

Disability rights: 73-74; Americans with Disabilities Act, 73; Disability Rights Education and Defense, 117

Domestic violence. *See* Violence against women

Downer, Carol, 33

Eating disorders: anorexia, 122; bulimia, 122, 123; definition of, 122; feminism and, 122-124; prevalence, 123. *See also* Body image

Education: representation, 93; sexual harassment, 203-204. *See also* Title IX

Emergency contraception, 178-179. *See also* Reproductive health

Ensler, Eve, 37, 154, 210-211
Equality, 15-16, 113
Equal Rights Amendment (ERA), 10, 31, 44-45

Feminism, 1, 6, 12-13, 224-225; definition of, 2; goals, xv; "I'm not a feminist but…," 7; media images, xv; myths of, 2-10; relevance, 7-8, 15-16; women of color, 47-48. *See also* Feminist movement; Women's movement
Feminist movement, 11, 27; first wave, 38, 40-42; gains of the movement, 11-12, 25; second wave, xiii; 38-39, 42-45; third wave, xiii, 45-48. *See also* Women's movement
Feminist Women's Health Center, 44, 148, 150, 159, 162, 184; vaginal and cervical self-exam, 150-152. *See also* Women's health movement
Fletcher, Joyce, 101-102
Friedan, Betty, xiv, 31-32

Gay marriage, 253n11; Defense of Marriage Act (DOMA), 80; Freedom to Marry Day, 79, 87; Massachusetts ruling, 79; religion, 78-79. *See also* Same-sex marriage
Glass ceiling. *See* Work
GLBTQQI, 74-81; adoption, 177; definition of, 6; feminism and, 48, 66; hate crimes, 253n12; sexuality, 154-155; timeline of rights, 75-77; violence, 188, 204-206. *See also* Homophobia; Sexuality; Violence against women
Grassroots: activism, 209; definition of, 16; global, 207-208. *See also* Activism
Grieco, Helen, 49, 54

Health: medical costs, 9, 177. *See also* Emergency contraception; Reproductive health; Women's health movement
Homophobia, 77, 204-206, 225; definition of, 204
hooks, bell, 63
Huerta, Delores, xi, 31, 221

Katz, Jackson, 82, 200-201, 215
Kivel, Paul, *Uprooting Racism*, 64-65

McIntosh, Peggy, 65; white privilege, 63-64
Media: activism, 103-104, 115; creating and earning effective media, 239-242; guidelines to a good interview, 235-237; how to write a press release, 233-234; media for women, 26, 104, 214; representation, 93, 102-104; working with, 22-24
Meyerson, Debra, 101-102
Military: representation, 93; service, 186
"Morning-after pill." *See* Emergency contraception

National Organization for Men Against Sexism (NOMAS), 83, 253n14
National Organization for Women (NOW), xiii, 22, 32, 43, 58, 96, 119, 184; California NOW, xiii, xiv, 6, 57, 103; NOW Foundation and "Love Your Body Day" campaign, 143, 146; *NOW v. Scheidler*, 172-173; 2003 Women with Disabilities and Allies Forum, 74
New Moon magazine, 141

Olson, Alix, 142, 224-225

Patriarchy, definition of, 3-4
Paul, Alice, 30, 40, 44, 221
Pelosi, Nancy, 38, 94-95, 96
Plan B. *See* Emergency contraception
Politics: political representation, 9, 93, 94-98; voter registration, 17, 95, 115

Racism, 60-65, 225; activism, 67-68; definition of, 59; feminism and women's movement, 41-42, 59, 65-67; unlearning racism, 63-65, 67-68
Rape, 192-199, 200-201; categories of, 193-194; definition of, 192; history, 195; myths of, 192-193; rape kits, 198, 211; "victim-blaming," 195-199; as a weapon of war, 37, 207. *See also* Violence against women
Religion: abortion, 167; Civil Rights Act of 1964, 105; feminism, 104-107; gay marriage, 78-79; representation, 93, 105; "We Are Church," 106, 121; women's response to religion, 106-107
Reproductive health: birth control, 31, 32; *Eisenstadt v. Baird*, 43; GLBTQQI, 176-177; *Griswold v. Connecticut*, 32, 43; menstruation, 153-154; midwives/midwifery, 149, 167-168; race/racism, 175-176; *Roe v. Wade*, 34, 43, 46, 149; sterilization, 175; unnecessary procedures, 175-176; vaginal and cervical self-exam, 150-152. *See also* Abortion
Richards, Amy, 37, 47, 103
Riot Grrls, 46

Same-sex marriage, 76. *See also* Gay marriage
Schlafly, Phyllis, 44
Seneca Falls, 29, 40
Severson, Kristen, 77-78

Sex education: abstinence, 155; Bush administration, 156; HIV/AIDS, 155, 156; international comparisons, 157-158; in schools, 155-158; sexually transmitted infections, 155; social attitudes, 157; Waxman report, 156
Sexism, 42, 225, 251n3
Sexual harassment. *See* Violence against women
Sexuality, 7, 154-155
SisterSong, 85-86
Stanton, Elizabeth Cady, 29, 30, 41, 95, 220; and *The Women's Bible*, 30
Suffrage, 38, 40; Alice Paul and hunger strikes, 40; fashion, 124-125; first wave of feminism, 40-42; Nineteenth Amendment, 29, 30, 40; suffragists, 94-95
Sweatshop labor: 134-140; definition, 137-138; status, 134, 138. *See also* Women globally; Work

Take Back the Night, 22, 209-210, 212
Third Wave Feminism, third wavers, third wave feminists. *See* Feminism; Feminist movement; Women's movement
Third Wave Foundation, 36, 46, 58, 92, 219
Title IX, 1, 42, 107-113, 251n1; body image, 127; challenges to, 111-112; compliance, 109-110, 254n26; definition of, 107-108; professional sports, 111-112; sexual harassment, 108, 204; single-sex classes, 108; status of, 112-113
Truth, Sojourner, 29, 41, 220

United Farm Workers, xi, 251n1-2

Vaid, Urvashi, 77

Violence against women: 9; cycle of, 189-190; definition of, 187; global, 52, 206-208; intimate partner violence, 187-192; media, 185-187, 200-201; men, 199-202; *Men Stopping Rape*, 201, 210; sexual harassment, 9, 35, 42, 202-204, 223; statistics of, 187, 190; teen violence, 191-192; video games, 200, 260n41; Violence Against Women Act (VAWA), 37, 209-210; White Ribbon Campaign, 201, 217. *See also* Take Back the Night; Women globally

Walker, Rebecca, 36, 46, 47, 223
Wells, Ida B., 30, 41, 221
Women: in history, 27, 28-38; as warriors, 186; who have made a difference, 220-223
Women globally, 41-42, 51-53, 252n5; fashion and the market place, 134-140; leaders, 97-98; trafficking, 208; violence, 52, 206-208. *See also* CEDAW
Women's health movement, 44, 177-178; Boston Women's Health Collective, 44, 154; National Black

Women's Health Project (Black Women's Health Imperative), 44; National Women's Health Network, 44, 154; women-centered health care, 147, 148-149; women's health agenda, 148, 177. *See also* Feminist Women's Health Center
Women's movement: xiv, xv; chronology, 28-38; criticism, 39; first wave, 38, 40-42; gains of the movement, 11-12; intergenerational partnership and mentoring, xiii, 48-51, 54, 68-72; men, 81-85; second wave, 38-39, 42-45; third wave, 39-40, 45-48; waves of the movement, 38-48. *See also* Feminist movement
Women's studies, xiv, 43
Work: Equal Pay Act, 31, 33; glass ceiling, 99, 101-102; and life integration issues, 8, 99-102; livable wage, 136-137; pay equity, 9-10; representation, 9, 93, 99-102; sexual harassment, 202-203; Wal-Mart, 114. *See also* Sweatshop labor

Zines, 46-47, 89

About the Author

MEGAN SEELY is a third-wave feminist and activist. She was the youngest person ever elected president of California National Organization for Women and served two terms, from 2001 to 2005. An activist from a very young age, she has been involved in community organizing, protests, marches, street theater, hunger strikes, rallies, and campaigns on the local, state and national levels. She lives and teaches in northern California. Her Web site is www.fightlikeagirl.org